James M. Hiatt

The political Manual

Comprising numerous important Documents connected with the political History of

America

James M. Hiatt

The political Manual
Comprising numerous important Documents connected with the political History of America

ISBN/EAN: 9783337079635

Printed in Europe, USA, Canada, Australia, Japan

Cover: Foto ©Suzi / pixelio.de

More available books at **www.hansebooks.com**

THE
POLITICAL MANUAL,

COMPRISING

NUMEROUS IMPORTANT DOCUMENTS

CONNECTED WITH THE

POLITICAL HISTORY OF AMERICA,

COMPILED FROM OFFICIAL RECORDS, WITH BIOGRAPHICAL
SKETCHES AND COMMENTS.

BY J. M. HIATT.

INDIANAPOLIS, IND.:
ASHER & ADAMS, Publishers.
1864.

Entered according to Act of Congress in the year 1864, by

ASHER & ADAMS,

In the Clerk's office of the District Court for the District of Indiana.

FORMATION OF THE ORIGINAL UNION.

On Monday, the 5th of September, 1774, there were assembled at Carpenter's Hall, in the city of Philadelphia, a number of men who had been chosen and appointed by the several colonies in North America to hold a Congress for the purpose of discussing certain grievances imputed against the mother-country. This Congress resolved on the next day that each colony should have one vote only. On Tuesday, the 2d July, 1776, the Congress resolved, "That these United Colonies are, and of right ought to be, Free and Independent States," etc., etc.; and on Thursday, the 4th July, the whole Declaration of Independence having been agreed upon, it was publicly read to the people. Shortly after, on the 9th September, it was resolved that the words "United Colonies" should be no longer used, and that the "UNITED STATES OF AMERICA" should thenceforward be the style and title of the Union. On Saturday, the 15th November, 1777, "Articles of Confederation and Perpetual Union of the United States of America" were agreed to by the state delegates, subject to the ratification of the state legislatures severally. Eight of the states ratified these articles on the 9th July, 1778; one on the 21st July; one on the 24th July; one on the 26th November of the same year; one on the 22d February, 1779; and the last one on the 1st March, 1781. Here was a bond of union between thirteen independent states, whose delegates in Congress legislated for the general welfare, and executed certain powers, so far as they were permitted by the articles aforesaid. The following are the names of the Presidents of the Continental Congress from 1774 to 1788:

Peyton Randolph, Virginia................................	5th Sept., 1774
Henry Middleton, South Carolina....................	22d Oct., 1774
Peyton Randolph, Virginia................................	10th May, 1775
John Hancock, Massachusetts..........................	24th May, 1776
Henry Laurens, South Carolina........................	1st Nov., 1777
John Jay, New York...	10th Dec., 1778
Samuel Huntingdon, Connecticut.....................	28th Sep., 1779
Thomas McKean, Delaware...............................	10th July, 1781
John Hanson, Maryland.....................................	5th Nov., 1781
Elias Boudinot, New Jersey..............................	4th " 1782
Thomas Mifflin, Pennsylvania..........................	3d " 1783

Richard Henry Lee, Virginia.......................... 30th Nov., 1784
Nathaniel Gorham, Massachusetts.................. 6th Jan., 1786
Arthur St. Clair, Pennsylvania........................ 2d Feb., 1787
Cyrus Griffin, Virginia.................................. 22d Jan., 1788

The seat of government was established as follows: at Philadelphia, Pa., commencing September 5, 1774, and May 10, 1775; at Baltimore, Md., December 20, 1776; at Philadelphia, Pa., March 4, 1777; at Lancaster, Pa., September 27, 1777; at York, Pa., September 30, 1777; at Philadelphia, Pa., July 2, 1778; at Princeton, N. J., June 30, 1783; at Annapolis, Md., November 26, 1783; at Trenton, N. J., November 1, 1784; and at New York City, N. Y., Jan. 11, 1785.

On the 4th March, 1789, the present Constitution, which had been adopted by a convention and ratified by the requisite number of states, went into operation.

POPULATION OF THE UNITED STATES AT DECENNIAL PERIODS.

Census Years.	White Persons.	Colored Persons.			Total Population.
		Free.	Slave.	Total.	
1790...	3,172,464	59,466	697,897	757,363	3,929,827
1800...	4,304,489	108,395	893,041	1,001,436	5,305,925
1810...	5,862,004	186,446	1,191,364	1,377,810	7,239,814
1820...	7,861,937	238,156	1,538,038	1,776,194	9,638,131
1830...	10,537,378	319,599	2,009,043	2,328,642	12,866,020
1840...	14,195,695	386,303	2,487,455	2,873,758	17,069,453
1850...	19,553,068	434,495	3,204,313	3,638,808	23,191,876
1860...	26,964,930	487,970	3,953,760	4,441,730	31,443,322

DECLARATION OF INDEPENDENCE.

IN CONGRESS, TUESDAY, JULY 4, 1776.

Agreeably to the order of the day, the Congress resolved itself into a committee of the whole, to take into their further consideration the Declaration; and after some time the President resumed the chair, and Mr. Harrison reported that the committee had agreed to a declaration, which they desired him to report. (The committee consisted of Jefferson, Franklin, John Adams, Sherman, and R. R. Livingston.)
The Declaration being read, was agreed to, as follows:

A DECLARATION

BY THE REPRESENTATIVES OF THE UNITED STATES OF AMERICA, IN CONGRESS ASSEMBLED.

When, in the course of human events, it becomes necessary for one people to dissolve the political bands which have connected them with another, and to assume among the powers of the earth, the separate and equal station to which the laws of nature and of nature's God entitle them, a decent respect to the opinions of mankind requires that they should declare the causes which impel them to the separation.

We hold these truths to be self-evident, that all men are created equal; that they are endowed by their Creator with certain unalienable rights; that among these, are life, liberty, and the pursuit of happiness. That to secure these rights, governments are instituted among men, deriving their just powers from the consent of the governed; that, whenever any form of government becomes destructive of these ends, it is the right of the people to alter or to abolish it, and to institute a new government, laying its foundation on such principles, and organizing its powers in such form, as to them shall seem most likely to effect their safety and happiness. Prudence, indeed, will dictate that governments long established, should not be changed for light and transient causes; and, accordingly, all experience hath shown, that mankind are more disposed to suffer, while evils are sufferable, than to right themselves by abolishing the forms to which they are accustomed. But, when a long train of abuses and usurpations, pursuing invariably the same object, evinces a design to reduce them under absolute despotism, it is their right, it is their duty, to throw off such government, and to provide new guards for their future security. Such has been the patient sufferance of these colonies, and such is now the necessity which constrains them to alter their former systems of government. The history of the present King of Great Britain is a history of repeated injuries and usurpations, all having, in direct object, the establishment of an absolute tyranny over these states. To prove this, let facts be submitted to a candid world:

He has refused his assent to laws the most wholesome and necessary for the public good.

He has forbidden his Governors to pass laws of immediate and pressing importance, unless suspended in their operation till his assent should be obtained; and when so suspended, he has utterly neglected to attend to them.

He has refused to pass other laws for the accommodation of large districts of people, unless those people would relinquish the right of representation in the legislature; a right inestimable to them, and formidable to tyrants only.

He has called together legislative bodies at places unusual, uncomfortable, and distant from the depository of their public records, for the sole purpose of fatiguing them into compliance with his measures.

He has dissolved representative houses repeatedly, for opposing, with manly firmness, his invasions on the rights of the people.

He has refused, for a long time after such dissolutions, to cause others to be elected; whereby the legislative powers, incapable of annihilation, have returned to the people at large for their exercise; the state remaining, in the mean time, exposed to all the danger of invasion from without, and convulsions within.

He has endeavored to prevent the population of these states; for that purpose, obstructing the laws for naturalization of foreigners; refusing to pass others to encourage their emigration hither, and raising the conditions of new appropriations of lands.

He has obstructed the administration of justice, by refusing his assent to laws for establishing judiciary powers.

He has made judges dependent on his will alone, for the tenure of their offices, and the amount and payment of their salaries.

He has erected a multitude of new offices, and sent hither swarms of officers to harass our people, and eat out their substance.

He has kept among us, in times of peace, standing armies, without the consent of our legislature.

He has affected to render the military independent of, and superior to, the civil power.

He has combined, with others, to subject us to a jurisdiction foreign to our constitution, and unacknowledged by our laws; giving his assent to their acts of pretended legislation:

For quartering large bodies of armed troops among us;

For protecting them, by a mock trial, from punishment, for any murders which they should commit on the inhabitants of these states;

For cutting off our trade with all parts of the world;

For imposing taxes on us without our consent;

For depriving us, in many cases, of the benefits of trial by jury.

For transporting us beyond seas to be tried for pretended offences.

For abolishing the free system of English laws in a neighboring province, establishing therein an arbitrary government, and enlarging its boundaries, so as to render it at once an example and fit instrument for introducing the same absolute rule into these colonies;

For taking away our charters, abolishing our most valuable laws, and altering, fundamentally, the powers of our governments;

For suspending our own legislatures, and declaring themselves invested with power to legislate for us in all cases whatsoever.

He has abdicated government here, by declaring us out of his protection, and waging war against us.

He has plundered our seas, ravaged our coasts, burnt our towns, and destroyed the lives of our people.

He is, at this time, transporting large armies of foreign mercenaries to complete the works of death, desolation, and tyranny, already begun, with circumstances of cruelty and perfidy scarcely paralleled in the most barbarous ages, and totally unworthy the head of a civilized nation.

He has constrained our fellow-citizens, taken captive on the high seas, to bear arms against their country, to become the executioners of their friends and brethren, or to fall themselves by their hands.

He has excited domestic insurrections amongst us, and has endeavored to bring on the inhabitants of our frontiers, the merciless Indian savages, whose known rule of warfare is an undistinguished destruction, of all ages, sexes, and conditions.

In every stage of these oppressions, we have petitioned for redress, in the most humble terms; our repeated petitions have been answered only by repeated injury. A prince, whose character is thus marked by every act which may define a tyrant, is unfit to be the ruler of a free people.

Nor have we been wanting in attention to our British brethren. We have warned them, from time to time, of attempts made by their legislature to extend an unwarrantable jurisdiction over us. We have reminded them of the circumstances of our emigration and settlement here. We have appealed to their native justice and magnanimity, and we have conjured them, by the ties of our common kindred, to disavow these usurpations, which would inevitably interrupt our connections and correspondence. They, too, have been deaf to the voice of justice and consanguinity. We must, therefore, acquiesce in the necessity, which denounces our separation, and hold them, as we hold the rest of mankind, enemies in war—in peace, friends.

We, therefore, the representatives of the UNITED STATES OF AMERICA, in GENERAL CONGRESS assembled, appealing to the Supreme Judge of the World for the rectitude of our intentions, do, in the name, and by the authority of the good people of these colonies, solemnly publish and declare, That these United Colonies are, and of right ought to be, FREE AND INDEPENDENT STATES; that they are absolved from all allegiance to the British crown, and that all political connection between them and the State of Great Britain, is, and ought to be, totally dissolved; and that, as *FREE AND INDEPENDENT STATES*, they have full power to levy war, conclude peace, contract alliances, establish commerce, and to do all other acts and things which INDEPENDENT STATES may of right do. And for the support of this Declaration, with a firm reliance on the protection of DIVINE PROVIDENCE, we mutually pledge to each other, our lives, our fortunes, and our sacred honor.

The foregoing Declaration was, by order of Congress, engrossed, and signed by the following members:

JOHN HANCOCK.

New Hampshire.

JOSIAH BARTLETT,
WILLIAM WHIPPLE,
MATTHEW THORNTON.

Massachusetts Bay.

SAMUEL ADAMS,
JOHN ADAMS,
ROBERT TREAT PAYNE,
ELBRIDGE GERRY.

Rhode Island.

STEPHEN HOPKINS,
WILLIAM ELLERY.

Connecticut.

ROGER SHERMAN,
SAMUEL HUNTINGTON,
WILLIAM WILLIAMS,
OLIVER WOLCOTT.

New York.

WILLIAM FLOYD,
PHILIP LIVINGSTON,
FRANCIS LEWIS,
LEWIS MORRIS.

New Jersey.

RICHARD STOCKTON,
JOHN WITHERSPOON,
FRANCIS HOPKINSON,
JOHN HART,
ABRAHAM CLARK.

Pennsylvania.

ROBERT MORRIS,
BENJAMIN RUSH,
BENJAMIN FRANKLIN,
JOHN MORTON,
GEORGE CLYMER,
JAMES SMITH,
GEORGE TAYLOR,
JAMES WILSON,
GEORGE ROSS.

Delaware.

CÆSAR RODNEY,
GEORGE READ,
THOMAS M'KEAN.

Maryland.

SAMUEL CHASE,
WILLIAM PACA,
THOMAS STONE,
CHARLES CARROLL, of Carrollton.

Virginia.

GEORGE WYTHE,
RICHARD HENRY LEE,
THOMAS JEFFERSON,
BENJAMIN HARRISON,
THOMAS NELSON, Jun.,
FRANCIS LIGHTFOOT LEE,
CARTER BRAXTON.

North Carolina.

WILLIAM HOOPER,
JOSEPH HEWES,
JOHN PENN.

South Carolina.

EDWARD RUTLEDGE,
THOMAS HEYWARD, Jun.,
THOMAS LYNCH, Jun.,
ARTHUR MIDDLETON.

Georgia.

BUTTON GWINNETT,
LYMAN HALL,
GEORGE WALTON.

CONSTITUTION

OF THE

UNITED STATES OF AMERICA.

We, the People of the United States, in order to form a more perfect Union, establish justice, insure domestic tranquility, provide for the common defence, promote the general welfare, and secure the blessings of liberty to ourselves and our posterity, do ordain and establish this Constitution for the United States of America.

ARTICLE 1.

SECTION 1. All the legislative powers herein granted shall be vested in a Congress of the United States, which shall consist of a Senate and House of Representatives.

SEC. 2. The House of Representatives shall be composed of members chosen every second year by the people of the several States, and the electors in each State shall have the qualifications requisite for electors of the most numerous branch of the State Legislature.

No person shall be a Representative who shall not have attained to the age of twenty-five years, and been seven years a citizen of the United States, and who shall not, when elected, be an inhabitant of that State in which he shall be chosen.

Representatives and direct taxes shall be apportioned among the several States which may be included within this Union, according to their respective numbers, which shall be determined by adding to the whole number of free persons, including those bound to service for a term of years, and excluding Indians not taxed, three-fifths of all other persons. The actual enumeration shall be made within three years after the first meeting of the Congress of the United States, and within every subsequent term of ten years, in such manner as they shall by law direct. The number of Representatives shall not exceed one for every thirty thousand, but each State shall have at least one Representative; and until such enumeration shall be made, the State of New

Hampshire shall be entitled to choose three, Massachusetts eight, Rhode Island and Providence Plantations one, Connecticut five, New York six, New Jersey four, Pennsylvania eight, Delaware one, Maryland six, Virginia ten, North Carolina five, South Carolina five, and Georgia three.

When vacancies happen in the representation from any State, the Executive authority thereof shall issue Writs of Election to fill such vacancies.

The House of Representatives shall choose their Speaker and other officers; and shall have the sole power of impeachment.

SEC. 3. The Senate of the United States shall be composed of two Senators from each State, chosen by the Legislature thereof, for six years; and each Senator shall have one vote.

Immediately after they shall be assembled in consequence of the first election, they shall be divided as equally as may be into three classes. The seats of the Senators of the first class shall be vacated at the expiration of the second year, of the second class at the expiration of the fourth year, and of the third class at the expiration of the sixth year, so that one-third may be chosen every second year; and if vacancies happen by resignation, or otherwise, during the recess of the Legislature of any State, the Executive thereof may make temporary appointments until the next meeting of the Legislature, which shall then fill such vacancies.

No person shall be a Senator who shall not have attained to the age of thirty years, and been nine years a citizen of the United States, and who shall not, when elected, be an inhabitant of that State for which he shall be chosen.

The Vice President of the United State shall be President of the Senate, but shall have no vote, unless they be equally divided.

The Senate shall choose their other officers, and also a President *pro tempore*, in the absence of the Vice President, or when he shall exercise the office of President of the United States.

The Senate shall have the sole power to try all impeachments. When sitting for that purpose, they shall be on oath or affirmation. When the President of the United States is tried, the Chief Justice shall preside; and no person shall be convicted without the concurrence of two-thirds of the members present.

Judgment in cases of impeachment shall not extend further than to removal from office, and disqualification to hold and enjoy any office of honor, trust or profit under the United States; but the party convicted shall nevertheless be liable and subject to indictment, trial, judgment and punishment, according to law.

SEC. 4. The times, places and manner of holding elections for Senators and Representatives, shall be prescribed in each State by the Legislature thereof; but the Congress may at any time by law make or alter such regulations, except as the places of choosing Senators.

The Congress shall assemble at least once in every year, and such meeting shall be on the first Monday in December, unless they shall by law appoint a different day.

Sec. 5. Each House shall be the judge of the elections, returns, and qualifications of its own members, and a majority of each shall constitute a quorum to do business; but a smaller number may adjourn from day to day, and may be authorized to compel the attendance of absent members, in such manner and under such penalties as each House may provide.

Each House may determine the Rules of its Proceedings, punish its members for disorderly behavior, and, with the concurrence of two-thirds, expel a member.

Each House shall keep a Journal of its Proceedings, and from time to time publish the same, excepting such parts as may in their judgment require secrecy; and the yeas and nays of the members of either House on any question shall, at the desire of one-fifth of those present, be entered on the journal.

Neither House, during the session of Congress, shall, without the consent of the other, adjourn for more than three days, nor to any other place than that in which the two Houses shall be sitting.

Sec. 6. The Senators and Representatives shall receive a compensation for their services, to be ascertained by law and paid out of the treasury of the United States. They shall in all cases, except treason, felony, and breach of the peace, be priviliged from arrest during their attendance at the session of their respective Houses, and in going to and returning from the same; and for any speech or debate in either House, they shall not be questioned in any other place.

No Senator or Representative shall, during the time for which he was elected, be appointed to any civil office under the authority of the United States, which shall have been created, or the emoluments whereof shall have been increased during such time; and no person holding any office under the United States shall be a member of either House during his continuance in office.

Sec. 7. All bills for raising revenue shall originate in the House of Representatives; but the Senate may propose or concur with amendments as on other bills.

Every bill which shall have passed the House of Representatives and the Senate, shall, before it becomes a law, be presented to the President of the United States: If he approve, he shall sign it; but if not, he shall return it, with his objections, to that House in which it shall have originated, who shall enter the objections at large on their Journal, and proceed to reconsider it. If, after such reconsideration, two-thirds of that House shall agree to pass the bill, it shall be sent, together with the objections, to the other House, by which it shall likewise be reconsidered, and if approved by two-thirds of that House, it shall become a law. But in all such cases the votes of both Houses shall be determined by yeas and nays, and the names of the persons voting for and against the bill shall be entered on the Journal of each House respectively. If any bill shall not be returned by the President within ten days (Sundays excepted) after it shall have been presented to him, the same shall be law, in like manner as if he had signed it, unless the Congress, by their adjournment, prevent its return, in which case it shall not be a law.

Every order, resolution, or vote to which the concurrence of the Senate and House of Representatives may be necessary (except on a question of adjournment) shall be presented to the President of the United States; and before the same shall take effect, shall be approved by him; or, being disapproved by him, shall be repassed by two-thirds of the Senate and House of Representatives, according to the rules and limitations prescribed in the case of a bill.

SEC. 8. The Congress shall have Power—

To lay and collect Taxes, Duties, Imposts and Excises, to pay the debts and provide for the common defence and general welfare of the United States; but all Duties, Imposts and Excises shall be uniform throughout the United States;

To borrow money on the credit of the United States;

To regulate commerce with foreign nations, and among the several States, and with the Indian tribes;

To establish an uniform rule of naturalization, and uniform laws on the subject of bankruptcies throughout the United States;

To coin money, regulate the value thereof and of foreign coin, and fix the standard of weights and measures;

To provide for the punishment of counterfeiting the securities and current coin of the United States;

To establish post offices and post roads;

To promote the progress of science and useful arts, by securing for limited times to authors and inventors the exclusive right to their respective writings and discoveries;

To constitute tribunals inferior to the Supreme Court;

To define and punish piracies and felonies committed on the high seas, and offences against the law of nations;

To declare war, grant letters of marque and reprisal, and make rules concerning captures on land and water;

To raise and support armies, but no appropriation of money to that use shall be for a longer term than two years;

To provide and maintain a navy;

To make rules for the government and regulation of the land and naval forces;

To provide for calling forth the militia to execute the laws of the Union, suppress insurrections and repel invasions;

To provide for organizing, arming, and disciplining the militia, and for governing such part of them as may be employed in the service of the United States, reserving to the States respectively the appointment of the officers, and the authority of training he militia according to the discipline prescribed by Congress;

To exercise exclusive legislation, in all cases whatsoever, over such district (not exceeding ten miles square) as may, by cession of particular States, and the acceptance of Congress, become the Seat of the Government of the United States, and to exercise like authority over all places purchased by the consent of the Legislature of the State in which the same shall be, for the erection of forts, magazines, arsenals, dock yards, and other needful buildings; and

To make all laws which shall be necessary and proper for carrying into execution the foregoing powers, and all other Powers vested by this Constitution in the Government of the United States, or in any department or officer thereof.

SEC. 9. The migration or importation of such persons as any of the States now existing shall think proper to admit, shall not be prohibited by the Congress prior to the year one thousand eight hundred and eight, but a tax or duty may be imposed on such importation, not exceeding ten dollars for each person.

The privilege of the Writ of Habeas Corpus shall not be suspended, unless when, in cases of rebellion or invasion, the public safety may require it.

No bill of attainder or ex post facto law shall be passed.

No capitation, or other direct, tax shall be laid, unless in proportion to the census or enumeration hereinbefore directed to be taken.

No tax or duty shall be laid on articles exported from any State.

No preference shall be given by any regulation of commerce or revenue to the ports of one State over those of another; nor shall vessels bound to or from one State, be obliged to enter, clear, or pay duties in another.

No money shall be drawn from the treasury but in consequence of appropriations made by law; and a regular statement and account of the receipts and expenditures of all public money shall be published from time to time.

No title of nobility shall be granted by the United States: And no person holding any office of profit or trust under them shall, without the consent of the Congress, accept of any present, emolument, office, or title, of any kind whatever, from any king, prince, or foreign State.

Sec. 10. No State shall enter into any treaty, alliance, or confederation; grant letters of marque or reprisal; coin money; emit bills of credit; make anything but gold and silver coin a tender in payment of debts; pass any bill of attainder, ex post facto law, or law impairing the obligation of contracts, or grant any title of nobility.

No State shall, without the consent of the Congress, lay any imposts or duties on imports or exports, except what may be absolutely necessary for executing its inspection laws; and the net produce of all duties and imposts, laid by any State on imports or exports, shall be for the use of the treasury of the United States; and all such laws shall be subject to the revision and control of the Congress.

No State shall, without the consent of Congress, lay any duty of tonnage, keep troops, or ships of war in time of peace, enter into any agreement or compact with another State, or with a foreign power, or engage in war, unless actually invaded, or in such imminent danger as will not admit of delay.

ARTICLE II.

Section 1. The Executive Power shall be vested in a President of the United States of America. He shall hold his office during the term of four years, and, together with the Vice President, chosen for the same term, be elected as follows:

Each State shall appoint, in such manner as the Legislature thereof may direct, a number of electors, equal to the number of Senators and Representatives to which the State may be entitled in the Congress; but no Senator or Representative, or person holding an office of trust or profit under the United States, shall be appointed an elector.

[The electors shall meet in their respective States, and vote by ballot for two persons, of one at least shall not be an inhabitant of the same State with themselves. And they shall make a list of all the persons voted for, and of the number of votes for each; which list they shall sign and certify, and transmit sealed to the seat of the Government of the United States, directed to the President of the Senate. The President of the Senate shall, in the presence of the Senate and House of Representatives, open all the certificates, and the votes shall then be counted. The person having the greatest number of votes shall be the President, if such number be a majority of the whole number of electors appointed; and if there be more than one who have such majority, and have an equal number of votes, then the House of Representatives shall immediately choose by ballot one of them for President; and if no person have a majority, then from the five highest on the list the said House shall in like manner choose the President. But in choosing the President, the votes shall be taken by States, the representation from each State having one vote. A quorum for this purpose shall consist of a member or members from two-thirds of the States, and a majority of all the States shall be necessary to a choice. In every case, after the choice of the President, the person having the greatest number of votes of the electors shall be the Vice President. But if there should remain two or more who have equal votes, the Senate shall choose from them by ballot the Vice President.*]

The Congress may determine the time of choosing the electors, and the day on which they shall give their votes; which day shall be the same throughout the United States.

No person except a natural born citizen, or a citizen of the United States, at the time of the adoption of this Constitution, shall be eligible to the office of President; neither shall any person be eligible to that office who shall not have attained to the age of thirty-five years, and been fourteen years a resident within the United States.

In case of the removal of the President from office, or of his death, resignation, or inability to discharge the powers and duties of the said office, the same shall devolve on the Vice President, and the Congress may by law provide for the case of removal, death, resignation, or inability, both of the President and Vice President, declaring what officer shall then act as President, and such officer shall act accordingly, until the disability be removed, or a President shall be elected.

The President shall, at stated times, receive for his services a compensation, which shall neither be increased nor diminished during the period for which he shall have been elected, and he shall not receive within that period any other emolument from the United States, or any of them.

Before he enter on the execution of his office, he shall take the following oath or affirmation:

"I do solemnly swear (or affirm) that I will faithfully execute the office of President of the United States, and will, to the best of my ability, preserve, protect and defend the Constitution of the United States."

SEC. 2. The President shall be Commander-in-Chief of the Army and Navy of the United States, and of the militia of the several States, when called into the actual service of the United States; he may require the opinion, in writing, of the principal

---

*This clause has been superceded and annuled by the 12th amendment.

officer in each of the Executive Departments, upon any subject relating to the duties of their respective offices; and he shall have power to grant reprieves and pardons for offences against the United States, except in cases of impeachment.

He shall have power, by and with the advice and consent of the Senate, to make treaties, provided two-thirds of the Senate present concur; and he shall nominate, and by and with the advice and consent of the Senate, shall appoint Ambassadors, other public Ministers and Consuls, Judges of the Supreme Court, and all other officers of the United States, whose appointments are not herein otherwise provided for, and which shall be established by law; but the Congress may by law vest the appointment of such inferior officers as they think proper in the President alone, in the Courts of Law, or in the Heads of Departments.

The President shall have power to fill up all vacancies that may happen during the recess of the Senate, by granting commissions, which shall expire at the end of their next session.

Sec. 3. He shall from time to time give to the Congress information of the state of the Union, and recommend to their consideration such measures as he shall judge necessary and expedient; he may, on extraordinary occasions, convene both Houses, or either of them; and in case of disagreement between them, with respect to the time of adjournment, he may adjourn them to such time as he shall think proper; he shall receive Ambassadors and other public Ministers; he shall take care that the laws be faithfully executed, and shall commission all the officers of the United States.

Sec. 4. The President, Vice President, and all Civil Officers of the United States, shall be removed from office on impeachment for, and conviction of, Treason, Bribery, or other high Crimes and Misdemeanors.

ARTICLE III.

Section 1. The judicial power of the United States shall be vested in one Supreme Court, and in such inferior Courts as the Congress may from time to time ordain and establish. The Judges, both of the Supreme and inferior Courts, shall hold their offices during good behavior, and shall, at stated times, receive for their services a compensation, which shall not be diminished during their continuance in office.

Sec. 2. The judicial power shall extend to all cases, in Law and Equity, arising under this Constitution, the Laws of the United States, and Treaties made, or which shall be made, under their authority; to all cases affecting Ambassadors, other public Ministers, and Consuls; to all cases of admirality and maritime jurisdiction; to controversies to which the United States shall be a party; to controversies between two or more States; between a State and citizens of another State; between citizens of different States; between citizens of the same State claiming lands under grants of different States, and between a State, or the citizens thereof, and foreign States, citizens or subjects.

In all cases affecting Ambassadors, other public Ministers and Consuls, and those in which a State shall be a party, the Supreme Court shall have original jurisdiction. In all the other cases before mentioned, the Supreme Court shall have appellate jurisdiction, both as to law and fact, with such exceptions and under such regulations as the Congress shall make.

The trial of all crimes, except in cases of Impeachment, shall be by jury; and such trial shall be held in the State where the said crimes shall have been committed; but when not committed within any State, the trial shall be at such place or places as the Congress may by law have directed.

SEC. 3. Treason against the United States shall consist only in levying war against them, or adhering to their enemies, giving them aid and comfort. No person shall be convicted of treason unless on the testimony of two witnesses to the same overt act, or on confession in open Court.

The Congress shall have power to declare the punishment of treason, but, no Attainder of Treason, shall work corruption of blood, or forfeiture, except during the life of the person attainted.

ARTICLE IV.

SECTION 1. Full faith and credit shall be given in each State to the public acts, records, and judicial proceedings of every other State. And the Congress may by general laws prescribe the manner in which such acts, records, and proceedings shall be proved, and the effect thereof.

SEC. 2. The citizens of each State shall be entitled to all privileges and immunities of citizens in the several States.

A person charged in any State with treason, felony, or other crime, who shall flee from justice, and be found in another State, shall, on demand of the executive authority of the State from which he fled, be delivered up, to be removed to the State having jurisdiction of the crime.

No person held to service or labor in one State, under the laws thereof, escaping into another, shall, in consequence of any law or regulation therein, be discharged from such service or labor, but shall be delivered up on claim of the party to whom such service or labor may be due.

SEC. 3. New States may be admitted by the Congress into this Union; but no new State shall be formed or erected within the jurisdiction of any other State; nor any State be formed by the junction of two or more States, or parts of States, without the consent of the Legislatures of the States concerned, as well as of the Congress.

The Congress shall have power to dispose of and make all needful rules and regulations respecting the territory or other property belonging to the United States; and nothing in this Constitution shall be so construed as to prejudice any claims of the United States, or any particular State.

SEC. 4. The United States shall guarantee to every State in this Union a republican form of Government, and shall protect each of them against invasion; and on application of the Legislature, or of the Executive (when the Legislature can not be convened,) against domestic violence.

ARTICLE V.

The Congress, whenever two-thirds of both House shall deem it necessary, shall propose amendments to the Constitution, or, on the application of the Legislatures of two-thirds of the several States, shall call a Convention for proposing amendments, which, in either case, shall be valid to all intents and purposes. as part of this Constitution, when ratified by the Legislatures of three-fourths of the several States, or by Conventions in three-fourths thereof, as the one or the other mode of ratification may be proposed by the Congress; *Provided*, that no amendment which may be made prior to the year one thousand eight hundred and eight shall in any manner affect the first and fourth clauses in the ninth section of the first article; and that no State, without its consent, shall be deprived of its equal suffrage in the Senate.

ARTICLE VI.

All debts contracted and engagements entered into before the adoption of this Constitution, shall be as valid against the United States, under this Constitution, as under the Confederation.

This Constitution and the laws of the United States which shall be made in pursuance thereof; and all Treaties made, or which shall be made, under the authority of the United States, shall be the supreme law of the land; and the Judges in every State shall be bound thereby, any thing in the Constitution or laws of any State to the contrary notwithstanding.

The Senators and Representatives before mentioned, and the members of the several State Legislatures, and all executive and judicial officers, both of the United States and of the several States, shall be bound by oath or affirmation to support this Constitution; but no religious test shall ever be required as a qualification to any office or public trust under the United States.

ARTICLE VII.

The ratification of the Conventions of nine States shall be sufficient for the establishment of this Constitution between the States so ratifying the same.

DONE in Convention, by the unanimous consent of the States present, the seventeenth day of September, in the year of our Lord one thousand seven hundred and eighty-seven, and of the Independence of the United States of America the twelfth. In Witness whereof, we have hereunto subscribed our names.

GEO. WASHINGTON,
Pres't and Deputy from Virginia.

New Hampshire.
JOHN LANGDON, NICHOLAS GILMAN.

Massachusetts.
NATHANIEL GORHAM, RUFUS KING.

Connecticut.
WM. SAML. JOHNSON, ROGER SHERMAN.

New York.
ALEXANDER HAMILTON.

New Jersey.
WIL. LIVINGSTON, DAVID BREARLEY,
WM. PATERSON, JONA. DAYTON.

Pennsylvania.
B. FRANKLIN, THOMAS MIFFLIN,
ROBT. MORRIS, GEO. CLYMER,
THO. FITZSIMONS, JARED INGERSOLL,
JAMES WILSON, GOUV. MORRIS.

Delaware.
GEO. READ, GUNNING BEDFORD, JUN'R,
JOHN DICKINSON, RICHARD BASSETT.
JACO. BROOM,

Maryland.
JAMES M'HENRY, DAN. OF ST. THOS. JENIFER.
DANL. CARROLL,

Virginia.
JOHN BLAIR, JAMES MADISON, JR.

North Carolina.
WM. BLOUNT, RICH'D DOBBS SPAIGHT.
HU. WILLIAMSON.

South Carolina.
J. RUTLEDGE, CHARLES COTESWORTH PINCKNEY,
CHARLES PINCKNEY, PIERCE BUTLER.

Georgia.
WILLIAM FEW, ABR. BALDWIN.
  Attest: WILLIAM JACKSON, *Secretary.*

ARTICLES,

In addition to, and amendment of, the Constitution of the United States of America, proposed by Congress, and ratified by the Legislatures of the several States, pursuant to the fifth article of the original Constitution.

ARTICLE I.

Congress shall make no law respecting an establishment of religion, or prohibiting the free exercise thereof; or abridging the freedom of speech or of the press; or the right of the people peaceably to assemble, and to petition the Government for a redress of grievances.

ARTICLE II.

A well-regulated Militia being necessary to the security of a free State, the right of the people to keep and bear arms shall not be infringed.

ARTICLE III.

No soldier shall, in time of peace, be quartered in any house, without the consent of the owner, nor in time of war, but in a manner to be prescribed by law.

ARTICLE IV.

The right of the people to be secure in their persons, houses, papers, and effects, against unreasonable searches and seizures, shall not be violated, and no warrant shall issue but upon probable cause, supported by oath or affirmation, and particularly describing the place to be searched, and the persons or things to be seized.

ARTICLE V.

No person shall be held to answer for a capital, or otherwise infamous crime, unless on a presentment or indictment of a Grand Jury, except in cases arising in the land or naval forces, or in the militia, when in actual service in time of war or public danger; nor shall any person be subject for the same offence to be twice put in jeopardy of life or limb; nor shall be compelled in any criminal case to be a witness against himself, nor be deprived of life, liberty, or property, without due process of law; nor shall private property be taken for public use without just compensation.

ARTICLE VI.

In all criminal prosecutions, the accused shall enjoy the right to a speedy and public trial, by an impartial jury of the State and district wherein the crime shall have been committed, which district shall have been previously ascertained by law and to be informed of the nature and cause of the accusation to be confronted with the witnesses against him; to have compulsory process for obtaining witnesses in his favor, and to have the assistance of counsel for his defence.

ARTICLE VII.

In suits at common law, where the value in controversy shall exceed twenty dollars, the right of trial by jury shall be preserved, and no fact tried by a jury shall be otherwise re-examined in any Court of the United States, than according to the rules of the common law.

ARTICLE VIII.

Excessive bail shall not be required, nor excessive fines imposed, nor cruel and unusual punishments inflicted.

ARTICLE IX.

The enumeration in the Constitution of certain rights, shall not be construed to deny or disparage others retained by the people.

ARTICLE X.

The powers not delegated to the United States by the Constitution, nor prohibited by it to the States, are reserved to the States respectively, or to the people.

ARTICLE XI.

The judicial power of the United States shall not be construed to extend to any suit in law or equity, commenced or prosecuted against one of the United States by citizens of another State, or by citizens or subjects of any foreign State.

ARTICLE XII.

The Electors shall meet in their respective States, and vote by ballot for President and Vice-President, one of whom, at least, shall not be an inhabitant of the same State with themselves; they shall name in their ballot the person voted for as President, and in distinct ballots the person voted for as Vice-President, and they shall make distinct lists of all persons voted for as President, and all persons voted for as Vice President, and of the number of votes for each, which lists they shall sign and certify, and transmit sealed to the seat of government of the United States, directed to the President of the Senate:—The President of the Senate shall, in presence of the Senate and House of Representatives, open all the certificates, and the votes shall then be counted; The person having the greatest number of votes for President, shall be the President, if such number be a majority of the whole number of Electors appointed; and if no person have such majority, then from the persons having the highest numbers, not exceeding three, on the list of those voted for as President, the House of Representatives shall choose immediately by ballot the President. But in choosing the President, the votes shall be taken by States, the representation from each State having one; a quorum for this purpose shall consist of a member or members from two-thirds of the States, and a majority of all the States shall be necessary to a choice. And if the House of Representatives shall not choose a President whenever the right of choice shall devolve upon them, before the fourth day of March next following, then the Vice-President shall act as President, as in the case of the death or other constitutional disability of the President. The person having the greatest number of votes as Vice-President, shall be the Vice-President, if such number be a majority of the whole number of Electors appointed; and if no person have a majority, then, from the two highest numbers on the list, the Senate shall choose the Vice-President; a quorum for the purpose shall consist of two-thirds of the whole number of Senators, and a majority of the whole number shall be necessary to a choice. But no person constitutionally ineligible to the office of President, shall be eligible to that of Vice-President of the United States.

The Constitution was adopted on the 17th of September, 1787, by the Convention appointed in pursuance of the Resolution of the Congress of the Confederation, of the 21st February, 1787, and ratified by the Conventions of the several States, as follows:

By Convention of	Delaware	7th December, 1787
"	" Pennsylvania	12th December, 1787
"	" New Jersey	18th December, 1787
"	" Georgia	2d January, 1788
"	" Connecticut	9th January, 1788
"	" Massachusetts	6th February, 1788
"	" Maryland	28th April, 1788
"	" South Carolina	23d May, 1788
"	" New Hampshire	21st June, 1788
"	" Virginia	26th June, 1788
"	" New York	26th July, 1788
"	" North Carolina	21st November, 1789
"	" Rhode Island	29th May, 1790

The first ten of the Amendments were proposed on the 25th September, 1789, and ratified by the constitutional number of States on the 15th December, 1791; the eleventh, on the 8th January, 1798; and the twelfth, on the 25th September, 1804.

WASHINGTON'S ADDRESSES.

There were not many occasions during his public career that Washington was called upon to exercise his abilities as a writer or an orator; but when such occasion did occur, he always acquitted himself with a degree of perspicuity and modesty which may be said to have been characteristic of himself alone. The addresses which follow mark, as it were, four distinct epochs in the history of this unexampled man:—the first, when he accepted the command of the armies by which our national independence was achieved; the second, when he surrendered his commission, after having driven the foes of freedom from his beloved country; the third, when he assumed the responsible duties of president, in which office his high qualities for civil government were as conspicuous as had been his military talents in the field; and fourth, when he resigned his great trust, and took leave of the people in his imperishable "Farewell Address," an inestimable legacy, which can not be too frequently conned by every American who values his birthright.

WASHINGTON'S ELECTION AS COMMANDER-IN-CHIEF.

On the 15th of June, 1775, Washington was unanimously elected by Congress to "command all the Continental forces raised, or to be raised, for the defence of American liberty," and when he appeared in his place the next day, the President of that body acquainted him with his election, in a well-timed address, "and requested that he should accept of that employment;" to which Washington replied as follows:

"Mr. President: Though I am truly sensible of the high honor done me, in this appointment, yet I feel great distress, from consciousness that my abilities and military experience may not be equal to the extensive and important trust: However, as the Congress desire it, I will enter upon the momentous duty, and exert every power I possess in their service, and for support of the glorious cause. I beg they will accept my most cordial thanks for this distinguished testimony of their approbation.

"But, lest some unlucky event should happen, unfavorable to

my reputation, I beg it may be remembered, by every gentleman in the room, that I, this day, declare, with the utmost sincerity, I do not think myself equal to the command I am honored with.

"As to pay, sir, I beg leave to assure the Congress, that, as no pecuniary consideration could have tempted me to accept this arduous employment, at the expense of my domestic ease and happiness, I do not wish to make any profit from it. I will keep an exact account of my expenses. Those, I doubt not they will discharge, and that is all I desire."

WASHINGTON'S RESIGNATION OF HIS COMMISSION.

The War of the Revolution having terminated auspiciously, Washington took leave of his officers and army at New York, and repaired to Annapolis, Md., where Congress was then in session. On the 20th of December, 1783, he transmitted a letter to that body, apprising them of his arrival, with the intention of resigning his commission, and desiring to know whether it would be most agreeable to receive it in writing or at an audience. It was immediately resolved that a public entertainment be given him on the 22d, and that he be admitted to an audience on the 23d, at 12 o'clock. Accordingly he attended at that time, and, being seated, the President informed him that Congress were prepared to receive his communications. Whereupon he arose, and spoke as follows:

"MR. PRESIDENT: The great events on which my resignation depended having at length taken place, I have now the honor of offering my sincere congratulations to Congress, and of presenting myself before them, to surrender into their hands the trust committed to me, and to claim the indulgence of retiring from the service of my country.

"Happy in the confirmation of our independence and sovereignty, and pleased with the opportunity afforded the United States of becoming a respectable nation, I resign with satisfaction the appointment I accepted with diffidence: a diffidence in my abilities to accomplish so arduous a task; which however was superseded by a confidence in the rectitude of our cause, the support of the supreme power of the Union, and the patronage of Heaven.

"The successful termination of the war has verified the most sanguine expectations; and my gratitude for the interposition of Providence, and the assistance I have received from my countrymen, increases with every review of the momentous contest.

"While I repeat my obligations to the army in general, I

should do injustice to my own feelings not to acknowledge, in this place, the peculiar services and distinguished merits of the gentlemen who have been attached to my person during the war. It was impossible the choice of confidential officers to compose my family should have been more fortunate. Permit me, sir, to recommend, in particular, those who have continued in the service to the present moment, as worthy of the favorable notice and patronage of Congress.

"I consider it an indispensable duty to close this last act of my official life by commending the interests of our dearest country to the protection of Almighty God, and those who have the superintendence of them to his holy keeping.

"Having now finished the work assigned me, I retire from the great theatre of action, and bidding an affectionate farewell to this august body, under whose orders I have so long acted, I here offer my commission, and take my leave of all the employments of public life."

WASHINGTON'S INAUGURAL ADDRESS.

In accordance with previous arrangements, General Washington met Congress in New York on the 30th of April, 1789, for the purpose of being inaugurated as the first President of the United States. The oath of office having been administered by the Chancellor of the State of New York, in presence of the Senate and House of Representatives, the President delivered the following Inaugural Address:

"*Fellow-Citizens of the Senate, and of the House of Representatives:*

"Among the vicissitudes incident to life, no event could have filled me with greater anxieties than that of which the notification was transmitted by your order, and received on the 14th day of the present month. On the one hand, I was summoned by my country, whose voice I can never hear but with veneration and love, from a retreat which I had chosen with the fondest predilection, and, in my flattering hopes, with an immutable decision, as the asylum of my declining years; a retreat which was rendered every day more necessary, as well as more dear to me, by the addition of habit to inclination, and of frequent interruptions in my health, to the gradual waste committed on it by time. On the other hand, the magnitude and difficulty of the trust to which the voice of my country called me, being sufficient to awaken in the wisest and most experienced of her citizens a distrustful scrutiny into his qualifications, could not but overwhelm with despondency one, who, inheriting inferior endowments from nature, and unpracticed in the duties of civil administration, ought to be peculiarly conscious of his own deficiencies. In this conflict of emotions, all I dare aver, is, that it has been my faithful study to collect my duty from a just appreciation of every circumstance by which it might be affected. All I dare hope, is, that if, in executing this task, I have been too much swayed by a grateful remembrance of former instances, or by an affectionate sensibility to this transcendent proof of the confidence of my fellow-citizens, and have thence too little consulted my incapacity as well as disinclination for the weighty and untried cares before me; my error will be palliated by the motives which misled me, and its consequences be judged by my country, with some share of the partiality in which they originated.

"Such being the impressions under which I have, in obedience to the public summons, repaired to the present station, it would be peculiarly improper to omit, in this first official act, my fervent supplications to that Almighty Being who rules over the universe—who presides in the councils of nations—and whose providential aids can supply every human defect, that his benediction may consecrate to the liberties and happiness of the people of the United States, a government instituted by themselves for these essential purposes; and may enable every instrument employed in its administration to execute with success the functions allotted to his charge. In tendering this homage to the Great Author of every public and private good, I assure myself that it expresses your sentiments not less than my own; nor those of my fellow-citizens at large, less than either. No people can be bound to acknowledge and adore the invisible hand which conducts the affairs of men, more than the people of the United States. Every step by which they have advanced to the character of an independent nation, seems to have been distinguished by some token of providential agency; and in the important revolution just accomplished in the system their united government, the tranquil deliberations, and voluntary consent of so many distinct communities, from which the event has resulted, can not be compared with the means by which most governments have been established, without some return of pious gratitude, along with an humble anticipation of the future blessings which the past seem to presage. These reflections, arising out of the present crisis, have forced themselves too strongly on my mind to be suppressed. You will join with me, I trust, in thinking that there are none, under the influence of which the proceedings of a new and free government can more auspiciously commence.

"By the article establishing the executive department, it is made the duty of the President 'to recommend to your consideration such measures as he shall judge necessary and expedient.' The circumstances under which I now meet you will acquit me from not entering into that subject, farther than to refer to the great constitutional charter under which you are assembled; and which, in defining your powers, designates the objects to which your attention is to be given. It will be more consistent with those circumstances, and far more congenial with the feelings which actuate me, to substitute, in place of a recommendation of particular measures, the tribute that is due to the talents, the rectitude, and the patriotism, which adorn the characters selected to devise and adopt them. In these honorable qualifications I behold the surest pledges that, as on one side, no local prejudices or attachments, no separate views, nor party animosities, will misdirect the comprehensive and equal eye which ought to watch over this great assemblage of communities and interests; so, on another, that the foundations of our national policy will be laid in the pure and immutable principles of private morality; and the pre-eminence of free government be exemplified by all the attributes which can win the affections of its citizens, and command the respect of the world. I dwell on this prospect with every satisfaction which an ardent love for my country can inspire: since there is no truth more thoroughly established, than that there exists in the economy and course of nature an indissoluble union between virtue and happiness—between duty and advantage—between the genuine maxims of an honest and magnanimous policy, and the solid rewards of public prosperity and felicity; since we ought to be no less persuaded that the propitious smiles of Heaven can never be expected on a nation that disregards the eternal rules of order and right, which Heaven itself has ordained; and since the preservation of the sacred fire of liberty, and the destiny of the republican model of government, are justly considered as deeply, perhaps as finally, staked on the experiment entrusted to the hands of the American people.

"Besides the ordinary objects submitted to your care, it will remain with your judgment to decide, how far an exercise of the occasional power delegated by the fifth article of the Constitution is rendered expedient at the present juncture, by the nature of objections which have been urged against the system, or by the degree of inquietude which has given birth to them. Instead of undertaking particular recommendations on this subject, in which I could be guided by no lights derived from official opportunities, I shall again give way to my entire confidence in your discernment and pursuit of the public good; for, I assure myself, that whilst you carefully avoid every alteration which might endanger the benefits of an united and effective government, or which ought to await the future lessons of experience, a reverence for the characteristic rights of freemen, and a regard for the public harmony, will sufficiently influence your deliberations on the question, how far the former can be more impregnably fortified, or the latter be safely and advantageously promoted.

"To the preceding observations I have one to add, which will be most properly addressed to the House of Representatives. It concerns myself, and will, therefore, be as brief as possible. When I was first honored with a call into the service of my country, then on the eve of an arduous struggle for its liberties, the light in which I contemplated my duty required that I should renounce every pecuniary compensation. From this resolution I have in no instance departed; and being still under the impressions which produced it, I must decline, as inapplicable to myself, any share in the personal emoluments which may be indispensably included in a permanent provision for the executive department; and must accordingly pray that the pecuniary estimates for the station in which I am placed, may, during my continuance in it, be limited to such actual expenditures as the public good may be thought to require.

"Having thus imparted to you my sentiments, as they have been awakened by the occasion which brings us together, I shall take my present leave; but not without resorting once more to the benign Parent of the human race, in humble supplication, that, since he has been pleased to favor the American people with opportunities for deliberating in perfect tranquility, and dispositions for deciding, with unparalleled unanimity, on a form of government for the security of their Union, and the advancement of their happiness, so his Divine blessing may be equally conspicuous in the enlarged views, the temperate consultations, and the wise measures, on which the success of this government must depend.

WASHINGTON'S FAREWELL ADDRESS.

Friends and Fellow-Citizens:

The period for a new election of a citizen to administer the Executive Government of the United States being not far distant, and the time actually arrived when your thoughts must be employed in designating the person who is to be clothed with that important trust, it appears to me proper, especially as it may conduce to a more distinct expression of the public voice, that I should now apprise you of the resolution I have formed, to decline being considered among the number of those out of whom a choice is to be made.

I beg you, at the same time, to do me the justice to be assured that this resolution has not been taken without a strict regard to all the considerations appertaining to the relation which binds a dutiful citizen to his country; and that, in withdrawing the tender of service, which silence, in my situation might imply, I am influenced by no diminution of zeal for your future interest; no deficiency of grateful respect for your past kindness; but am supported by a full conviction that the step is compatible with both.

The acceptance of, and continuance hitherto in, the office to which your suffrages have twice called me, have been a uniform sacrifice of inclination to the opinion of duty, and to a deference for what appeared to be your desire. I constantly hoped that it would have been much earlier in my power, consistently with motives which I was not at liberty to disregard, to return to that retirement from which I had been reluctantly drawn. The strength of my inclination to do this, previous to the last election, had even led to the preparation of an address to declare it to you; but mature reflection on the then perplexed and critical posture of our affairs with foreign nations, and the unanimous advice of persons entitled to my confidence, impelled me to abandon the idea.

I rejoice that the state of your concerns, external as well as internal, no longer renders the pursuit of inclination incompatible with the sentiment of duty or propriety; and am persuaded, whatever partiality may be retained for my services, that, in the present circumstances of our country, you will not disapprove my determination to retire.

The impressions with which I undertook the arduous trust were explained on the proper occasion. In the discharge of this trust, I will only say, that I have with good intentions contributed towards the organization and administration of the Government the best exertions of which a very fallible judgment was capable. Not unconscious in the outset of the inferiority of my qualifications, experience, in my own eyes—perhaps still more in the eyes of others—has strengthened the motives to diffidence of myself; and every day the increasing weight of years admonishes me, more and more, that the shade of retirement is as necessary to me as it will be welcome. Satisfied that if any circumstances have given peculiar value to my services, they were temporary, I have the consolation to believe that, while choice and prudence invite me to quit the political scene, patriotism does not forbid it.

In looking forward to the moment which is intended to terminate the career of my public life, my feelings do not permit me to suspend the deep acknowledgment of that debt of gratitude which I owe to my beloved country for the many honors it has conferred upon me; still more for the steadfast confidence with which it has supported me; and for the opportunities I have thence enjoyed of manifesting my inviolable attachment, by services faithful and persevering, though in usefulness unequal to my zeal. If benefits have resulted to our country from these services, let it always be remembered to your praise, and as an instructive example in our annals that, under circumstances in which the passions, agitated in every direction, were liable to mislead; amidst appearances sometimes dubious, vicissitudes of fortune often discouraging; in situations in which, not unfrequently, want of success has countenanced the spirit of criticism—the constancy of your support was the essential prop of the efforts, and a guarantee of the plans, by which they were effected. Profoundly penetrated with this idea, I shall carry it with me to my grave, as a strong incitement to unceasing vows, that Heaven may continue to you the choicest tokens of its beneficence; that your union and brotherly affection may be perpetual; that the free Constitution, which is the work of your hands, may be sacredly maintained; that its administration, in every department, may be stamped with wisdom and virtue; that, in fine, the happiness of the people of these States, under the auspices of liberty, may be made complete, by so careful a preservation and so prudent a use of this blessing as will acquire to them the glory of recommending it to the applause, the affection, and the adoption of every nation which is yet a stranger to it.

Here, perhaps, I ought to stop; but a solicitude for your welfare, which can not end but with my life, and the apprehension of danger natural to that solicitude, urge me, on an occasion like the present, to offer to your solemn contemplation, and to recommend to your frequent review, some sentiments which are the result of much reflection, of no inconsiderable observation, and which appear to me all-important to the permenancy of our felicity as a people. These will be afforded to you with the more freedom, as you can only see in them the disinterested warnings of a parting friend, who can possibly have no personal motive to bias his counsel; nor can I forget, as an encouragement to it, your indulgent reception of my sentiments or a former and not dissimilar occasion.

Interwoven as is the love of liberty with every ligament of of your hearts, no recommendation of mine is necessary to fortify or confirm the attachment.

The unity of government, which constitutes you one people, is also now dear to you. It is justly so; for it is a main pillar in the edifice of your real independence—the support of your tranquility at home, your peace abroad, of your safety, of your prosperity, of that very liberty which you so highly prize. But as it is easy to foresee that, from different causes and from different quarters, much pains will be taken, many artifices employed, to weaken in your minds the conviction of this truth; as this is the point in your political fortress against which the batteries of internal and external enemies will be most constantly and actively (though often covertly and insidiously) directed—it is of infinite moment that you should properly estimate the immense value of your National Union to your collective and individual happiness; that you should cherish a cordial, habitual and immoval attachment to it; accustoming yourselves to think and speak of it as of the palladium of your political safety and prosperity; watching for its preservation with jealous anxiety; discountenancing whatever may suggest even a suspicion that it can, in any event, be abandoned; and indignantly frowning upon the first dawning of every attempt to alienate any portion of our country from the rest, or to enfeeble the sacred ties which now link together the various parts.

For this you have every inducement of sympathy and interest Citizens by birth or choice, of a common country, that country has a right to concentrate your affections. The name of *American*, which belongs to you in your national capacity, must always exalt the just pride of patriotism, more than any appellation derived from local discriminations. With slight shades of difference, you have the same religion, manners, habits, and political principles. You have, in a common cause, fought and triumphed together; the independence and liberty you possess are the work of joint counsels and joint efforts—of common dangers, sufferings and successes.

But these considerations, however powerfully they address themselves to your sensibility, are greatly outweighed by those which apply more immediately to your interest; here every portion of our country finds the most commanding motives for carefully guarding and preserving the union of the whole.

The North, in an unrestrained intercourse with the South, protected by the equal laws of a common government, finds, in the productions of the latter, great additional resources of maritime and commercial enterprise, and prescious materials of manufacturing industry. The South, in the same intercourse, benefiting by the agency of the North, sees its agriculture grow and its commerce expand. Turning partly into its own channels the seamen of the North, it finds its particular navigation invigorated; and while it contributes, in different ways, to nourish and increase the general mass of the national navigation, it looks forward to the protection of a maritime strength to which itself is unequally adapted. The East, in like intercourse with the West, already finds, and in the progressive improvement of interior communication, by land and water, will more and more find, a valuable vent for the commodities which it brings from abroad, or manufactures at home. The West derives from the East supplies requisite to its growth and comfort; and what is perhaps of still greater consequence, it must, of necessity, owe the secure enjoyment of indispensable outlets for its own productions, to the weight, influence, and the future maritime strength of the Atlantic side of the Union, directed by an indissoluble community of interest as one nation. Any other tenure by which the West can hold this essential advantage, whether derived from its own separate strength, or from an apostate and unnatural connection with any foreign power, must be intrinsically precarious.

While, then, every part of our country thus feels an immediate and particular interest in UNION, all the parts combined can not fail to find, in the united mass of means and efforts, greater strength, greater resource, proportionately greater security from external danger, a less frequent interruption of their peace by foreign nations; and what is of inestimable value, they must derive from union an exemption from those broils and wars between themselves, which so frequently afflict neighboring countries, not tied together by the same government; which their own rivalships alone would be sufficient to produce, but which opposite foreign alliances, attachments, and intrigues, would stimulate and embitter. Hence, likewise, they will avoid the necessity of those overgrown military establishments, which, under any form of government, are inauspicious to liberty, and which are to be regarded as particularly hostile to republican liberty; in this sense it is that your union ought to be considered as a main prop of your liberty, and that the love of the one ought to endear to you the preservation of the other.

These considerations speak a persuasive language to every reflecting and virtuous mind, and exhibit the continuance of the Union as a primary object of patriotic desire. Is there a doubt, whether a common government can embrace so large a sphere? Let experience solve it. To listen to mere speculation, in such a case, were criminal. We are authorized to hope, that a proper organization of the whole, with the auxiliary agency of governments for the respective subdivisions, will afford a happy issue to the experiment. It is well worth a fair and full experiment. With such powerful and obvious motives to Union, affecting all parts of our country, while experience shall not have demonstrated its impracticability, there will always be reason to distrust the patriotism of those who, in any quarter, may endeavor to weaken its bands.

In contemplating the causes which may disturb our Union, it occurs, as a matter of serious concern, that any ground should have been furnished for characterizing parties by geographical discriminations—Northern and Southern—Atlantic and Western; whence designing men may endeavor to excite a belief that there is a real difference of local interests and views. One of the expedients of party to acquire influence within particular districts, is to misrepresent the opinions and aims of other districts. You can not shield yourself too much against the jealousies and heart-burnings which spring from these misrepresentations; they tend to render alien to each other those who ought to be bound together by fraternal affection. The inhabitants of our western country have lately had a useful lesson on this head; they have seen in the negotiation of the Executive, and in the unanimous ratification by the Senate, of the treaty with Spain, and in the universal satisfaction at that event throughout the United States, a decisive proof how unfounded were the suspicions propagated among them of a policy in the General Government, and in the Atlantic States, unfriendly to their interests in regard to the Mississippi; they have been witnesses to the formation of two treaties—that with Great Britian, and that with Spain—which secure to them every thing they could desire in respect to our foreign relations, towards confirming their prosperity. Will it not be their wisdom to rely for the preservation of these advantages on the Union by which they were procured? Will they not henceforth be deaf to those advisers, if such there are, who would sever them from their brethren, and connect them with aliens?

To the efficacy and permanency of your Union, a Government

for the whole is indispensable. No alliance, however strict between the parts, can be an adequate substitute; they must inevitably experience the infractions and interruptions which all alliances, in all time, have experienced. Sensible of this momentous truth, you have improved upon your first essay, by the adoption of a Constitution of Government better calculated than your former for an intimate Union, and for the efficacious management of your common concerns. This Government, the offspring of our own choice, uninfluenced and unawed, adopted upon full investigation and mature deliberation, completely free in its principles, in the distribution of its powers, uniting security with energy, and containing within itself a provision for its own amendment, has a just claim to your confidence and your support. Respect its authority, compliance with its laws, acquiescence in its measures, are duties enjoined by the fundamental maxims of true liberty. The basis of our political systems, is the right of the people to make and to alter their constitutions of Government: but the Constitution which at any time exists, till changed by an explicit and authentic act of the whole people, is sacredly obligatory upon all. The very idea of the power and the right of the people to establish Government, pre-supposes the duty of every individual to obey the established Government.

All obstructions to the execution of the laws, all combinations and associations, under whatever plausible character, with the real design to direct, control, counteract, or awe the regular deliberation and action of the constituted authorities, are destructive to this fundamental principle, and of fatal tendency. They serve to organize faction, to give it an artificial and extraordinary force, to put in the place of the delegated will of the nation, the will of a party, often a small but artful and enterprising minority of the community; and, according to the alternate triumphs of different parties, to make the public administration the mirror of the ill-concerted and incongruous projects of faction, rather than the organ of consistent and wholesome plans, digested by common counsels, and modified by mutual interests.

However combinations and associations of the above description may now and then answer popular ends, they are likely, in the course of time and things, to become potent engines, by which cunning, ambitious, and unprincipled men, will be enabled to subvert the power of the people, and to usurp for themselves the reins of Government; destroying, afterwards, the very engines which had lifted them to unjust dominion.

Towards the preservation of your Government, and the permanency of your present happy state, it is requisite, not only that you steadily discountenance irregular oppositions to its acknowledged authority, but also that you resist with care the

spirit of innovation upon its principles, however specious the pretexts. One method of assault may be to effect, in the forms Constitution, alterations which will impair the energy of the system, and thus to undermine what can not be directly overthrown. In all the changes to which you may be invited, remember that time and habit are at least as necessary to fix the true character of Governments as of other human institutions; that experience is the surest standard by which to test the real tendency of the existing constitution of a country; that facility in changes, upon the credit of mere hypothesis and opinion, exposes to perpetual change, from the endless variety of hypothesis and opinion; and remember, especially, that for the efficient management of your common interests, in a country so extensive as ours, a Government of as much vigor as is consistent with the perfect security of liberty, is indispensable. Liberty itself will find in such a Government, with powers properly distributed and adjusted, its surest guardian. It is indeed, little else than a name, where the Government is too feeble to withstand the enterprises of faction, to confine each member of the society within the limits prescribed by the laws, and to maintain all in the secure and tranquil enjoyment of the rights of person and property.

I have already intimated to you the danger of parties in the State, with particular reference to the founding of them on geographical discriminations. Let me now take a more comprehensive view, and warn you, in the most solemn manner, against the baneful effects of the spirit of party generally.

This spirit, unfortunately, is inseperable from our nature, having its root in the strongest passions of the human mind. It exists under different shapes, in all Governments, more or less stifled, controlled, or repressed; but in those of the popular form it is seen in its greatest rankness, and is truly their worst enemy.

The alternate domination of one faction over another, sharpened by the spirit of revenge, natural to party dissention, which, in different ages and countries, has perpetrated the most horrid enormities, is itself a frightful despotism. But this leads, at length, to a more formal and permanent despotism. The disorders and miseries which result, gradually incline the minds of men to seek security and repose in the absolute power of an individual; and, sooner or later, the chief of some prevailing faction, more able or more fortunate than his competitors, turns this disposition to the purposes of his own elevation on the ruins of public liberty.

Without looking forward to an extremity of this kind, (which, nevertheless, ought not to be entirely out of sight,) the common and continual mischiefs of the spirit of party are sufficient to make it the interest and duty of a wise people to discourage and restrain it.

It serves always to distract the public counsels, and enfeeble the public administration. It agitates the community with ill-founded jealousies and false alarms; kindles the animosities of one part against another; foments, occasionally, riot and insurrection. It opens the door to foreign influence and corruption, which find a facilitated access to the Government itself, through the channels of party passions. Thus the policy and the will of one country are subjected to the policy and will of another

There is an opinion that parties, in free countries, are useful checks upon the administration of the Government, and serve to keep alive the spirit of liberty. This, within certain limits, is probably true; and in Governments of a monarchical cast, patriotism may look with indulgence, if not with favor, upon the spirit of party. But in those of the popular character, in Governments purely elective, it is a spirit not to be encouraged. From their natural tendency, it is certain there will always be enough of that spirit for every salutary purpose. And there being constant danger of excess, the effort ought to be, by force of public opinion, to mitigate and assuage it. A fire not be quenched, it demands a uniform vigilance to prevent its bursting into a flame, lest, instead of warming, it should consume.

It is important, likewise, that the habits of thinking, in a free country, should inspire caution in those intrusted with its administration to confine themselves within their respective constitutional spheres, avoiding in the exercise of one department, to encroach upon another. The spirit of encroachment tends to consolidate the powers of all the departments in one, and thus to create, whatever the form of Government, a real despotism. A just estimate of that love of power, and proneness to abuse it which predominates in the human heart, is sufficient to satisfy us of the truth of this position. The necessity of reciprocal checks in the exercise of political power, by dividing and distributing it into different depositories, and constituting each the guardian of public weal, against invasions by the others, has been evinced by experiments, ancient and modern; some of them in our own country, and under our own eyes. To preserve them must be as necessary as to institute them. If, in the opinion of the people, the distribution or modification of the constitutional powers be, in any particular, wrong, let it be corrected by an amendment in the way which the Constitution designates. But let there be no change by usurpation; for though this, in one instance, may be the instrument of good, it is the customary weapon by which free Governments are destroyed. The precedent must always greatly overbalance, in permanent evil, any partial or transient benefit which the use can, at any time, yield.

Of all the dispositions and habits which lead to political prosperity, religion and morality, are indispensable supports. In vain would that man claim the tribute of patriotism, who should labor to subvert these great pillars of human happiness, these firmest props of the duties of men and citizens. The mere politician, equally with the pious man, ought to respect and to cherish them. A volume could not trace all their connections with private and public felicity. Let it simply be asked, where is the security for property, for reputation, for life, if the sense of religious obligation desert the oaths which are the instruments of investigation in the courts of justice? And let us with caution indulge the supposition, that morality can be maintained without religion. Whatever may be conceded to the influence of refined education on minds of peculiar structure, reason and experience both forbid us to expect that national morality can prevail in exclusion of religious principles.

It is substantially true, that virtue or morality is a necessary spring of popular Government. The rule, indeed, extends with more or less force to every species of free Government. Who, that is a sincere friend to it, can look with indifference upon attempts to shake the foundation of the fabric?

Promote, then, as an object of primary importance, institutions for the general diffusion of knowledge. In proportion as the structure of a Government gives force to public opinion, it is essential that public opinion should be enlightened.

As a very important source of strength and security, cherish public credit. One method to preserve it is to use it as sparingly as possible; avoiding occasions of expense by cultivating peace, but remembering also that timely disbursements to prepare for danger, frequently prevent much greater disbursements to repel it; avoiding, likewise, the accumulation of debt, not only by shunning occasions of expense, but by vigorous exertions in time of peace to discharge the debts which unavoidable wars may have occasioned; not ungenerously throwing upon posterity the burden which we ourselves ought to bear. The execution of these maxims belongs to your representatives, but it is necessary that public opinion should co-operate. To facilitate to them the performance of their duty, it is essential that you should practically bear in mind, that towards the payment of debts there must be revenue; that to have revenue there must be taxes; that no taxes can be devised, which are not more or less inconvenient and unpleasant; that the intrinsic embarrassment inseparable from the selection of the proper objects (which is always a choice of difficulties,) ought to be a decisive motive for a candid construction of the conduct of the Government in making it, and for a spirit of acquiescence in the measures for obtaining revenue, which the public exigencies may at that time dictate.

Observe good faith and justice towards all nations; cultivate peace and harmony with all; religion and morality enjoin this conduct; and can it be that good policy does not equally enjoin it? It will be worthy of a free, enlightened, and, at no distant period, a great nation, to give to mankind the magnanimous and too novel example of a people always guided by an exalted justice and benevolence. Who can doubt that, in the course time and things, the fruits of such a plan would richly repay any temporary advantages which might be lost by a steady adherence to it? Can it be that Providence has not connected the permanent felicity of a nation with its virtue? The experiment, at least, is recommended by every sentiment which enobles human nature. Alas! is it to be rendered impossible by its vices?

In the execution of such a plan, nothing is more essential than that permanent inveterate antipathies against particular nations, and passionate attachment for others, should be excluded; and that, in place of them, just and amicable feelings towards all should be cultivated. The nation which indulges towards another an habitual hatred, or an habitual fondness, is, in some degree, a slave. It is a slave to its animosity or its affection; either of which is sufficient to lead it astray from its duty and its interest. Antipathy in one nation against another, disposes each more readily to offer insult and injury, to lay hold of slight causes of umbrage, and to be haughty and intractable, when accidental or trifling occasions of dispute occur. Hence frequent collisions, obstinate, envenomed and bloody contests. The nation, prompted by ill-will and resentment, sometimes impels to war the Government, contrary to the best calcations of policy. The Government sometimes participates in the national propensity, and adopts, through passion, what reason would reject; at other times it makes the animosity of the nation subservient to projects of hostility, instigated by pride, ambition, and other sinister and pernicious motives. The peace often, sometimes perhaps the liberty, of nations has been the victim.

So, likewise, a passionate attachment of one nation to another produces a variety of evils. Sympathy for the favorite nation, facilitating the illusion of an imaginary common interest, in cases where no real common interest exists, and infusing into one the enmities of the other, betrays the former into a participation in the quarrels and wars of the latter, without adequate inducement or justification. It leads also to concessions to the favorite nation of privileges denied to others, which is apt doubly to injure the nation making the concessions; by unnecessarily parting with what ought to have been retained, and by exciting jealousy, ill-will, and a disposition to retaliate, in the parties from whom equal privileges are withheld; and it gives to ambitious, corrupted, or deluded citizens (who devote themselves to the favorite nation) facility to betray, or sacrifice the interest of their own country, without odium; sometimes even with popularity; gilding with the appearance of a virtuous sense of obligation, a commendable deference for public opinion, or a laudable zeal for public good the base or foolish compliances of ambition, corruption or infatuation.

As avenues to foreign influence in innumerable ways, such attachments are particularly alarming to the truly enlightened and independent patriot. How many opportunities do they afford to tamper with domestic factions, to practice the art of seduction, to mislead public opinion, to influence or awe the public councils! Such an attachment of a small or weak, towards a great and powerful nation, dooms the former to be the satelite of the latter.

Against the insidious wiles of foreign influence (I conjure you to believe me, fellow-citizens,) the jealousy of a free people ought to be *constantly* awake; since history and experience prove that foreign influence is one of the most baneful foes of Republican Government. But that jealousy, to be useful, must be impartial; else it becomes the instrument of the very influence to be avoided, instead of a defence against it. Excessive partiality for one foreign nation, and excessive dislike for another, cause those whom they actuate to see danger only on one side, and serve to veil, and even second, the arts of influence on the other. Real patriots, who may resist the intrigues of the favorite, are liable to become suspected and odious; while its tools and dupes usurp the applause and confidence of the people, to surrender their interests.

The great rule of conduct for us, in regard to foreign nations, is, in extending our commercial relations, to have with them as little political connection as possible. So far as we have already formed engagements, let them be fulfilled with perfect good faith. Here let us stop.

Europe has a set of primary interests, which to us have none, or a very remote relation. Hence she must be engaged in frequent controversies, the causes of which are essentially foreign to our concerns. Hence, therefore, it must be unwise in us to implicate ourselves, by artificial ties, in the ordinary vicissitudes of her politics, or the ordinary combinations and collisions of her friendships or enmities.

Our detached and distant situation invites and enables us to pursue a different course. If we remain one people, under an efficient Government, the period is not far off when we may defy material injury from external annoyance; when we may take such an attitude as will cause the neutrality we may at any time resolve upon, to be scrupulously respected; when belligerent nations, under the impossibility of making acquisitions upon us, will not lightly hazard the giving us provocation; when we may choose peace or war, as our interest, guided by justice, shall counsel.

Why forego the advantages of such a peculiar situation? Why quit our own to stand upon foreign ground? Why, by interweaving our destiny with that of any part of Europe, entangle our peace and prosperity in the toils of European ambition, rivalship, interest, humor or caprice?

It is our true policy to steer clear of permanent alliances with any portion of the foreign world; so far, I mean, as we are now at liberty to do it; for let me not be understood as capable of patronising infidelity to existing engagements. I hold the maxim no less applicable to public than to private affairs, that honesty is always the best policy. I repeat it, therefore, let those engagements be observed in their genuine sense. But, in my opinion, it is unnecessary, and would be unwise to extend them.

Taking care always to keep ourselves, by suitable establishments, on a respectable defensive posture, we may safely trust to temporary alliances for extraordinary emergencies.

Harmony, and a liberal intercourse with all nations, are recommended by policy, humanity, and interest. But even our commercial policy should hold an equal and impartial hand; neither seeking nor granting exclusive favors or preferences; consulting the natural course of things; diffusing and diversifying, by gentle means, the streams of commerce, but forcing nothing; establishing, with powers so disposed, in order to give trade a stable course, to define the rights of our merchants, and to enable the Government to support them, conventional rules of intercourse, the best that present circumstances and mutual opinions will permit, but temporary, and liable to be, from time to time, abandoned or varied, as experience and circumstances shall dictate; constantly keeping in view, that it is folly in one nation to look for disinterested favors from another; that it must pay, with a portion of its independence, for whatever it may accept under that character; that by such acceptance it may place itself in the condition of having given equivalents for nominal favors, and yet of being reproached with ingratitude for not giving more. There can be no greater error than to expect, or calculate upon, real favors from nation to nation. It is an illusion which experience must cure, which a just pride ought to discard.

In offering to you, my countrymen, these counsels of an old and affectionate friend, I dare not hope they will make the strong and lasting expression I could wish; that they will con trol the usual current of the passions, or prevent our nation from running the course which has hitherto marked the destiny of nations; but if I may even flatter myself that they may be productive of some partial benefit, some occasional good; that they may now and then recur to moderate the fury of party spirit, to warn against the mischiefs of foreign intrigues, to guard against the impostures of pretended patriotism; this hope will be a full recompense for the solicitude for your welfare by which they have been dictated.

How far, in the discharge of my official duties, I have been guided by the principles which have been delineated, the public records, and other evidences of my conduct, must witness to you and the world. To myself, the assurance of my own conscience is, that I have at least believed myself to be guided by them.

In relation to the still subsisting war in Europe, my proclamation of the 22d of April, 1793, is the index to my plan. Sanctioned by your approving voice, and by that of your Representatives in both Houses of Congress, the spirit of that measure has continually governed me, uninfluenced by any attempts to deter or divert me from it.

After deliberate examination, with the aid of the best lights I could obtain, I was well satisfied that our country, under all the circumstances of the case, had a right to take, and was bound in duty and interest to take, a neutral position. Having taken it, I determined, as far as should depend upon me, to maintain it with moderation, perseverance, and firmness.

The considerations which respect the right to hold this conduct, it is not necessary on this occasion to detail. I will only observe, that, according to my understanding of the matter, that right, so far from being denied by any of the belligerent powers, has been virtually admitted by all.

The duty of holding a neutral conduct may be inferred, without any thing more, from the obligation which justice and humanity impose on every nation, in cases in which it is free to act, to maintain inviolate the relations of peace and amity towards other nations.

The inducements of interest, for observing that conduct, will best be referred to your own reflections and experience. With me, a predominant motive has been to endeavor to gain time to our country to settle and mature its yet recent institutions, and to progress, without interruption, to that degree of strength and consistency which is necessary to give it, humanly speaking, the command of its own fortunes.

Though in reviewing the incidents of my administration, I am unconscious of intentional error; I am, nevertheless, too sensible of my defects not to think it probable that I may have committed many errors. Whatever they may be, I fervently beseech the Almighty to avert or mitigate the evils to which they may tend. I shall also carry with me the hope, that my country will never cease to view them with indulgence; and that, after forty-five years of my life dedicated to its service with an upright zeal, the faults of incompetent abilities will be consigned to oblivion, as myself must soon be to the mansions of rest.

Relying on its kindness in this, as in other things, and actuated by that fervent love towards it which is so natural to a man who views in it the native soil of himself and his progenitors, I anticipate, with pleasing expectation, that retreat in which I promise myself to realize, without alloy, the sweet enjoyment of partaking, in the midst of my fellow-citizens, the benign influence of good laws under a free Government—the ever favorite object of my heart—and the happy reward, as I trust, of our mutual cares, labors, and dangers.

GEORGE WASHINGTON.

United States, 17th September, 1796.

HISTORY OF THE STATES.

VIRGINIA.

"The Old Dominion," so distinguished as being the native State of the Father of American Liberty, and the "Mother of Presidents," really seemed at one time, to be peculiarly favorable to the birth and development of statesmen. It has furnished no less than five Presidents, among whom are Washington, Monroe, Madison, and Jefferson. It was the first Colony, on the Continent, settled by the English. In 1607, a company formed under the patronage of James I., obtained a grant to make settlements in America, between the 34th and 38th degrees of north latitude. In May, 1607, a colony of one hundred and five persons, under direction of this company, arrived off the coast of South Virginia. Their intention had been to form a settlement on Roanoke, now in North Carolina; but being driven north by a violent storm, they discovered and entered the mouth of Chesapeake Bay. Passing up this Bay they named its Capes—Henry and Charles, in honor of the King's two sons. They were commanded by Capt. Christopher Newport, an experienced and distinguished navigator. Passing up James River, they arrived at a Peninsula, upon which they landed and established Jamestown.

After promulgating a code of laws which had been formed by the London company, Capt. Newport sailed for England, leaving the colony under the care of Capt. John Smith, whose subsequent relations to the settlement became so important,. and without whose efforts the enterprise would doubtless have proved a failure. The colonists seem to have been very poorly adapted to the labor required at their hands. Too many of them were *gentlemen*, and came, it appears, only to enrich themselves by gathering gold, which, they had heard, was very abundant.

Through a series of difficulties, which it is rarely the lot of man to encounter, this colony progressed; the settlers awhile quarreling among themselves, and awhile contending against savages and famine, for bare existence, until the period of the Revolution, in which it was one of the first colonies to take active part, furnishing to the young Republic many of its most efficient military chieftains and statesmen. It ratified the Constitution June 26th, 1788. After the Revolution its course was for many years one of great prosperity. But, unfortunately, the year 1861 found the majority of its statesmen arrayed against the Government, on the side of secession, and on the 15th of April, 1861, she seceded from the Union. On the 17th of June, 1861, all the counties lying between the Allegheny Mountains and the Ohio river, were, by a convention held at Wheeling, declared independent of the old State government, and were organized into a new State, called West Virginia, which remains loyal. The Capital of the old State was selected as the seat of government of the so-called Confederate States of America.

MASSACHUSETTS.

Massachusetts was settled in the year 1620, by the Puritans. These people, having been severely persecuted in England, had previously taken refuge in Holland; but for various reasons, they determined, after remaining in Holland a season, to emigrate to the New World. Unfortunately, they started at a very unpropitious season of the year, arriving at New England in the winter. The severity of the climate, their scarcity of food at times, operated seriously against their comfort and progress. It is said that they were frequently threatened with starvation. At one time the entire company had but one pint of Indian corn, which being divided equally among them, allowed to each person eight grains. But, unlike the early settlers of Virginia, they were all working men, and good economists. From the time of the landing at Plymouth up to 1691, this, first, settlement was known as the Plymouth Colony. Meantime, another settlement had been formed, styled the Massachusetts Colony. Both were for some years under the control of a London company. In 1691, Massachusetts and Plymouth Colonies were united, and thenceforward their history is one. The people of Massachusetts were, during the early part of their colonial existence, sorely vexed, at times, by the Indians, especially by the Pequods. They, unfortunately, had imbibed, during their own persecutions, too much of the spirit of conscription, and, although themselves refugees from religious bigotry, sullied much of their history prior to the Revolution by punishing what they called heresy in the Quakers and Baptists. During 1774—1775, Massachusetts took a very prominent part in favor of Colonial rights, and was the first State to manifest the spirit of resentment toward Great Britain. Its history during the War for Independence is one of glory. It adopted the Constitution June 6th, 1788.

NEW HAMPSHIRE.

This State was a part of Massachusetts up to the year 1680. It was, however, settled in 1624, the first settlement being formed at Dover by the English. In 1680 it was erected into a separate colony, and its first legislative assembly met this year. John Mason was its first Governor. It suffered severely from Indian wars, and its progress, during the first years of its existence, was slow. In 1742 it contained only six hundred persons liable to taxation. Its first Constitution was formed in 1683. It suffered from the effects of an insurrection in 1686, although prior and subsequent to this affair, it seems to have been one of the most peaceful and quiet of the colonies. It is distinguished for its excellent pastures, towering hills and fine cattle. The White Mountains are the highest in New England. It took a prominent and active part in the Revolution. It ratified the Constitution June 21st, 1788, since which time it has been highly prosperous. Its present population is 326,073. Its course during the Rebellion has been highly commendable.

MARYLAND.

In 1632, Sir George Calvert (Lord Baltimore) visited America, explored a tract of country lying on the Chesapeake Bay, belonging to what was then called South Virginia, and returned to England to procure a grant for it. But before the patent was made out, he died, and it was given to his son, Cecil. The province was named, by King Charles I., in the patent, in honor of his Queen, Henrietta Maria. A part of the province appears to have been included in the grant made some time afterward to Wm. Penn, and to have caused much contention between the successors of Penn and Baltimore.

In March, 1634, Leonard Calvert, the brother of Cecil, arrived at the mouth of the Potomac river, bringing with him two hundred emigrants, most of whom were Roman Catholic Gentlemen. Leaving the vessel, he ascended in a pinnace as far as Piskataqua, an Indian village nearly opposite Mount Vernon. The Indian Sachem gave him full liberty to settle there if he chose; but not deeming it safe, he began a settlement lower down on a branch of the Potomac, at the Indian town of Yoacomoco. The settlement was called St. Marys.

Maryland made a very fortunate beginning. The colonists arrived in time to make a crop for that year. Their neighbors in Virginia supplied them with cattle and protected them in great part from the Indians, while their own kind and consistent course materially promoted their happy relations with the savages.

The charter which had been granted them was very liberal, ceding to them the full power of legislation, without any interference on the part of the Crown. In 1635 they made laws for their government, which were somewhat modified in 1639. In 1650 they had an upper and lower legislative assembly, as had their Virginia neighbors.

Ten or twelve years after its settlement, Maryland was disturbed by an insurrection, headed by one Clayborne; but this difficulty was soon settled. It played a conspicuous part in the Revolution, and adopted the Constitution April 28th, 1788. Its progress has been fair, its present population being 687,049. Its geographical position and the mixed political character of its people caused it to assume a rather dubious attitude at the commencement of the Rebellion of 1861. Some of its best statesmen, however, were among the most uncompromising friends of the Union.

NEW YORK.

Captain Henry Hudson, the famous voyager, discovered what is now New York, together with a considerable extent of territory contiguous to it, in the year 1609. Although an Englishman by nativity, Hudson was at this time employed by the Dutch, (Hollanders) who, consequently, claimed the territory. Meantime the English set up a claim to it, as being a part of North Virginia. They also claimed it on account of Hudson being an Englishman. The Dutch, however, determined to hold it, and in 1610 opened a trade with the natives of Manhattan Island, on the spot where the City of New York now stands. They erected a fort on or near the site of Albany, named the country in general, New Netherlands, and the station at Manhattan, New Amsterdam. The Dutch retained the country until the year 1664.

It seems that up to this time they claimed not only the present territory of New York, but also that of Connecticut and New Jersey. The liberal governments of the surrounding colonies stood in great contrast with the despotic one imposed by the Dutch Government upon their American colonists. And when, in 1664, an English squadron despatched by James, Duke of York, with instructions to take possession of the province of New Netherlands, appeared before New Amsterdam, the inhabitants were willing to capitulate without resistance. Peter Styvesant, their Governor, and an able executive, made vain efforts to rouse them to defence and was forced to surrender. The English Government was now acknowledged over the whole of New Netherlands, the Capital receiving the name of New York, as well as the province. From this time forward to the

Revolutionary War, New York remained in the hands of the English, and was under the control of a very arbitrary succession of Governors. The progress of the colony was steady, in numbers, wealth and civilization. It took an active part in the Revolution, and adopted the Constitution July 26th, 1788. After this it outstripped every other State in the Union in every thing pertaining to wealth and greatness, save education, in which matter no State can compare with Massachusetts. At the commencement of the great Rebellion, this noble State showed herself truly worthy to be ranked as the Empire State. She has furnished the Government more money than any other State. Her population is 3,880,735.

CONNECTICUT.

In the year 1633, the Puritans of Massachusetts, having heard very flattering reports of the valley of Connecticut, resolved to make an effort to settle it. Accordingly, a company of them sailed for the Connecticut river, taking with them the frame of a house. Meantime the Dutch, claiming the territory as theirs, built a fort on the river where Hartford now stands, to prevent the emigrants from passing up. The Yankees, however, with that steady perseverance which has always marked their course, proceeded on their way, paying no attention to the Dutch fort, whose only demonstration was an unexecuted threat to fire on the emigrants if they passed it. Landing where Farmington river enters the Connecticut, they founded the town of Windsor. Other settlements were subsequently formed at Westerfield, Hartford, and Watertown. The first general Court was held at Hartford, in the year 1636. The province suffered severely from the depredations of the Pequod Indians, with which tribe a great and decisive battle was ultimately fought on the river Mystic, in the year 1636.* During this year the towns of Windsor, Hartford, and Wethersfield, met in convention and formed a Government, electing John Haynes the first Governor of the colony.

Its course from this period forward was one of great prosperity. It stood in the front rank during the war for Independence, and in no case was ever known to flinch from duty. It ratified the Constitution June 9th, 1788. Its present population is 460,147.

At the commencement of the Rebellion in 1861, its voice was for the Union and the Government of the Fathers. Its aid in behalf of freedom has been earnest and efficient.

---

*This battle resulted in the destruction of the Pequod tribe.

RHODE ISLAND.

In June, 1636, Roger Williams, an earnest, enthusiastic advocate of religious liberty in the broadest sense, having been banished by the Puritans of Massachusetts from that colony, went to what is now known as Rhode Island, purchased the present site of Providence of the Narigansett Indians, and founded a colony, of which he was at once pastor, teacher and father. He donated land to any whom he thought worthy, and Providence Plantation, as it was long called, became an asylum for persecuted Christians of all denominations, especially the Baptists. The first settlement in Rhode Island, proper, was formed by William Codington in the year 1636. Up to 1640, the citizens of Rhode Island made their own laws in general convention. But, in 1644, Roger Williams, with the aid of Gov. Vane, of Massachusetts, procured a charter for two settlements, under the name of Rhode Island and Providence Plantations. The Constitution framed under this charter was a good one, and lasted until the year 1818. For many years the legislative assembly of this colony met twice a year.

Rhode Island is distinguished as the smallest State in the Union. It did noble service in the war for Independence, but did not, for some reason, adopt the Constitution till the 29th of May, 1790. It has been a highly prosperous State; is distinguished for its good schools and large manufactories.

At the breaking out of the rebellion in 1861, it stepped nobly forward in defence of the Government, sending its own Governor to Washington at the head of a regiment of volunteers.

Its population is 174,620.

NEW JERSEY,

At first, formed a part of the Dutch province of New Netherlands. But soon after the latter came into the hands of the English, the territory of New Jersey was transferred to Lord Berkley and Sir George Carteret, by the Duke of York. The first permanent settlement was formed at Elizabethtown, in 1664, by emigrants from Long Island. Phillip Carteret arrived in the colony in 1665, and became its first Governor. The province had very little trouble with the Indians. Many emigrants from New England and New York soon arrived, and for a series of years the colony advanced in prosperity. It enjoyed the blessings flowing from a liberal form of government.

In the year 1685, the Duke of York became the King of England, under the title of James II., and disregarding his former pledges, assumed, in 1688, the government of New Jersey, placing it under the control of Sir Edmond Andros, whom he had already made Governor of New York and New England. This state of things was terminated by the revolution in England, but left New Jersey for years in a very precarious condition. In 1702, its proprietors having resigned their claims, it became a royal province, and was united to New York. In 1738, it became again a separate province, and so continued until the Revolution, in which it took a very active part in favor of liberty. It ratified the Constitution December 18th, 1787. Thence forward its career has been a highly prosperous one. Its strength has been put forth to aid in crushing the great rebellion. Population 672,075.

DELAWARE.

Gustavus Adolphus, King of Sweden, formed a plan of establishing colonies in America as early as the year 1626. But as he died on the field of Leutzen, during the German war in 1633, without carrying his scheme into effect, his minister took it up, and employed Peter Minuets, first Governor of New Netherlands, to carry it into effect. In 1638, a small Swedish colony arrived under the direction of Minuets, and settled on Christian Creek, near the present town of Wilmington. Notwithstanding the remonstrances of the Dutch Government of New Netherlands, who claimed the territory, the Swedes continued to extend their settlements from this time until they pre-empted all the territory from Cape Henlopen to the falls of the Delaware. At this time the colony was called New Sweden. In 1651, Gov. Styvesant, to check the aggressive movements of the Swedes, built a fort near the present site of New Castle, of which the Swedes afterwards obtained possession by strategem. Enraged at this movement, the Government of Holland ordered Styvesant to reduce the Swedes to submission, which he speedily accomplished with six hundred men, in 1655. The province was soon after annexed to New Netherlands. Delaware was, after it fell into the hands of the English, included in the grant made to William Penn, in 1692. It remained attached to Pennsylvania until 1691, when it was allowed a separate government. It was reunited to Pennsylvania in 1692. In 1703, it was again separated, having its own Legislature, though the same Governor presided over both colonies. The ancient forms of the government were preserved through the Revolutionary struggle. It ratified the Constitution December 7th, 1787.

Its position, at the commencement of the rebellion of 1861, was somewhat dubious. It, being a northerly slave State, was somewhat divided in regard to where its interests lay. It, however, finally came out somewhat decidedly for the Union, al, though its entire strength has not been exerted against the rebellion. Its population is 112,216.

THE CAROLINAS.

In the year 1563, the coast of Carolina was explored, and named after Charles IX. of France. The first attempt to settle it was made by the celebrated and accomplished Sir Walter Raleigh, in 1585, twenty two years before the settlement of Jamestown, and thirty-five years before the Puritans landed at Plymouth. This effort failed on account of the incapacity of the Governor appointed by Raleigh, and the ill-behavior of the colonists towards the natives.

The first successful attempt was made sometime between 1640 and 1650, under the direction of Gov. Berkley. The settlement was made in Albemarle county, by a few Virginia planters. In 1663, a large tract of land, lying between the 30th and the 36th degrees of north latitude, having the Atlantic Ocean for its eastern boundary, was conveyed by Charles II., to Lord Clarendon and associates, under whose auspices a settlement was made near the mouth of Cape Fear River, in the year 1665, by emigrants from Barbadoes. Sir James Yeomans was appointed Governor. A settlement was made at Port Royal, South Carolina, in 1670; and in 1671, a few persons located at what was then called Old Charleston, which place was abandoned in 1680, and the foundation of the present city of Charleston laid, several miles nearer the sea.

All the various settlements here mentioned went under the general name of Carolina until 1571, when a division was made, and the northern and southern portions were called by their distinctive names, North and South Carolina. These States were the scenes of many Revolutionary tragedies. South Carolina, in particular, although the home of Sumpter, and Marion, and Rutledge, was replete with tories, (royalists) who spared no effort to annoy the infant republic, and play into the hands of the British Government. South Carolina ratified the Constitution May 23d, 1778, but threatened to break the compact in 1832, and was only prevented by the stern will of President Jackson. After this the State did nothing worthy of note, until December 20th, 1860, when it seceded from the Union, taking the lead in the great rebellion. Present population 703,708.

North Carolina ratified the Constitution Nov. 21st, 1789, and seceded from the Union May 21st, 1861. Population 992,622.

PENNSYLVANIA.

The Old Keystone State, and one of the most wealthy and

prosperous in the Union, was settled by the Quakers, under the direction of Wm. Penn, at Philadelphia, in the year 1682. The founder of this colony showed himself a philosopher, a philanthropist, a thorough political economist, at the very commencement of his labors. He put the province under the government of a Council of Three and a House of Delegates, chosen by the freemen, who, according to his arrangement, were all those who acknowledged the existence of one God. He pursued such a course with the natives as won their confidence and esteem. No Qnaker was ever murdered by an Indian; and to this day the "sons of Wm. Penn" are everywhere respected by the savage. The treaty Penn made with the Indians was never violated. In framing the colonial government, he provided for the largest religious liberty, allowing every one to worship according to the dictates of his own conscience. Up to 1684 Delaware, as before mentioned, was included in Penn's grant. But about this time he procured a new charter, more strictly defining the rights and limits of Pennsylvania, and Delaware was detached. For seventy years prosperity smiled upon this colony, during much of which time Penn was, according to the historian, its governor, magistrate, preacher and teacher. It was troubled with no Indian wars till 1754, when Penn's example and teachings began to be forgotten. The population, owing to a considerable influx from Sweden, Germany, and some other countries, began, at a later date, to assume a more varied aspect; and when the colonies rebelled against the mother country, Pennsylvania contained sufficient "fighting" material to lend valuable assistance to the cause of liberty.

She adopted the Constitution December 12th, 1787, since which time her increase in wealth, and advancement in general improvement has been almost without a parallel. Her vast coal fields and rich iron mines constitute a source of eternal wealth. Upon the breaking out of the rebellion of 1861, her position in favor of the Union was well defined.

Her population is 2,906,115.

GEORGIA.

General James Oglethorpe, and a company of twenty-one others, received, in the year 1732, from George II., of England, a grant for all the land between the Savannah and the Altamaha rivers. In January, 1733, a company of one hundred and fourteen men, women and children, arrived at Charleston, S. C., destined for Georgia. They were kindly treated by the Charlestonians, and were greatly assisted by them in their labor of forming a colony. The first laws made for the province by the twenty-two grantees, prohibited the importation of rum, trade with the Indians, and the use of negroes. They also provided that lands should go back to the original owners in case the purchaser had no male heirs. Although the first, second and third of these provisions were undoubtedly wholesome, the fourth was highly objectionable, and tended very much to retard the progress of the colony. In the year 1740, General Oglethorpe, as commander in chief of the forces in Georgia, at the head of two thousand men, invaded Florida with the intention of forcibly annexing it to Georgia; but he was soon repelled from the territory, and returned home bootless. The Spanish, in turn, with two sail of vessels and three thousand men, invaded Georgia in 1742, and were likewise forced to return home thwarted. The progress of this colony was for many years very slow; the people manifesting that indolence and indifference which is still too prominent a characteristic of Georgians. It was mainly on the side of freedom during the revolution.

It ratified the Constitution January 9th, 1788. Since the revolution, the State has manifested but little life as compared with its sisters, and its secession from the Union, May 19th, 1861, was followed by speedy ruin.

VERMONT

The territory of which this State is composed began to be settled in the year 1731, but was for some years considered as a part of New Hampshire. It was also claimed at one time by New York, and a contest arose between that State and New Hampshire, which was adjusted by the King of England in a manner by no means satisfactory to the settlers. The result was a quarrel between Vermont and the Crown, in which the Green Mountain Boys, led by Col. Ethan Allen, resisted the officers of justice, as well as the New York militia, who were called out to sustain them. The province appears not to have had even a territorial government until 1777, at which time a convention of delegates met at Westminster, and declared themselves an independent State, under the name of New Connecticut. Previous to this time, however, they had rendered material aid to the revolution. It May, 1755, Col. Allen, at the head of two hundred and seventy men, reduced Fort Ticonderoga and Crown Point, and thus became complete master of Lake Champlain. During the whole period of the revolution the State did good service in the cause of liberty, although it remained independent. Some time subsequent to its declaration of independence its name was changed to Vermont. As it was not one of the original States, it did not ratify the Constitution, but, upon application, was admitted to the Union during the second session of Congress, in the year 1791. It has been a highly prosperous State, and added much to the luster of the Union in its palmly days of peace. It fully sustained its revolutionary reputation at the commencement of the rebellion of 1861. Its population is 315,098.

KENTUCKY,

Was settled in the year 1775 by Daniel Boone and a number of associates from North Carolina. The trials and adventures of these hardy pioneers, and especially those of Boone, constitute one of the most romantic leaves in the history of the West. For over two years, previous to 1775, Boone was busily employed in surveying Kentucky, building roads, and forts. One of the latter he erected at Boonsborough, to which place he removed his family in 1775. Boone said that his wife and daughter were the first white women who ever stood on the banks of the Kentucky river. For a number of years after Boone's settlement, he and his associatiates experienced many difficulties with the natives, Boone's daughter being at one time captured by the Indians, though shortly afterwards rescued by her father. But, notwithstanding the difficuities with the savages, the young territory grew rapidly in population and wealth, and on June 1st, 1792, was admitted to the Union. Having a fertile soil, and affording excellent pasturage, she has far outstripped most of her slave-holding sisters in general improvement.

Her position for some time after the commencement of the rebellion, was by no means promotive of her prosperty. Owing to her attempt to observe strict neutrality, she became the scene of many guerrilla outrages, and has suffered, perhaps, more than any other State during the struggle.

Her population is 1,115,684.

TENNESSEE,

Was, for some time, a part of North Carolina. It was made a territorial government in the year 1790, and was admitted into the Union in 1796. The first permanent white inhabitants of Tennessee went there in the year 1775, and built Fort Louden, now in Blount county. They were, in 1760, attacked by the savages, and two hundred persons were massacred. But, in 1767, the natives were reduced to submission by Col. Grant, and a treaty was made with them which encouraged emigration. Settlements were formed on Holston river in 1765, which although frequently attaked by the Indians, made very fair progress. Col. John Sevier, with the Tennessee militia and a few Virginia soldiers, gained a decisive victory over the savages, and from this time forward, though more or less harrassed by the Indians, the progress of the State, in population and improvement, was rapid. North Carolina gave up the territory in 1789, and in 1790 Congress recognized it as a separate province. It has great extent of territory and, up to 1861, was considered as among the greatest of the agricultural States. At this time, however, it was seduced by the voice of the siren, secession, and on the 24th of June, 1861, formally seceded from the Union. It should be stated, however, in justice to the State, that the eastern portion of it was generally loyal, and was only dragged out of the Union by force. Tennessee is now, (1864) occupied by the armies of the United States and is under a provisional government.

OHIO.

Ohio was admitted into the Union on the 29th of November, 1802; the State containing, at the time, 72,000 inhabitants, 12,000 more than was required in order to its admission. It was settled in the spring of 1788, one year after it, with a vast additional extent of North-Western territory, had been ceded, by Virginia, to the United States.

The year 1788 was a famous year from emigration. It witnessed the passage of no less than 20,000 persons down the Ohio river. The company which settled Ohio consisted of forty persons, under Gen. Rufus Putnam. They built a stockade fort at Marietta of sufficient strength to resist the attacks of the natives, cleared several acres of ground, and planted a crop. They were joined by twenty additional families in the autumn. Both these companies were New England people.

For a number of years they were not troubled by the savages, nor did any of their number trouble the Indians, except in one or two instances. The earliest settlers of Cincinnati arrived there, about twenty in number, in 1790. Until the year 1795 the attempts made to settle most parts of Ohio were attended with great difficulties, on account of Indian wars. Marietta, however, formed an exception to this rule. After the great victory which Gen. Wayne achieved over the savages during Washington's administration, the population increased rapidly. Unembarrassed by any centralizing or aristocratic institutions, possessed of the finest natural resources, and vitalized by an enterprising population, Ohio, after its admission into the Union, made an advancement of which any State might well be proud. In population it is the third State in the Union, numbering 2,390,502.

At the breaking out of the rebellion Ohio took its position staunchly for the Union, and has done much during the war for the restoration of the authority of the Government over the seceded States.

LOUISIANA

Was ceded by Spain to France in the year 1802, and was bought by the United States, of the latter power, in 1803, at a cost of $15,000,000. Gov. Clayborne took possession of it the same year. It was settled by the French, at Iberville, in 1699, and was admitted into the Union April 8th, 1812. It is an important State, in that it holds the keys of entrance to the mouth of the Mississippi. In the year 1860, nearly one-half its population was slave. It seceded from the Union on the 26th of January, 1861. Its most important towns are now (1864) occupied by the Federal forces. Its population in 1860 was 708,002. It has been a very forward State in the great rebellion.

INDIANA.

About the year 1690, a French settlement, the first in Indiana, was made at Vincennes, that place being within the territory claimed, at that time, by the French, upon priority of discovery by La Salle. Indiana was long the residence of various Indian tribes, and the theatre of Indian wars. By the terms of the treaty of the peace of 1763, it, with the rest of the North-Western Territory, was ceded to Great Britain. It was still claimed by the Indians, but, by various treaties, extensive tracts were obtained for settlement. The Indians, however, retained possession of many parts of the State up to the year 1812, and to that portion known as the Indian Reserve, even later. It was erected into a territory in 1809, and on the 11th of December, 1816, was admitted into the Union. Its population—1,350,428—in the year 1860 is an indication of its progress. In the matter of education, Indiana is somewhat behind some of her Western sisters, but her efforts in behalf of the Government, during the great rebellion, shall halo her future with glory.

MISSISSIPPI.

The territory comprising the present States of Mississippi and Alabama having been divided, that portion lying next the river was, in 1817, admitted into the Union as a State, under the name Mississippi, while the eastern portion was organized as a territory, and named Alabama. The whole of this territory was explored, first by Ferdinand de Soto, and afterwards by La Salle. It suffered greatly during the wars of the Natchez Indians. The Choctaws, for a long time, retained possession of the northern portion of it, and were to some extent civilized. Mississippi was settled by the French in 1716, at Natchez. Its population—791,305—shows fair progress. On the 9th of January, 1861, it went the way of the seceding States, since which time its course, like theirs, has been downward.

ILLINOIS.

This most thriving and prosperous State came into the Union on the 3d of December, 1818. Until 1809, it was a part of Indiana, at which time it became a separate territory, and so remained till received into the Union. This State has been little disturbed by civil divisions, or by Indian wars. Its most serious troubles arose from the appearance, within its borders, of the Mormons, in 1838, and from attempts made to curb their irregularities. This singular people, believing themselves to be ill-treated, assembled to the number of 700 under their leaders, in a remote part of the State, and proposed fighting for their rights. But a body of 300 troops marched against and captured them. The whole sect was ultimately reduced to submission, and banished the State. It was explored by La Salle, and settled by the French at Kaskaskia,* in 1720. Its growth has been immense. Its population in 1860 was 1,711,951. It has been one of the most forward and glorious of the loyal States during the great rebellion.

ALABAMA

Was admitted to the Union on the 14th of December, 1819. It has a deep, rich soil, and in many places a healthful climate. It remained till the Revolution a mere hunting ground of the savages. From the peace of 1783 to 1802, it was claimed by Georgia, and lands were sold to settlers and speculators accordingly. In the year 1802, Georgia ceded all her western territory to the United States for $1,250,000. In 1800, the present State of Alabama became a part of Mississippi Territory—from which it was separated when Mississippi became a State. It was settled in 1711, at Mobile, by the French, being a part of the territory explored by La Salle in his Mississippi tour. It formally seceded from the Union January 11, 1861.

MAINE.

In the year 1638, the same year in which New Haven was

---

* Kaskaskia, the first capital of Illinois, is located on Kaskaskia River, and is the present site of Vandalia.

settled, Ferdinand Gorges procured a charter of the King of England for all the lands from the borders of New Hampshire on the south-west to Sagadahoc, on the Kenebeck river, on the north-east, under the name of the Province of Maine. It remained a separate province till 1652, when it became a part of Massachusetts. Various attempts were made between 1785 and 1802 to form it into an independent State; but these efforts failed. In 1819 a large majority of the people were in favor of separating from Massachusetts. A convention was called, a Constitution prepared and adopted, and in 1820, Maine was received into the Union. It is by no means an agricultural State, but its extensive fisheries and great lumber trade have greatly enriched it, and its progress in morality has, perhaps, been superior to that of any other State. It is the only State in the Union that has an efficient prohibitory liquor law. It proved itself true to the Government in 1861, and there is no danger of its ever ceasing to be so.

It was settled in 1625, at Bristol, by the English. Its population is 628,279.

MISSOURI.

This great, though crippled, State was admitted into the Union on the 10th of August, 1821. It, with all the territory then belonging to the United States, west of the Mississippi, was included in the purchase of Louisiana, made in 1803. Louisiana afterwards was divided into Orleans Territory, Louisiana proper, and Missouri Territory. In 1819, Missouri Territory was divided into Arkansas on the south, and Missouri on the north; and it was about this time that the latter took the requisite steps toward framing a State Constitution. It will be remembered that this is the State, the discussion of the propriety of the admission of which raised such a storm in Congress in 1820.

Being a border slave State, it was nearly equally divided on the question of secession in 1861, and thus, like Kentucky, has been overrun by both Southern and Northern troops during the Rebellion, and has been the scene of much blood-shed and ruin. It was settled in 1764, at St. Louis, by the French. Its population is 1,182,012.

FLORIDA.

The Peninsular States, discovered and explored by Ponce de Leon, a voyager with Columbus, and whose name was suggested to the discoverer by the abundance and beauty of its wild flora, was, from 1512 to 1819. with the exception of the interval between 1763 and 1783, a province of Spain. The first attempt to settle it was made in the year 1565, at St. Augustine, which is said to be the oldest town in America, by the Spaniards. This effort was attended with many difficulties, the colonists contending, for the first few years, alternately with the horrors of savage warfare and famine, at times being forced to subsist on roots and acorns. In 1819 it was transferred to the United States by treaty, which treaty was, after much delay, ratified by Spain, and with still more delay by the United States. Possession of the colony was granted the Government in July, 1821. The Territory contained, in 1840, a population of 54,477, and on the 3d of March, 1845, became a State and was received into the Union. Florida was the theater of the Seminole war, which cost the United States so much blood and treasure. It went the way of the seceding States, January 7th, 1861. Florida, like the Indian's gun, has "cost more than she has come to." Her population. in 1860, was 140,425.

ARKANSAS.

This State lies south of Missouri, and was once attached to it. It has a fine climate and prolific soil. The first settlement of whites within its limits was made at Arkansas Post, in the year 1685. The earlier inhabitants were French. Its progress, for many years, was very slow. It was not until about the year 1829 that the tide of emigration began to flow from the Atlantic States in that direction. Little Rock, the early seat of government and the present Capital, was laid out in the year 1820, during which year the first steamboat ascended the Arkansas river. The boat was eight days in going from New Orleans to the village of Arkansas—a distance of scarcely one hundred miles above the mouth of the Arkansas river. The State once contained the remnants of several powerful tribes of Indians. By a treaty made between the Cherokees and the United States, the former agreed to give up all their lands east of the Mississippi river, and to retire to a region guaranteed to them in the present State of Arkansas.

The State was admitted into the Union on the 15th of June, 1836. It seceded May 6th, 1861, and has since been the retreat of guerrillas, and the scene of some sanguinary battles.

MICHIGAN

Was admitted into the Union January 26th, 1837. It had the requisite population (60,000) before this, but there were some difficulties in the way of its admission. In 1837 it contained

200,000; in 1840, 212,267, and in 1850, 851,470. The territory, when first discovered by the whites, contained a tribe of Indians called Hurons by the French, and Iroquois by the Indians themselves. Many of them were converted to Christianity, by the untiring labors of Catholic Missionaries, as early as 1648. It was not, however, till 1670 that the French took possession of the territory. It was a portion of the extensive tract explored by the assiduous, daring La Salle. Its progress, while it belonged to the French, was very slow. It was not until 1763, when, by treaty, it was ceded to Great Britain, that much was done in the way of civilizing and improving it. Comparatively little, in fact, was done until 1783, when the territory was ceded by England to the United States. Until 1800 it was, for purposes of Government, considered a part of the Great North Western Territory. After Ohio, Indiana, and Illinois had been severally detached, the remainder, in 1805, became a distinct territory, the first Governor of which was General Hull, by appointment of President Jefferson. Michigan suffered much from the war of 1812. For nearly two years nearly the whole territory was the theatre of sanguinary conflicts. It was exposed to the barbarity of the enemy and their Indian allies. Since then, however, its enterprising inhabitants have brought it up to a degree of improvement which few States of its age can boast. Its strength was offered the Government in 1861, and it continues as well as it began. Its population, in 1860, was 749,113.

IOWA.

This State derives its name from the Indians. It was included in the Louisiana purchase. It was first settled at Dubuque, by the French, in the year 1686. This settlement, however, does not seem to have been permanent, nor productive of any real good to the territory. In 1833 Burlington was settled by emigrants from the eastern States. It formed a part of Missouri from 1804 to 1821, when it was included in Michigan Territory. It subsequently belonged to Wisconsin Territory. It was admitted into the Union March 3d, 1845. It is a highly prosperous State, having a vast extent of rich soil and excellent pasturage. It is faithful to the Union; placed itself in the front rank at the commencement of the Rebellion.

TEXAS.

The territory of Texas was explored by Ponce de Leon and La Salle. After Mexico became independent of Spain, a grant which had been made to Moses Austin, a native of Connecticut, comprising a large tract of this province, was confirmed by the now Republic; and, being transferred by Moses Austin, at his death, to his son, Stephen, was subsequently enlarged by a further grant. Emigration from the United States was encouraged, and in 1830 nearly ten thousand Americans were settled in Texas. The prosperity of these inhabitants excited the jealousy of Mexico, and under the administration of Santa Anna, an unjust, oppressive policy was adopted toward Texas. Remonstrance proving useless, the people of the territory declared themselves independent. The Revolution began in 1835, by a battle at Gozales, in which five hundred Texans defeated over one thousand Mexicans. Other engagements followed, the result of which was the dispersion of the Mexican army. Santa Anna now redoubled his efforts, and appearing in March, 1835, with a force of eight thousand men, several bloody battles followed. On the 21st of April, having under his immediate command one thousand and five hundred men, he was met by Gen. Sam. Houston, with eight hundred men, and totally defeated, on the banks of the San Jacinto. Santa Anna, himself, was captured the next day in the woods, when he acknowledged the independence of Texas, though the Mexican Congress refused to ratify the act. Active hostilities, however, were now abandoned, and the independence of Texas was acknowledged by the United States, Great Britain and other European countries. It was in this condition of things that Texas was annexed to the United States. On the 24th of December, 1845, it was admitted into the Union, which act was ratified by the Texan Legislature, July 4th, 1846. But Mexico, still regarding Texas as a revolted province, refused to acknowledge the validity of this measure. The result was a war between Mexico and the United States, which terminated on the 2d of February, 1848, in a treaty by which the latter power, in consideration of the payment of a debt of $3,500,000, due from Mexico to the citizens of Texas, acquired New Mexico, Texas and California. The progress of Texas from this time till the eve of the great Rebellion, was almost unprecedented, no less than twenty-five thousand Germans having emigrated to that State in five years' time. These, however, owing to the jealousy aroused against them by their having demonstrated the superiority of free labor, even in a slave State, were obliged to migrate to Mexico in the year 1860. By this and other oppressive acts on the part of the advocates of slavery, Texas, purchased by the blood and treasure of the United States, was driven into the whirlpool of secession, March 4th, 1861. Its population, in 1860, was 604.215. The first settlement within its borders was made by the Spaniards, at St. Antonia de Bexar, in 1690.

WISCONSIN

Was admitted into the Union May 29th, 1848. It was a part of the extensive territory ceded by France to Great Britain in the treaty of 1763. At the close of the revolution it was given up by Great Britain to the United States. It was erected into a territory in 1836, the portion now forming the State of Iowa being detached in 1838. Its natural resources are extraordinary, the climate being very healthful, and the soil unsurpassed in fertility. It was settled in the year 1669, at Green Bay, by the French. It is thoroughly loyal to the Union. In 1860, it had a population of 775,881.

MINNESSOTA

Lies north of Iowa, and extends to the Canadian boundary. On the north-east it touches Lake Superior, and, to the West, is bounded by Dacotah Territory. It comprises the head waters of the Mississippi, and abounds in rivers and lakes, teeming with fish. Its soil is highly prolific, and its forests are among the finest in the world. Its name is derived from Minnisotah, the Indian name of St. Peter's river. Primarily discovered by La Salle, it, for some years, belonged to the French, and at a very early period was traversed by their traders and soldiers. It was ceded to Great Britain by the treaty of 1763, and to the United States at the peace of 1783. It received a territorial government in 1849, and was admitted into the Union in May, 1858. It has still, within its borders, several bands of the Chippewas, with whom considerable trouble has been experienced since the breaking out of the rebellion. It is, however, a thrifty, growing State, and is thoroughly loyal. It was settled in 1846, at St. Paul, by emigrants from the eastern States.

OREGON

Was admitted into the Union in the year 1859. It, primarily, included Washington Territory, and, with the latter, comprised the extensive tract lying between the British Possessions, on the north, and California, on the south; the Rocky Mountains on the east, and the Pacific Ocean on the west. The coasts of this region were discovered by the Spaniards in the 16th century. In 1792, Capt. Grey, of Boston, discovered and entered the Columbia river, and thus the United States acquired the right of sovereignty over the territory. The exploration of the country from the Missouri to the Columbia, by Lewis and Clark, government appointees, in 1804–5–6, strengthened this claim. The British, however, laid claim to the northern part of the territory, which gave rise to a threatening dispute between Great Britain and the United States. But the difficulty was adjusted by a treaty in 1846, establishing the boundary of 49°, north latitude. The State still contains the Flathead, Pend Oreille, Spokane, Shoshone, and other tribes of Indians, who are, for the most part, in the savage state, though the Christian Missionaries have done much in the way of civilizing a portion of them. The furs of this region, those of the badger, beaver, bear, fisher-fox, lynx, martin, mink, muskrat, &c., have long been a great source of revenue.

The American fur companies established trading posts in Oregon at an early period, that of Astoria being founded in 1810, under the aupices of the late John Jacob Astor, of New York. It was settled, at Astoria, by emigrants from the Eastern States, in the year 1811. Its population amounted to 52,465 in 1860.

KANSAS.

About the development of this young State cluster some of the most important events of American history. Its territorial organization, by the passage of the Kansas-Nebraska Bill, in 1854, reopened the agitation of the slavery question, which seeming to have acquired fresh vigor and virulence from the sleep it had enjoyed under the Missouri Compromise, thoroughly aroused the old animosities between the pro and anti-slavery elements of our national politics. From 1854 to 1857 it was the theater of political tragedies, the bare mention of which may well put the blush of shame upon even the most fool-hardy partizan; and the historian has well said that these dire afflictions might have been expected when the bill organizing Kansas Territory was passed. No sooner was it decided that this territory was open alike to the abolitionist and the slaveholder, than the Emigrant Aid Societies of New England and the pro-slavery organizations of the South began pouring streams of settlers into it of opposite political views, entertaining the most hostile feelings, each party toward the other, and as the legitimate result, came a civil war, which lasted about two years, and which, in some of its incidents would have shamed even savages.

The Territory made application to Congress in 1857, for a place in the Union, but the Constitution under which it asked admission (the one framed at Lecompton) was known to be a fraudulent affair, and, hence, Kansas was rejected. The discussion of this Constitution caused a permanent division of the Democratic party. The Constitution was rejected by the people of Kansas by a majority of 10,000. Kansas was, however, received into the Union in 1861, under a free State Constitution, formed at Topeka.

CALIFORNIA

Was admitted into the Union on the 7th of September, 1850. The alarming discussion which occurred upon the question of admission was what gave rise to the compromise measures of 1850, popularly styled the *Omnibus Bill.* The measures are presented in detail in another part of this work.

General Fremont, with a small but dauntless band of rangers, conquered California in 1846, having defeated on frequent occasions, vastly superior forces of Mexicans. Its resources as a farming country early attracted attention. But when, in February, 1848, it was published that gold in quantities had been found on a branch of the Sacramento, the swarm of emigrants which rushed in, comprising representatives from every State in the Union, and from nearly all the nations of Europe, was almost incalculable. From a small village, San Francisco was rapidly inflated to a large city. In many places towns sprang up like mush-roons. Owing to the fact that its population had been thrown hastily together, from so many places, and in consequence of the want of a government, California was, for some time, the scene of many dark crimes and hideous outrages. Never was the want of wholesome legal restraint more keenly felt than here. The Constitution of California was framed by a convention of delegates in 1849. It took a firm stand for the Union in 1861. The first settlement, within its limits, was made at San Diego, by the Spanish, in 1764. It furnishes, annually, to the Government, seventy to eighty millions of dollars in gold.

MISSOURI COMPROMISE OF 1820.

When Missouri applied for admission into the Union, a proposition was started in Congress to prohibit the introduction of slavery into the new State. This had the effect of arraying the South against the North—the slaveholding against the non-slaveholding States—and the whole subject of slavery became the exciting topic of debate throughout the country. The question was finally settled by a *Compromise*, which tolerated slavery in Missouri, but otherwise prohibited it in all the territory of the United States north and west of the northern limits of Arkansas.

As the principle then settled has often since been the prolific source of much sectional controversy and angry debate, and as it is desirable that every one should be familiar with the *real* provisions of the act by which Missouri was admitted, we have concluded to insert here so much of the law as is necessary to a full understanding of the subject. All the sections except the following relate entirely to the formation of the Missouri territory, in the usual form of territorial bills:

"Sec. 8. That in all that territory ceded by France to the United States, under the name of Louisiana, which lies north of thirty-six degrees and thirty minutes north latitude, not included within the limits of the State contemplated by this act, slavery and involuntary servitude, otherwise than in the punishment of crimes, whereof the parties shall be duly convicted, shall be, and is hereby, forever prohibited. *Provided always*, that any person escaping into the same, from whom labor or service is lawfully claimed, in any State or Territory of the United States, such fugitive may be lawfully reclaimed and conveyed to the person claiming his or her labor or service as aforesaid."

FUGITIVE SLAVE LAW OF 1850.

An Act to amend, and supplementary to, the Act entitled, "An Act respecting Fugitives from Justice, and persons escaping from the Service of their Masters," approved February 12, 1793.

Be it enacted by the Senate and House of Representatives of the United States of America in Congress assembled, That the persons who have been, or may hereafter be, appointed Commissioners, in virtue of any Act of Congress, by the Circuit Courts of the United States, and who, in consequence of such appointment, are authorized to exercise the powers that any justice of the peace, or other magistrate of any of the United States, may exercise in respect to offenders for any crime or offence against the United States, by arresting, imprisoning, or bailing the same, under and by virtue of the thirty-third section of the act of the twenty-fourth of September, seven hundred and eighty-nine, entitled, "An Act to establish the judicial courts of the United States," shall be, and are hereby, authorized and required to exercise and discharge all the powers and duties conferred by this Act.

SEC. 2. That the Superior Court of each organized territory of the United States shall have the same power to appoint Commissioners to take acknowledgments of bail and affidavits, and to take depositions of witnesses in civil causes, which is now possessed by the Circuit Court of the United States; and all Commissioners who shall hereafter be appointed for such purposes by the Superior Court of any organized territory of the United States, shall possess all the powers, and exercise all the duties, conferred by law upon the Commissioners appointed by the Circuit Courts of the United States for similar purposes, and shall moreover exercise and discharge all the powers and duties conferred by this Act.

SEC. 3. That the Circuit Courts of the United States, and the Superior Courts of each organized territory of the United States, shall from time to time enlarge the number of Commissioners with a view to afford reasonable facilities to reclaim fugitives from labor, and to the prompt discharge of the duties imposed by this Act.

SEC. 4. That the Commissioners above named shall have concurrent jurisdiction with the Judges of the Circuit and District Courts of the United States, in their respective circuits and districts within the several States, and the Judges of the Superior Courts of the territories, severally and collectively, in term-time and vacation; and shall grant certificates to such claimants, upon satisfactory proof being made, with authority to take and remove such fugitives from service or labor, under the restrictions herein contained, to the State or Territory from which such persons may have escaped or fled.

Sec. 5. That it shall be the duty of all marshals and deputy marshals to obey and execute all warrants and precepts issued under the provisions of this act, when to them directed; and should any marshal or deputy marshal refuse to receive such warrant, or other process, when tendered, or to use all proper means diligently to execute the same, he shall, on conviction thereof, be fined in the sum of one thousand dollars, to the use of such claimant, on the motion of such claimant, by the Circuit or District Court for the district of such marshal; and after arrest of such fugitive, by such marshal or his deputy, or whilst at any time in his custody, under the provisions of this act, should such fugitive escape, whether with or without the assent of such marshal or his deputy, such marshal shall be liable, on his official bond, to be prosecuted for the benefit of such claimant, for the full value of the service or labor of said fugitive in the State, Territory, or district whence he escaped; and the better to enable said Commissioners, when thus appointed, to execute their duties faithfully and efficiently, in conformity with the requirements of the Constitution of the United States, and of this Act, they are hereby authorized and empowered, within their counties respectively, to appoint, in writing under their hands, any one or more suitable persons, from time to time, to execute all such warrants and other process as may be issued by them in the lawful performance of their respective duties; with authority to such Commissioners, or the persons to be appointed by them, to execute process as aforesaid, to summon and call to their aid the bystanders, or *posse commitatus* of the proper county, when necessary to insure a faithful observance of the clause of the Constitution referred to, in conformity with the provisions of this Act; and all good citizens are commanded to aid and assist in the prompt and efficient execution of this law, whenever their services may be required, as aforesaid, for that purpose; and said warrants shall run, and be executed by said officers, anywhere in the State within which they are issued.

Sec. 6. That when a person held to service or labor in any State or Territory of the United States, has heretofore or shall hereafter escape into another State or Territory of the United States, the person or persons to whom such service or labor may be due, or his, her, or their agent or attorney, duly authorized by power of attorney, in writing acknowledged and certified under the seal of some legal officer or Court of the State or Territory in which the same may be executed, may pursue and reclaim such fugitive person, either by procuring a warrant from some one of the Courts, Judges, or Commissioners aforesaid, of the proper circuit, district or county, for the apprehension of such fugitive from service or labor, or by seizing and arresting such fugitive where the same can be done without process, and by taking or causing such person to be taken forthwith before such Court, Judge or Commissioner, whose duty it shall be to hear and determine the case of such claimant in a summary manner; and upon satisfactory proof being made, by deposition or affidavit, in writing, to be taken and certified by such Court, Judge or Commissioner, or by other satisfactory testimony, duly taken and certified by some Court, Magistrate, Justice of the Peace, or other legal officer authorized to administer an oath and take depositions under the laws of the State or Territory from which such person owing service or labor may have escaped, with a certificate of such magistracy, or other authority as aforesaid, with the seal of the proper Court or officer thereto attached, which seal shall be sufficient to establish the competency of the proof, and with proof, also by affidavit, of the identity of the person whose service or labor is claimed to be due as aforesaid, that the person so arrested does in fact owe service or labor to the person or persons claiming him or her, in the State or Territory from which such fugitive may have escaped as aforesaid, and that said person escaped, to make out and deliver to said claimant, his or her agent or attorney, a certificate setting forth the substantial facts as to the service or labor due from such fugitive to the claimant, and of his or her escape from the State or Territory in which such service or labor was due to the State or Territory in which he or she was arrested, with authority to such claimant, or his or her agent or attorney, to use such reasonable force and restraint as may be necessary, under the circumstances of the case, to take and remove such fugitive person back to the State or Territory whence he or she may have escaped as aforesaid. In no trial or hearing under this Act shall the testimony of such alleged fugitive be admitted in evidence; and the certificates in this and the first [fourth] section mentioned, shall be conclusive of the right of the person or persons in whose favor granted, to remove such fugitive to the State or Territory from which he escaped, and shall prevent all molestation of such person or persons by any process issued by any Court, Judge, Magistrate, or other person whomsoever.

SEC. 7. That any person who shall knowingly and willingly

obstruct, hinder, or prevent such claimant, his agent or attorney, or any person or persons lawfully assisting him, her or them, from arresting such a fugitive from service or labor, either with or without process as aforesaid, or shall rescue or attempt to rescue such fugitive from service or labor, from the custody of such claimant, his or her agent or attorney, or other person or persons lawfully assisting as aforesaid, when so arrested pursuant to the authority herein given, and declared, or shall aid, abet, or assist such person so owing service or labor as aforesaid, directly or indirectly, to escape from such claimant, his agent or attorney, or other person or persons legally authorized as aforesaid; or shall harbor or conceal such fugitive so as to prevent the discovery and arrest of such person, after notice or knowledge of the fact that such person was a fugitive from service or labor as aforesaid, shall, for either of said offences, be subject to a fine not exceeding one thousand dollars, and imprisonment not exceeding six months, by indictment and conviction before the District Court of the United States, for the district in which such offence may have been commited, or before the proper court of criminal jurisdiction, if committed within any one of the organized territories of the United States, and shall moreover forfeit and pay, by way of civil damages to the party injured by such illegal conduct, the sum of one thousand dollars, for each fugitive so lost as aforesaid, to be recovered as aforesaid, to be recovered by action of debt in any of the District or Territorial Courts aforesaid, within whose jurisdiction the said offence may have been committed.

Sec. 8. That the marshals, their deputies, and the clerks of the said District and Territorial Courts, shall be paid for their services the like fees as may be allowed to them for similar services in other cases; and where such services are rendered exclusively in the arrest, custody, and delivery of the fugitive to the claimant, his or her agent or attorney, or where such supposed fugitive may be discharged out of custody for the want of sufficient proof as aforesaid, then such fees are to be paid in the whole by such claimant, his agent or attorney; and in all cases where the proceedings are before a Commissioner, he shall be entitled to a fee of ten dollars in full for his services in each case, upon the delivery of the said certificate to the claimant, his or her agent or attorney; or a fee of five dollars in cases where the proof shall not, in the opinion of such Commissioner, warrant such certificate and delivery, inclusive of all services incident to such arrest and examination, to be paid in either case by the claimant, his or her agent or attorney. The person or persons authorized to execute the process to be issued by such Commissioner for the arrest and detention of fugitives from service or labor as aforesaid, shall also be entitled to a fee of five dollars each, for each person he or they may arrest and take before any such Commissioner, as aforesaid, at the instance and request of such claimant, with such other fees as may be deemed reasonable by such Commissioners for such other additional services as may be necessarily performed by him or them; such as attending at the examination, keeping the fugitive in custody, and providing him with food and lodging during his detention, and until the final determination of such Commissioner; and, in general, for performing such other duties as may be required by such claimant, his or her attorney or agent, or Commissioner in the premises. Such fees to be made up in conformity with the fees usually charged by the officers of the courts of justice within the proper district or county, as near as may be practicable, and paid by such claimants, their agents or attorneys, whether such supposed fugitives from service or labor be ordered to be delivered to such claimants by the final determination of such Commissioner or not.

Sec. 9. That, upon affidavit made by the claimant of such fugitive, his agent or attorney, after such certificate has been issued, that he has reason to apprehend that such fugitive will be rescued by force from his or her possession before he can be taken beyond the limits of the State in which the arrest is made, it shall be the duty of the officer making the arrest to retain such fugitive in his custody, and to remove him to the State whence he fled, and there to deliver him to said claimant, his agent or attorney. And to this end, the officer aforesaid is hereby authorized and required to employ so many persons as he may deem necessary to overcome such force, and to retain them in his service so long as circumstances may require. The said officer and his assistants while so employed to receive the same compensation, and to be allowed the same expenses as are now allowed by law for transportation of criminals, to be certified by the Judge of the district within which the arrest is made, and paid out of the treasury of the United States.

Sec. 10. That when any person held to service or labor in any State or Territory, or in the District of Columbia, shall escape therefrom, the party to whom such service or labor may be due, his, her, or their agent or attorney, may apply to any court of record therein, or Judge thereof in vacation, and make satisfactory proof to such court, or Judge in vacation, of the escape aforesaid, and that the person escaping owed service or labor to such party. Whereupon the court shall cause a record to be made of the matters so proved, and also a general description of the person so escaping, with such convenient certainty as may be; and a transcript of such record, authenticated by the attestation of the clerk and of the seal of the said court, being produced in any other State, Territory or District in which the person so escaping may be found, and being exhibited to any Judge, Commissioner, or other officer authorized by the law of the United States to cause persons escaping from service or labor to be delivered up, shall be held and taken to be full and conclusive evidence of the fact of the escape, and that the service or labor of the person escaping is due to the party in such record mentioned. And upon the production by the said party of other and further evidence if necessary, either oral or by affidavit, in addition to what is contained in the said record of the identity of the person escaping, he or she shall be delivered up to the claimant. And the said Court, Commissioner, Judge, or other person authorized by this Act to grant certificates to claimants of fugitives, shall, upon the production of the record and other evidences aforesaid, grant to such claimant a certificate of his right to take any such person identified and proved to be owing service or labor as aforesaid, which shall authorize such claimant to seize or arrest and transport such person to the State or Territory from which he escaped: *Provided*, That nothing herein contained shall be construed as requiring the production of a transcript of such record as evidence as aforesaid. But in its absence the claim shall be heard and determined upon other satisfactory proofs, competent in law.

Approved September 18, 1850.

[The above law was repealed by the 38th Congress, 1864.]

KANSAS AND NEBRASKA ACT OF 1854.

An Act to Organize the Territories of Nebraska and Kansas.

Be it enacted by the Senate and House of Representatives of the United States of America in Congress assembled, That all that part of the territory of the United States included within the following limits, except such portions thereof as are hereinafter expressly exempted from the operations of this Act, to-wit: beginning at a point on the Missouri river where the fortieth parallel of north latitude crosses the same; thence west on said parallel to the east boundary of the Territory of Utah on the summit of the Rocky Mountains; thence on said summit northward to the forty ninth parallel of north latitude; thence east on said parallel to the western boundary of the Territory of Minnesota; thence southward on said boundary to the Missouri river; thence down the main channel of said river to the place of beginning, be, and the same is hereby, created into a temporary government by the name of the Territory of Nebraska; and when admitted as a State or States, the said Territory, or any portion of the same, shall be received into the Union with or without slavery, as their Constitution may prescribe at the time of their admission: *Provided,* That nothing in this Act contained shall be construed to inhibit the Government of the United States from dividing said Territory into two or more Territories, in such manner and at such times as Congress shall deem convenient and proper, or from attaching any portion of said Territory to any other State or Territory of the United States: *Provided, further,* That nothing in this Act contained shall be construed to impair the rights of person or property now pertaining to the Indians in said Territory, so long as such rights shall remain unextinguished by treaty between the United States and such Indians, or to include any Territory which, by treaty with any Indian tribe, is not, without the consent of said tribe, to be included within the Territorial limits or jurisdiction of any State or Territory; but all such Territory shall be excepted out of the boundaries, and constitute no part of the Territory of Nebraska, until said tribe shall signify their assent to the President of the United States to be included within the said Territory of Nebraska, or to affect the authority of the Government of the United States to make any regulations respecting such Indians, their lands, property or other rights, by treaty, law, or otherwise, which it would have been competent to the Government to make if this Act had never passed.

Sec. 2. That the executive power and authority in and over said Territory of Nebraska shall be vested in a Governor, who shall hold his office for four years, and until his successor shall be appointed and qualified, unless sooner removed by the President of the United States. The Governor shall reside within said Territory, and shall be commander-in-chief of the militia thereof. He may grant pardons and respites for offences against the laws of said Territory, and reprieves for offences against the laws of the United States, until the decision of the President can be made known thereon; he shall commission all officers who shall be appointed to office under the laws of the said Territory, and shall take care that the laws be faithfully executed.

Sec. 3. That there shall be a Secretary of said Territory, who shall reside therein, and hold his office for five years, unless sooner removed by the President of the United States; he shall record and preserve all the laws and proceedings of the Legislative Assembly hereinafter constituted, and all the acts and proceedings of the Governor in his executive department; he shall transmit one copy of the laws and journals of the Legislative Assembly within thirty days after the end of each session, and one copy of the executive proceedings and official correspondence semi-annually, on the first days of January and July in each year, to the President of the United States, and two copies of the laws to the President of the Senate and to the Speaker of the House of Representatives, to be deposited in the libraries of Congress; and, in case of the death, removal, resignation, or absence of the Governor from the Territory, the Secretary shall be, and he is hereby duly authorized and required to execute and perform all the powers and duties of the Governor during such vacancy or absence, or until another Governor shall be duly appointed and qualified to fill such vacancy.

Sec. 4. That the legislative power and authority of said Territory shall be vested in the Governor and a Legislative Assembly. The Legislative Assembly shall consist of a Council and House of Representatives. The Council shall consist of thirteen members, having the qualifications of voters, as hereinafter prescribed, whose term of service shall continue two years. The House of Representatives shall, at its first session, consist of twenty-six members, possessing the same qualifications as prescribed for members of the Council, and whose term of service shall continue one year. The number of Representatives may be increased by the Legislative Assembly, from time to time. in proportion to the increase of qualified voters: *Provided*, That the whole number shall never exceed thirty-nine; an apportionment shall be made as nearly equal as practicable, among the several counties or districts, for the election of the Council and Representatives, giving each section of the Territory representation in the ratio of its qualified voters as nearly as may be. And the members of the Council and of the House of Representatives shall reside in, and be inhabitants of, the district or county, or counties, for which they may be elected respectively. Previous to the first election, the Governor shall cause a census or enumeration of the inhabitants and qualified voters of the several counties and districts of the Territory, to be taken by such persons and in such mode as the Governor shall designate and appoint; and the persons so appointed shall receive a reasonable compensation therefor. And the first election shall be held at such times and places, and be conducted in such manner, both as to the persons who shall superintend such election and the returns thereof, as the Governor shall appoint and direct; and he shall at the same time declare the number of members of the Council and House of Representatives to which each of the counties or districts shall be entitled under this Act. The persons having the highest number of legal votes in each of said Council districts for members of the Council, shall be declared by the Governor to be duly elected to the Council; and the persons having the highest number of legal votes for the House of Representatives, shall be declared by the Governor to be duly elected members of said House: *Provided*, That in case two or more persons voted for shall have an equal number of votes, and in case a vacancy shall otherwise occur in either branch of the Legislative Assembly, the Governor shall order a new election; and the persons thus elected to the Legislative Assembly shall meet at such place and on such day as the Governor shall appoint; but thereafter, the time, place, and manner of holding and conducting all elections by the people, and the apportioning the representation in the several counties or districts to the Council and House of Representatives, according to the number of qualified voters, shall be prescribed by law, as well as the day of the commencement of the regular sessions of the Legislative Assembly: *Provided*, That no session in any one year shall exceed the term of forty days, except the first session, which may continue sixty days.

Sec. 5. That every free white male inhabitant, above the age of twenty-one years, who shall be an actual resident of said territory, and shall possess the qualifications hereinafter prescribed, shall be entitled to vote at the first election, and shall be eligible to any office within the said territory; but the qualifications of voters, and of holding office, at all subsequent elections, shall be such as shall be prescribed by the Legislative Assembly: *Provided,* That the right of suffrage and of holding office shall be exercised only by citizens of the United States and those who shall have declared on oath their intention to become such, and shall have taken an oath to support the Constitution of the United States and the provisions of this act: *And provided further,* That no officer, soldier, seaman, or marine, or other person in the army or navy of the United States, or attached to troops in the service of the United States, shall be allowed to vote or hold office in said territory, by reason of being on service therein.

SEC. 6. That the legislative power of the Territory shall extend to all rightful subjects of legislation consistent with the Constitution of United States and the provisions of this Act; but no law shall be passed interfering with the primary disposal of the soil; no tax shall be imposed upon the property of the United States; nor shall the lands or other property of non-residents be taxed higher than the lands or other property of residents. Every bill which shall have passed the Council and House of Representatives of said Territory, shall, before it become a law, be presented to the Governor of the Territory; if he approve, he shall sign it; but if not, he shall return it with his objections to the House in which it originated, who shall enter the objections at large on their journal, and proceed to reconsider it. If, after such reconsideration, two-thirds of that House shall agree to pass the bill, it shall be sent, together with the objections, to the other House, by which it shall likewise be reconsidered, and if approved by two-thirds of that House, it shall become a law. But in all such cases the votes of both Houses shall be determined by yeas and nays, to be entered on the journal of each House respectively. If any bill shall not be returned by the Governor within three days (Sundays excepted) after it shall have been presented to him, the same shall be a law in like manner as if he had signed it, unless the Assembly, by adjournment, prevent its return, in which case it shall not be a law.

SEC. 7. That all township, district, and county officers, not herein otherwise provided for, shall be appointed or elected, as the case may be, in such manner as shall be provided by the Governor and Legislative Assembly of the Territory of Nebraska. The Governor shall nominate, and, by and with the advice and consent of the Legislative Council, appoint all officers not herein otherwise provided for; and in the first instance the Governor alone may appoint all said officers, who shall hold their offices until the end of the first session of the Legislative Assembly; and shall lay off the necessary districts for members of the Council and House of Representatives, and all other officers.

SEC. 8. That no member of the Legislative Assembly shall hold, or be appointed to, any office which may have been created, or the salary or emoluments of which shall have been increased, while he was a member, during the term for which he was elected, and for one year after the expiration of such term; but this restriction shall not be applicable to members of the first Legislative Assembly; and no person holding a commission or appointment under the United States, except postmasters, shall be a member of the Legislative Assembly, or shall hold any office under the government of said Territory.

SEC. 9. That the judicial power of said Territory shall be vested in a Supreme Court, District Courts, Probate Courts, and in Justices of the Peace. The Supreme Court shall consist of a Chief Justice and two Associate Justices, any two of whom shall constitute a quorum, and who shall hold a term at the seat of government of said Territory annually, and they shall hold their offices during the period of four years, and until their successors shall be appointed and qualified. The said Territory shall be divided into three judicial districts, and a District Court shall be held in each of said districts by one of the Justices of the Supreme Court, at such times and places as may be prescribed by law; and the said Judges shall, after their appointments, respectively reside in the district which be assigned them. The jurisdiction of the several courts herein provided for, both appellate and original, and that of the Probate Courts and of Justices of the Peace, shall be limited by law: *Provided*, That Justices of the Peace shall not have jurisdiction of the matter in controversy when the title or boundaries of land may be in dispute, or where the debt or sum claimed shall exceed one hundred dollars; and the said Supreme and District Courts, respectively, shall possess chancery as well as common law juristion. Each District Court, or the judge thereof, shall appoint its clerk, who shall also be the register in chancery, and shall keep his office at the place where the Court may be held. Writs of error, bills of exception, and appeals, shall be allowed in all cases from the final decision of said District Courts to the Supreme Court, under such regulations as may be prescribed by law; but in no case removed to the Supreme Court shall trial by jury be allowed by said Court. The Supreme Court, or the Justices thereof, shall appoint its own clerk, and every clerk shall hold his office at the pleasure of the Court for which he shall have been appointed. Writs of error, and appeals from the final decision of said Supreme Court, shall be allowed, and may be taken to the Supreme Court of the United States, in the same manner and under the same regulations as from the Circuit Courts of the United States, where the value of the property, or the amount in controversy. to be ascertained by the oath or affirmation of either party, or other competent witness, shall exceed one thousand dollars; except only that in all cases involving title to slaves, the said writs of error or appeals shall be allowed and decided by the said Supreme Court, without regard to the value of the matter, property, or title in controversy; and except also that a writ of error or appeal shall also be allowed to the Supreme Court of the United States, from the decisions of the said Supreme Court created by this Act, or of any judge thereof, or of the District Courts created by this Act, or of any Judge thereof, upon any writ of *habeas corpus*, involving the question of personal freedom: *Provided*, That nothing herein contained shall be construed to apply to or affect provisions of the "Act respecting fugitives from justice, and persons escaping from the service of their masters," approved February 12th, 1793, and the "Act to amend and supplementary to the aforesaid Act," approved September 18, 1850; and each of the said District Courts shall have and exercise the same jurisdiction in all cases arising under the Constitution and laws of the United States as is vested in the Circuit and District Courts of the United States; and the said Supreme and District Courts of the said Territory, and the respective judges thereof, shall and may grant writs of *habeas corpus* in all cases in which the same are granted by the judges of the United States in the District of Columbia; and the first six days of every term of said courts, or so much thereof as shall be necessary, shall be appropriated to the trial of causes arising under the said Constitution and laws, and writs of error and appeal in all such cases shall be made to the Supreme Court of said Territory, the same as in other cases. The said clerk shall receive in all such cases the same fees which the clerks of the District Courts of Utah Territory now receive for similar services.

SEC. 10. That the provisions of an Act entitled "an Act respecting fugitives from justices, and persons escaping from the service of their masters," approved February 12, 1793, and the provisions of the Act entitled "an Act to amend, and supplementary to, the aforesaid Act," approved September 18, 1850, be, and the same are hereby, declared to extend to and be in full force within the limits of said Territory of Nebraska.

SEC. 11. That there shall be appointed an attorney for said Territory, who shall continue in office for four years, and until his successor shall be appointed and qualified, unless sooner removed by the President, and who shall receive the same fees and salary as the attorney of the United States for the present Territory of Utah. There shall also be a marshal for the Territory appointed, who shall hold his office for four years, and until his successor shall be appointed and qualified, unless sooner removed by the President, and who shall execute all processes issuing from the said courts when exercising their jurisdiction as Circuit and District Courts of the United States; he shall perform the duties, be subject to the same regulations and penalties, and be entitled to the same fees as the marshal of the District Court of the United States for the present Territory of Utah, and shall, in addition, be paid two hundred dollars annually as a compensation for extra services.

Sec. 12. That the Governor, Secretary, Chief Justice, and Associate Justices, Attorney, and Marshal, shall be nominated, and, by and with the advice and consent of the Senate, appointed by the President of the United States. The Governor and Secretary to be appointed as aforesaid, shall, before they act as such, respectively take an oath or affirmation before the District Judge or some Justice of the Peace in the limits of said Territory, duly authorized to administer oaths and affirmations by the laws now in force therein, or before the Chief Justice or some Associate Justice of the Supreme Court of the United States, to support the Constitution of the United States, and faithfully to discharge the duties of their respective offices, which said oaths, when so taken, shall be certified by the person by whom the same shall have been taken; and such certificates shall be received and recorded by the said Secretary among the executive proceedings; and the Chief Justice and Associate Justices, and all other civil officers in said Territory, before they act as such, shall take a like oath or affirmation before the said Governor or Secretary, or some Judge or Justice of the Peace of the Territory who may be duly commissioned and qualified, which said oath or affirmation shall be certified and transmitted by the person taking the same to the Secretary, to be by him recorded as aforesaid; and afterwards, the like oath or affirmation shall be taken, certified, and recorded, in such manner and form as may be prescribed by law. The Governor shall receive an annual salary of two thousand five hundred dollars. The Chief Justice and Associate Justices shall receive an annual salary of two thousand dollars. The Secretary shall receive an annual salary of two thousand dollars. The said salaries shall be paid quarter-yearly, from the dates of the respective appointments, at the treasury of the United States; but no such payment shall be made until said officers shall have entered upon the duties of their respective appointments. The members of the Legislative Assembly shall be entitled to receive three dollars each per day during their attendance at the sessions thereof, and three dollars each for every twenty miles' travel in going to and returning from the said sessions, estimated according to the nearest usually traveled route; and an additional allowance of three dollars shall be paid to the presiding officer of each House for each day he shall so preside. And a chief clerk, one assistant clerk, a sergeant-at-arms, and door-keeper, may be chosen for each House; and the chief clerk shall receive $4 per day, and the said other officers $3 per day, during the session of the Legislative Assembly; but no other officers shall be paid by the United States: *Provided*, That there shall be but one session of the Legislature annually, unless, on an extraordinary occasion, the Governor shall think proper to call the Legislature together. There shall be appropriated, annually, the usual sum, to be expended by the Governor, to defray the contingent expenses of the Territory, including the salary of a Clerk of the Executive Department; and there shall also be appropriated, annually, a sufficient sum, to be expended by the Secretary of the Territory, and upon an estimate to be made by the Secretary of the Treasury of the United States, to defray the expenses of the Legislative Assembly, the printing of the laws, and other incidental expenses; and the Governor and Secretary of the Territory shall, in the disbursement of all moneys intrusted to them, be governed solely by the instructions of the Secretary of the Treasury of the United States, and shall, semi-annually, account to the said Secretary for the manner in which the aforesaid moneys shall have been expended; and no expenditure shall be made by said Legislative Assembly for objects not specially authorized by the Acts of Congress making the appropriations, nor beyond the sums thus appropriated for such objects.

Sec. 13. That the Legislative Assembly of the Territory of Nebraska shall hold its first session at such time and place in said Territory as the Governor thereof shall appoint and direct; and at said first session, or as soon thereafter as they shall deem expedient, the Governor and Legislative Assembly shall proceed to locate and establish the seat of government for said Territory at such place as they may deem eligible; which place, however, shall thereafter be subject to be changed by the said Governor and Legislative Assembly.

Sec. 14. That a delegate to the House of Representatives of the United States, to serve for the term of two years, who shall be a citizen of the United States, may be elected by the voters qualified to elect members of the Legislative Assembly, who shall be entitled to the same rights and privileges as are exercised and enjoyed by the delegates from the several other Territories of the United States to the said House of Representatives, but the delegate first elected shall hold his seat only during the term of the Congress to which he shall be elected. The first election shall be held at such time and places, and be conducted in such manner, as the Governor shall appoint and direct; and at all subsequent elections the times, places, and manner of holding the elections shall be prescribed by law. The person having the greatest number of votes shall be declared by the Governor to be duly elected, and a certificate thereof shall be given accordingly. That the Constitution, and all the laws of the United States which are not locally inapplicable, shall have the same force and effect within the said Territory of Nebraska as elsewhere within the United States, except the eighth section of the Act preparatory to the admission of Missouri into the Union, approved March sixth, eighteen hundred and twenty, which, being inconsistent with the principle of non-intervention by Congress with slavery in the States and Territories, as recognized by the legislation of eighteen hundred and fifty, commonly called the Compromise Measures, is hereby declared inoperative and void; it being the true intent and meaning of this Act not to legislate slavery into any Territory or State, nor to exclude it therefrom, but to leave the people thereof perfectly free to form and regulate their domestic institutions in their own way, subject only to the Constitution of the United States: *Provided*, That nothing herein contained shall be construed to revive or put in force any law or regulation which may have existed prior to the Act of sixth March, eighteen hundred and twenty, either protecting, establishing, prohibiting, or abolishing slavery.

Sec. 15. That there shall hereafter be appropriated, as has been customary for the territorial governments, a sufficient amount, to be expended under the direction of the said Governor of the Territory of Nebraska, not exceeding the sums heretofore appropriated for similar objects, for the erection of suitable public buildings at the seat of government, and for the purchase of a library, to be kept at the seat of government for the use of the Governor, Legislative Assembly, Judges of the Supreme Court, Secretary, Marshal, and Attorney of said Territory, and such other persons, and under such regulations, as shall be prescribed by law.

Sec. 16. That when the lands in said Territory shall be surveyed under the direction of the Government of the United States, preparatory to bringing the same into market, sections numbered sixteen and thirty-six, in each township in said Territory, shall be, and the same are hereby, reserved for the purpose of being applied to schools in said Territory, and in the States and Territories hereafter to be erected out of the same.

Sec. 17. That, until otherwise provided by law, the Governor of said Territory may define the judicial districts of said Territory, and assign the judges who may be appointed for said Territory to the several districts; and also appoint the times and places for holding courts in the several counties or subdivisions in each of said judicial districts by proclamation, to be issued by him; but the Legislative Assembly, at their first or any subsequent session, may organize, alter, or modify such judicial districts, and assign the judges, and alter the times and places of holding the courts, as to them shall seem proper and convenient.

SEC. 18. That all officers to be appointed by the President, by and with the advice and consent of the Senate, for the Territory of Nebraska, who, by virtue of the provisions of any law now existing, or which may be enacted during the present Congress, are required to give security for moneys that may be intrusted with them for disbursements, shall give security, at such time and place, and in such manner as the Secretary of Treasury may prescribe.

SEC. 19. That all that part of the territory of the United States included within the following limits, except such portions thereof as are hereinafter expressly exempted from the operations of this act, to-wit: beginning at a point on the western boundary of the State of Missouri, where the thirty-seventh parallel of north latitude crosses the same; thence west on said parallel to the eastern boundary of New Mexico; thence north on said boundary to latitude thirty-eight; thence following said boundary westward to the east boundary of the Territory of Utah, on the summit of the Rocky Mountains, thence northward on said summit to the fortieth parallel of latitude; thence east on said parallel to the western boundary of the State of Missouri; thence south with the western boundary of said State to the place of beginning, be, and the same is hereby, created into a temporary government by the name of the Territory of Kansas; and when admitted as a State or States, the said Territory, or any portion of the same, shall be received into the Union with or without slavery, as their Constitution may prescribe at the time of their admission: *Provided*, That nothing in this Act contained shall be construed to inhibit the Government of the United States from dividing said Territory into two or more Territories, in such manner and at such times as Congress shall deem convenient and proper, or from attaching any portion of said Territory to any other State or Territory of the United States: *Provided further*, That nothing in this Act contained shall be so construed as to impair the rights of persons or property now pertaining to the Indians in said Territory, so long as such rights shall remain unextinguished by treaty between the United States and such Indians, or to include any territory which, by treaty with any Indian tribe, is not, without the consent of said tribe, to be included within the territorial limits or jurisdiction of any State or Territory; but all such territory shall be excepted out of the boundaries, and constitute no part of the Territory of Kansas, until said tribe shall signify their assent to the President of the United States to be included within the said Territory of Kansas, or to affect the authority of the Government of the United State to make any regulation respecting such Indians, their lands, property, or other rights, by treaty, law, or otherwise, which it would have been competent to the government to make if this act had never passed.

[With the single exception of the location of the seat of government for Kansas at Fort Leavenworth, provided for in section 31, the ensuing sixteen sections, relative to the organization and government of the Territory, are precisely similar to the sections already recited, providing for the government of Nebraska Territory. The final section of the act, which has a general reference to both Territories, is as follows:]

SEC. 37. *And be it further enacted,* That all treaties, laws, and other engagements made by the Government of the United States with the Indian tribes inhabiting the Territories embraced within this act, shall be faithfully and rigidly observed, notwithstanding anything contained in this act; and that the existing agencies and superintendencies of said Indians be continued, with the same powers and duties which are now prescribed by law, except that the President of the United States may at his discretion change the location of the office of superintendent.

ORDINANCE OF 1787.

IN CONGRESS, JULY 13, 1787.

An Ordinance for the government of the territory of the United States, northwest of the river Ohio.

Be it ordained, by the United States in Congress assembled, that the said Territory, for the purpose of temporary government, be one district; subject, however, to be divided into two districts, as future circumstances may, in the opinion of Congress, make it expedient.

Be it ordained, by the authority aforesaid, that the estates both of resident and non-resident proprietors in the said Territory, dying intestate, shall descend to, and be distributed among their children, and the descendants of a deceased child, in equal parts; the descendants of a deceased child or grand-child, to take the share of their deceased parent, in equal parts, among them, and where there shall be no children or descendants, then in equal parts to the next of kin, in equal degree; and among collaterals, the children of a deceased brother or sister of the intestate shall have, in equal parts, among them, their deceased parents share; and there shall in no case be a distinction between kindred of the whole and half blood; saving in all cases to the widow of the intestate her third part of the real estate for life, and one-third part of the personal estate; and this law relative to descents and dower shall remain in full force until altered by the Legislature of the district. And until the Governor and judges shall adopt laws as hereinafter mentioned, estates in the said territory may be devised or bequeathed by wills in writing, signed and sealed by him or her, in whom the estate may be (being of full age,) and attested by three witnesses; and real estates may be conveyed by lease and release, or bargain and sale, signed, sealed and delivered by the person, being of full age, in whom the estate may, and attested by two witnesses, provided such wills be duly proved, and such conveyances be acknowledged, or the execution thereof duly proved, and be recorded within one year after proper magistrates, courts, and registers shall be appointed for that purpose, and personal property may be transferred by delivery, saving, however, to the

(85)

French and Canadian inhabitants, and other settlers of the Kaskaskias, Saint Vincents, and the neighboring villages, who have heretofore professed themselves citizens of Virginia, their laws and customs now in force among them, relative to descent and conveyance of property.

Be it ordained, by the authority aforesaid, that there shall be appointed, from time to time, by Congress, a Governor, whose commission shall continue in force for the term of three years, unless sooner revoked by Congress; he shall reside in the district, and have a freehold estate therein, in one thousand acres of land, while in the exercise of his office. There shall be appointed, from time to time, by Congress, a Secretary, whose commission shall continue in force for four years, unless sooner revoked; he shall reside therein, and have a freehold estate therein, in five hundred acres of land, while in the exercise of his office; it shall be his duty to keep and preserve the acts and laws passed by the Legislature, and the public records of the district, and the proceedings of the Governor in his executive department, and transmit authentic copies of such acts and proceedings, every six months, to the Secretary of Congress. There shall also be appointed a court, to consist of three judges, any two of whom to form a court, who shall have a common law jurisdiction, and reside in the district, and have each therein a freehold estate in five hundred acres of land, while in the exercise of their offices; and their commissions shall continue in force during good behavior.

The Governor and judges, or a majority of them, shall adopt and publish in the district such laws of the original States, criminal and civil, as may be necessary, and best suited to the circumstances of the district, and report them to Congress, from time to time, which laws shall be in force in the district until the organization of the General Assembly therein, unless disapproved by Congress; but afterwards, the Legislature shall have authority to alter them as they shall think fit.

The Governor, for the time being, shall be commander-in-chief of the militia, appoint and commission all officers in the same, below the rank of general officers. All general officers shall be appointed and commissioned by Congress.

Previous to the organization of the General Assembly, the Governor shall appoint such magistrates and other civil officers, in each county or township, as he shall find necessary for the preservation of the peace and good order in the same. After the General Assembly shall be organized, the powers and duties of magistrates and other civil officers shall be regulated and defined by the said Assembly; but all magistrates and other civil officers, not herein otherwise directed, shall, during the continuance of this temporary government, be appointed by the Governor.

For the prevention of crimes and injuries, the laws to be adopted or made, shall have force in all parts of the district, and for the execution of process, criminal and civil, the Governor shall make proper divisions thereof; and shall proceed, from time to time, as circumstances may require, to lay out the parts of the district in which the Indian titles shall have been extinguished, into counties and townships, subject, however, to such alterations as may hereafter be made by the Legislature.

So soon as there shall be five thousand free male inhabitants, of full age, in the district, upon giving proof thereof to the governor, they shall receive authority, with time and place, to elect representatives from their counties or townships, to represent them in the General Assembly; *Provided*, That for every five hundred free male inhabitants there shall be one representative, and so on progressively with the number of free male inhabitants, shall the right of representation increase, until the number of representatives shall amount to twenty-five, after which the number and proportion of representatives shall be regulated by the Legislature; *Provided*, That no person be eligible or qualified to act as a representative, unless he shall have been a citizen of one of the United States three years and be a resident in the district, or unless he shall have resided in the district three years, and in either case shall likewise hold in his own right, in fee simple, two hundred acres of land within the same; *Provided*, also, that a freehold in fifty acres of land in the district, having been a citizen of one of the States, and being resident in the district, or the like freehold and two years residence in the district, shall be necessary to qualify a man as an elector of a representative.

The representative thus elected, shall serve for the term of two years, and in case of the death of a representative, or removal from office, the Governor shall issue a writ to the county or township for which he was a member, to elect another in his stead, to serve for the residue of the term.

The General Assembly, or Legislature, shall consist of the Governor, Legislative Council, and a House of Representatives. The Legislative Council shall consist of five members, to continue in office five years, unless sooner removed by Congress, any three of whom to be a quorum, and the members of the Council, shall be nominated and appointed in the following manner, to-wit: as soon as representatives shall be elected, the Governor shall appoint a time and place for them to meet together, and, when met, they shall nominate ten persons, residents in the district, and each possessed of a freehold in five hundred acres of land, and return their names to Congress, five of whom

Congress shall appoint and commission to serve as aforesaid; and whenever a vacancy shall happen in the Council, by death or removal from office, the House of Representatives shall nominate two persons qualified as aforesaid, for each vacancy, and return their names to Congress, one of whom Congress shall appoint and commission for the residue of the term; and every five years, four months at least before the expiration of the time of service of the Council, the said House shall nominate ten persons qualified as aforesaid, and return their names to Congress, five of whom Congress shall appoint and commission to serve as members of the Council five years, unless sooner removed. And the Governor, Legislative Council and House of Representatives, shall have authority to make laws in all cases for the good government of the district, not repugnant to the principles and articles in this ordinance established and declared. And all bills having passed by a majority in the House, and by a majority in the Council, shall be referred to the Governor for his assent; but no bill or legislative act whatever, shall be of any force without his assent. The Governor shall have power to convene, prorogue and dissolve the assembly, when in his opinion it shall be expedient.

The Governor, Judges, Legislative Council, Secretary, and such other officers as Congress shall appoint in the district, shall take an oath or affirmation of fidelity, and of office—the Governor before the President of Congress, and all other officers before the Governor. As soon as a Legislature shall be formed in the District, the Council and House, assembled in one room, shall have authority by joint ballot to elect a delegate to Congress, who shall have a seat in Congress, with the right of debating, but not of voting, during this temporary government.

And for extending the fundamental principles of civil and religious liberty, which form the basis whereon these republics, their laws and constitutions, are erected; to *fix and establish those principles as the basis of all laws, constitutions and governments, which* FOREVER *hereafter shall be formed in the said territory;* to provide also for the establishment of States, and for their admission to a share in the federal council on an equal footing with the original States, at as early periods as may be consistent with the general interest:

It is hereby ordained and declared, by the authority aforesaid, that the following articles shall be considered as articles of compact between the original States, and the people and States in the said Territory, and forever remain unalterable, unless by common consent, viz:

ARTICLE I. No person, demeaning himself in a peaceable and orderly manner, shall ever be molested on account of his mode of worship or religious sentiments in the said territory.

ART. II. The inhabitants of the said territory shall always be entitled to the benefit of the writ of *habeas corpus*, and of the trial by jury; of a proportionate representation of the people in the Legislature, and of judicial proceedings according to the course of the common law; all persons shall be bailable unless for capital offences, where the proof shall be evident, or the presumption great; all fines shall be moderate, and no cruel or unusual punishments shall be inflicted; no man shall be deprived of his liberty or property, but by the judgment of his peers, or the law of the land; and should the public exigencies make it necessary for the common preservation to take any person's property, or to demand his particular services, full compensation shall be made for the same; and in the just preservation of rights and property, it is understood and declared, that no law ought ever to be made, or have force in the said territory, that shall in any manner whatever, interfere with, or affect private contracts or engagements, *bona fide*, and without fraud previously formed.

ART. III. Religion, morality, and knowledge, being necessary to good government and the happiness of mankind, schools and the means of education shall forever be encouraged. The utmost good faith shall always be observed toward the Indians; their lands and property shall never be taken from them without their consent; and in their property, rights, and liberty, they never shall be invaded or disturbed, unless in just and lawful wars authorized by Congress; but laws founded in justice and humanity, shall, from time to time, be made, for preventing wrongs being done to them, and for preserving peace and friendship with them.

ART. IV. The said Territory, and the States which may be formed therein, shall forever remain a part of this Confederacy of the United States of America, subject to the articles of confederation,* and to such alterations therein, as shall be constitutionally made; and to all the acts and ordinances of the United States in Congress assembled, conformable thereto. The inhabitants and settlers in the said Territory, shall be subject to pay a part of the federal debts contracted, or to be contracted, and a proportional part of the expenses of government, to be apportioned on them, by Congress, according to the same common rule and measure by which apportionments thereof shall be made on the other States; and the taxes for paying their proportion, shall be laid and levied by the authority and direction of the Legislatures of the district, or districts, or new States, as in the original States, within the time agreed upon by the United States in Congress assembled. The Legislatures of those dis-

---

*This ordinance was drawn up before the Constitution was formed.

tricts, or new States, shall never interfere with the primary disposal of the soil by the United States in Congress assembled, nor with any regulations Congress may find necessary for securing the title in such soil to the *bona fide* purchasers. No tax shall be imposed on lands the property of the United States; and in no case shall non-resident proprietors be taxed higher than residents. The navigable waters leading into the Mississippi and St. Lawrence, and the carrying places between the same shall be common highways, and forever free, as well to the inhabitants of the said territory, as to the citizens of the United States, and those of any other States that may be admitted into the confederacy, without any tax, impost or duty therefor.

ART. V. There shall be formed in the said Territory, not less than three, nor more than five States; and the boundaries of the States, as soon as Virginia shall alter her act of session and consent to the same, shall become fixed and established as follows, to-wit: The western State shall be bounded by the Mississippi, the Ohio, and Wabash rivers; a direct line drawn, from the Wabash and Post Vincents due north to the territorial line between the United States and Canada, and by the said territorial line to the Lake of the Woods and Mississippi. The middle State shall be bounded by the said direct line, the Wabash from Post Vincents to the Ohio, by the Ohio, by a direct line drawn due north from the mouth of the Great Miami to the said territorial line, and by said territorial line. The eastern State shall be bounded by the last mentioned direct line, the Ohio, Pennsylvania, and the said territorial line; *Provided*, however, and it is further understood and declared, that the boundaries of these three States shall be subject so far to be altered, and if Congress shall hereafter find it expedient, they shall have authority to form one or two States in that part of the said territory which lies north of an east and west line drawn through the southerly bend or extreme of Lake Michigan; and whenever any of the said States shall have sixty thousand free inhabitants therein, such States shall be admitted by its delegates, into the Congress of the United States, on an equal footing with the original States, in all respects whatsoever; and shall be at liberty to form a permanent constitution and State government; *Provided*, the constitution and government so to be formed, shall be republican, and in conformity to the principles contained in these articles; and so far as it can be consistent with the general interest of the confederacy, such admission shall be allowed at an earlier period, and when there may be a less number of free inhabitants in the State than sixty thousand.

ART. VI. There shall be neither slavery nor involuntary servitude in the said territory, otherwise than in the punishment of crimes whereof the party shall have been duly convicted;

Provided, always, that any person escaping into the same, from whom labor or service is lawfully claimed in any of the original States, such fugitive may be lawfully reclaimed and conveyed to the person claiming his or her labor or service as aforesaid.

Be it ordained, by the authority aforesaid, that the resolutions of the 23d of April, 1784, relative to the subject of this ordinance, be, and the same are hereby repealed and declared null and void.

NOTE.—By this ordinance, Virginia ceded to the United States the territory now composing the States of Ohio, Indiana, Illinois, Wisconsin and Michigan, making the ordinance the fundamental law of these States.

ELECTORAL VOTES

FOR
PRESIDENT AND VICE-PRESIDENT OF THE UNITED STATES.

Election for the First Term, commencing March 4, 1789, and terminating March 3, 1793.

No. of Electors from each State.	STATES.	George Washington, of Virginia.	John Adams, of Massachusetts.	Samuel Huntington, of Connecticut.	John Jay, of New York.	John Hancock, of Massachusetts.	R. H. Harrison, of Maryland.	George Clinton, of New York.	John Rutledge, of South Carolina.	John Milton, of Georgia.	James Armstrong, of Georgia.	Edward Telfair, of Georgia.	Benjamin Lincoln, of Massachusetts.
5	New Hampshire	5	5	....	....	....	....	....	....	....	....	....	....
10	Massachusetts	10	10	....	....	....	....	....	....	....	....	....	....
7	Connecticut	7	5	2	....	....	....	....	....	....	....	....	....
6	New Jersey	6	1	....	5	....	....	....	....	....	....	....	....
10	Pennsylvania	10	8	....	....	2	....	....	....	....	....	....	....
3	Delaware	3	....	....	3	....	....	....	....	....	....	....	....
6	Maryland	6	....	....	....	....	6	....	....	....	....	....	....
10	Virginia	10	5	....	1	1	....	3	....	....	....	....	....
7	South Carolina	7	....	....	....	1	....	....	6	....	....	....	....
5	Georgia	5	....	....	....	....	....	....	....	2	1	1	1
69	Whole No. Electors	69	34	2	9	4	6	3	6	2	1	1	1
	Majority 35												

The first Congress under the Constitution was convened at the "Federal Hall," situated at the head of Broad, fronting on Wall street, (where the Custom House now stands,) in the city of New York, on the first Wednesday, being March 4, 1789—Senators and Representatives having been elected from the eleven States which had ratified the Constitution; but, owing to the absence of a quorum, the House was not organized till the 1st of April, and, for a like reason, the Senate was not organized till the 6th; when the latter body "proceeded by ballot to the choice of a President, for the sole purpose of opening and counting the [electoral] votes for President of the United States." John Langdon, of New Hampshire, was chosen President *pro tem.* of the Senate, and Samuel Alyne Otis, of Massachusetts, Secretary; after which, proper measures were taken to notify the successful individuals of their election.

George Washington took the oath of office, as President, and entered upon his duties April 30, 1789. (For his Inaugural Address, see p. 28.

John Adams, Vice-President, entered upon his duties in the Senate April 21, 1789, and took the oath of office June 3, 1789.

Election for the Second Term, commencing March 4, 1793, and terminating March 3, 1797.

No. of Electors from each State	STATES.	George Washington, of Virginia.	John Adams, of Massachusetts.	George Clinton, of New York.	Thomas Jefferson, of Virginia.	Aaron Burr, of New York.
6	New Hampshire	6	6			
16	Massachusetts	16	16			
4	Rhode Island	4	4			
9	Connecticut	9	9			
3	Vermont	3	3			
12	New York	12		12		
7	New Jersey	7	7			
15	Pennsylvania	15	14	1		
3	Delaware	3	3			
8	Maryland	8	8			
21	Virginia	21		21		
4	Kentucky	4			4	
12	North Carolina	12		12		
8	South Carolina	8	7			1
4	Georgia	4		4		
132	Whole No. of Electors	132	77	50	4	1
	Majority............67					

George Washington, re-elected President, took the oath of office for a second term, and entered upon his duties March 4, 1793.

John Adams, re-elected Vice President, took the oath of office, and entered upon his duties in the Senate December 2, 1793.

After the expiration of his second Presidential term, Washington retired to the tranquil shades of Mount Vernon, fondly indulging the hope that the remainder of his days would be peacefully enjoyed in his much cherished home; but these pleasing anticipations were not allowed to remain long undisturbed. In 1798 the conduct of the French Directory and its emissaries led to frequent difficulties with this country, which were calculated to provoke a war; and the opinion was universally entertained that he who had formerly so well acquitted himself, must be again called to the command of our armies. Accordingly, early in July, the rank and title of Lieutenant-General and Commander-in-Chief of all the armies raised, or to be raised, in the United States," was conferred upon him; and the Secretary of War, Mr. McHenry, immediately waited upon him to tender the commission. In a letter to President Adams, accepting this "new proof of public confidence," he makes a reservation that he shall not be called into the field until the army is in a situation to require his presence, and adds: "I take the liberty also to mention, that I must decline having my acceptance considered as drawing after it any immediate charge upon the public, and that I cannot receive any emoluments annexed to the appointment, before entering into a situation to incur expense."

Election for the Third Term, commencing March 4, 1797, and terminating March 3, 1801.

No. of Electors from each State	STATES.	John Adams, of Massachusetts.	Thomas Jefferson, of Virginia.	Thos. Pinckney, of South Carolina.	Aaron Burr, of New York.	Samuel Adams, of Massachusetts.	Oliver Ellsworth, of Connecticut.	John Jay, of New York.	George Clinton, of New York.	S. Johnston, of North Carolina.	James Iredell, of North Carolina.	Geo. Washington, of Virginia.	C. C. Pinckney, of South Carolina.	John Henry, of Maryland.
6	New Hampshire	6	....	....	....	....	6	....	....	....	....	....	....	....
16	Massachusetts..	16	....	13	....	....	1	....	....	2	....	....	....	....
4	Rhode Island..	4	....	....	....	....	4	....	....	....	....	....	....	....
9	Connecticut ...	9	....	4	....	....	....	5	....	....	....	....	....	....
4	Vermont	4	....	4	....	....	....	....	....	....	....	....	....	....
12	New York	12	....	12	....	....	....	....	....	....	....	....	....	....
7	New Jersey....	7	....	7	....	....	....	....	....	....	....	....	....	....
15	Pennsylvania..	1	14	2	13	....	....	....	....	....	....	....	....	....
3	Delaware......	3	....	3	....	....	....	....	....	....	....	....	....	....
11	Maryland.....	7	4	4	3	....	....	....	....	....	....	....	....	2
21	Virginia	1	20	1	1	15	....	....	3	....	....	1	....	....
4	Kentucky	....	4	....	4	....	....	....	....	....	....	....	....	....
12	North Carolina.	1	11	1	6	....	....	....	....	....	3	1	....	....
8	South Carolina.	....	8	8	....	....	....	....	....	....	....	....	1	....
4	Georgia........	....	4	....	....	....	....	....	4	....	....	....	....	....
3	Tennessee.....	....	3	....	3	....	....	....	....	....	....	....	....	....
139	No. of Electors.	71	68	59	30	15	11	5	7	2	3	2	1	2
	Majority.....70													

John Adams, elected President, took the oath of office, and entered upon his duties, March 4, 1797.

Thomas Jefferson, elected Vice President, took the oath of office, and entered upon his duties in the Senate, March 4, 1797.

The administration of Mr. Adams encountered the most virulent opposition, both domestic and foreign. France, still in the confusion following her revolution, made improper demands on our country, which not being complied with, she commenced seizing American property on the high seas. Our people, taking different sides, were about equally divided—some approving and others deprecating the course pursued by France. Letters of marque and reprisal were issued by our government, and a navy was raised with surprising promptitude. This had the desired effect, peace being thereby secured; and the aggressor was taught that the Americans were friends in peace, but were not fearful of war when it could not be honorably averted.

The Indians on our western frontiers also caused much trouble; but at length, being severely chastised by General Wayne, they sued for peace, which was granted in 1795.

In 1800 the seat of government was removed from Philadelphia to Washington City, which had been designated by Washington, under a law of Congress, as the most central situation.

Election for the Fourth Term, commencing March 4, 1801, and terminating March 3, 1805.

No. of Electors from each State.	STATES.	Thomas Jefferson, of Virginia.	Aaron Burr, of New York.	John Adams, of Massachusetts.	C. C. Pinckney, of South Carolina.	John Jay, of New York.
6	New Hampshire....................................	....	....	6	6	....
16	Massachusetts.....................................	....	....	16	16	....
4	Rhode Island.......................................	....	....	4	3	1
9	Connecticut..	....	....	9	9	....
4	Vermont..	....	....	4	4	....
12	New York...	12	12	....	....	....
7	New Jersey...	....	....	7	7	....
15	Pennsylvania.......................................	8	8	7	7	....
3	Delaware...	....	....	3	3	....
10	Maryland...	5	5	5	5	....
21	Virginia..	21	21	....	....	....
4	Kentucky...	4	4	....	....	....
12	North Carolina.....................................	8	8	4	4	....
3	Tennessee..	3	3	....	....	....
8	South Carolina.....................................	8	8	....	....	....
4	Georgia...	4	4	....	....	....
138	No. of Electors....................................	73	73	65	64	1
	Majority..................................... 70					

The electoral vote for Thos. Jefferson and Aaron Burr being equal, no choice was made by the people, and on the 11th of February, 1801, the House of Representatives proceeded to the choice of President in the manner prescribed by the Constitution. On the first ballot eight States voted for Thos. Jefferson, six for Aaron Burr, and the votes of two States were divided. The balloting continued till the 17th of February, when the thirty-fifth ballot, as had all previously, resulted the same as the first. After the thirty-sixth ballot, the Speaker declared that the votes of ten States had been given for Thos. Jefferson, the votes of four States for Aaron Burr, and the votes of two States in blank; and that, consequently, Thomas Jefferson had been elected for the term of four years.

Thomas Jefferson, thus elected President, took the oath of office, and entered upon his duties, March 4, 1801.

In his inaugural address, Mr. Jefferson used the following memorable expression: "We have called by different names brethren of the same principle. We are all republicans: we are all federalists. If there be any among us who would wish to dissolve this Union, or to change its republican form, let them stand, undisturbed, as monuments of the safety with which ERROR OF OPINION MAY BE TOLERATED, WHERE REASON IS LEFT FREE TO COMBAT IT."

Aaron Burr, elected Vice-President, took the oath of office, and entered upon his duties in the Senate, March 4, 1801.

Election for the Fifth Term, commencing March 4, 1805, and terminating March 3, 1809.

No. of Electors from each State.	STATES.	Thomas Jefferson, of Virginia.	Charles C. Pinckney, of South Carolina.	George Clinton, of New York.	Rufus King, of New York.
7	New Hampshire	7	....	7	....
19	Massachusetts	19	....	19	....
4	Rhode Island	4	....	4	....
9	Connecticut	....	9	....	9
6	Vermont	6	....	6	....
19	New York	19	....	19	....
8	New Jersey	8	....	8	....
20	Pennsylvania	20	....	20	....
3	Delaware	....	3	....	3
11	Maryland	9	2	9	2
24	Virginia	24	....	24	....
14	North Carolina	14	....	14	....
10	South Carolina	10	....	10	....
6	Georgia	6	....	6	....
5	Tennessee	5	....	5	....
8	Kentucky	8	....	8	....
3	Ohio	3	....	3	....
176	Whole No. of Electors	162	14	162	14
	Majority	89			

Thomas Jefferson, elected President, took the oath of office for a second term, and entered upon his duties March 4, 1805.

George Clinton, elected Vice-President, took the oath of office, and entered upon his duties in the Senate, March 4, 1805.

Among the most important acts of Mr. Jefferson's administration was the purchase of Louisiana from France for $15,000,000, which territory was surrendered to our Government in December, 1803.

In November, 1808, the celebrated "ORDERS IN COUNCIL," were issued by the British Government, which prohibited all trade with France and her allies; and, as a retaliatory measure, in December following Bonaparte issued his "MILAN DECREE," interdicting all trade with England and her colonies—thus subjecting almost every American vessel on the ocean to capture. In requital for these tyrannous proceedings, and that England and France might both feel their injustice, Congress decreed an embargo; but as this failed to obtain from either power an acknowledgment of our rights, and was also ruinous to our commerce with other nations, it was repealed in March, 1809.

Election for the Sixth Term, commencing March 4, 1809, and terminating March 3, 1813.

No. of Electors from each State.	STATES	PRESIDENT.			VICE-PRESIDENT.			
		James Madison, of Virginia.	George Clinton of New York.	C. C. Pinckney, of South Carolina.	George Clinton, of New York.	James Madison, of Virginia.	James Monroe, of Virginia.	John Langdon, of New Hampshire.	Rufus King, of New York.
7	New Hampshire.................	....	....	7	....	....	....	....	7
19	Massachusetts..................	....	....	19	....	....	....	....	19
4	Rhode Island....................	....	....	4	....	....	....	....	4
9	Connecticut......................	....	....	9	....	....	....	....	9
6	Vermont..........................	6	....	....	....	....	....	6	....
19	New York.........................	13	6	....	13	3	3	....	....
8	New Jersey......................	8	....	....	8	....	....	....	....
20	Pennsylvania....................	20	....	....	20	....	....	....	....
3	Delaware.........................	....	....	3	....	....	....	....	3
11	Maryland.........................	9	....	2	9	....	....	....	2
24	Virginia..........................	24	....	....	24	....	....	....	....
14	North Carolina..................	11	....	3	11	....	....	....	3
10	South Carolina..................	10	....	....	10	....	....	....	....
6	Georgia...........................	6	....	....	6	....	....	....	....
7	Kentucky.........................	7	....	....	7	....	....	....	....
5	Tennessee........................	5	....	....	5	....	....	....	....
3	Ohio...............................	3	....	....	....	....	....	3	....
175	Whole No. of Electors.........	122	6	47	113	3	3	9	47
	Majority....................88								

James Madison took the oath of office, as President, and entered upon his duties March 4, 1809.

George Clinton, elected Vice President, took the oath of office, and attended in the Senate, March 4, 1809.

Our national position, especially in regard to England and France, was certainly a very perplexing one when Mr. Madison came to the Presidency. We were not only threatened by enemies abroad, but were harassed by a savage foe on our western frontier, probably urged on by British influence, and led by the famous chief Tecumseh and his brother the Prophet. These last were finally subdued in 1811; but our European foes were more troublesome. After all peaceful means had failed to check the aggressions of England, and when at length "patience had ceased to be a virtue," war was declared against that country, June 19, 1812. The events of that war it is not within our province to record; and it is sufficient to say, that they greatly elevated the American character in the estimation of both friends and enemies.

7

Election for the Seventh Term, commencing March 4, 1813, and terminating March 3, 1817.

No. of Electors from each State.	STATES.	PRESID'T. James Madison, of Virginia.	PRESID'T. De Witt Clinton, of New York.	V. PRES'T. Elbridge Gerry, of Massachusetts.	V. PRES'T. Jared Ingersoll, of Pennsylvania.
8	New Hampshire..........	....	8	1	7
22	Massachusetts..........	....	22	2	20
4	Rhode Island............	....	4	....	4
9	Connecticut.............	....	9	....	9
8	Vermont.................	8	....	8	....
29	New York................	....	29	....	29
18	New Jersey..............	....	8	....	8
25	Pennsylvania............	25	....	25	....
14	Delaware................	....	4	....	4
11	Maryland................	6	5	6	5
25	Virginia.................	25	....	25	....
15	North Carolina..........	15	....	15	....
11	South Carolina..........	11	....	11	....
8	Georgia..................	8	....	8	....
12	Kentucky................	12	....	12	....
8	Tennessee...............	8	....	8	....
7	Ohio.....................	7	....	7	....
3	Louisiana................	3	....	3	....
217	Whole No. of Electors...	128	89	131	86
	Majority............109				

James Madison, elected President for a second term. [There is no notice on the Journals of Congress of his having taken the oath.]

Elbridge Gerry, elected Vice-President, attended in the Senate on the 24th of May, 1813, and exhibited a certificate of his having taken the oath of office prescribed by law, which was read.

The war into which the country had been forced was brought to a close by the treaty of Ghent, which was signed December 24, 1814; but this treaty had scarcely been ratified, when it became necessary to commence another war for the protection of American commerce and seamen against Algerine piracies. In May, 1815, a squadron under Commodore Decatur sailed for the Mediterranean, where the naval force of Algiers was cruising for American vessels. After capturing two of the enemy's best frigates in that sea, Decatur proceeded to the Bay of Algiers, and there dictated a treaty which secured the United States from any further molestation from that quarter. Similar treaties were also concluded with the other Barbary powers.

Election for the Eighth Term, commencing March 4, 1817, and terminating March 3, 1821.

No. of Electors from each State.	STATES.	PRESID'T. James Monroe, of Virginia.	PRESID'T. Rufus King, of New York.	VICE-PRESIDENT. D. D. Tompkins, of New York.	VICE-PRESIDENT. John E. Howard, of Maryland.	VICE-PRESIDENT. James Ross, of Pennsylvania.	VICE-PRESIDENT. John Marshall, of Virginia.	VICE-PRESIDENT. Rob't G. Harper, of Maryland.
8	New Hampshire	8	....	8	....	....	....	....
22	Massachusetts	....	22	....	22	....	....	....
4	Rhode Island	4	....	4	....	....	....	....
9	Connecticut	....	9	....	....	5	4	....
8	Vermont	8	....	8	....	....	....	....
29	New York	29	....	29	....	....	....	....
8	New Jersey	8	....	8	....	....	....	....
25	Pennsylvania	25	....	25	....	....	....	....
3	Delaware	....	3	....	....	....	....	3
8	Maryland	8	....	8	....	....	....	....
25	Virginia	25	....	25	....	....	....	....
15	North Carolina	15	....	15	....	....	....	....
11	South Carolina	11	....	11	....	....	....	....
8	Georgia	8	....	8	....	....	....	....
12	Kentucky	12	....	12	....	....	....	....
8	Tennessee	8	....	8	....	....	....	....
8	Ohio	8	....	8	....	....	....	....
3	Louisiana	3	....	3	....	....	....	....
3	Indiana	3	....	3	....	....	....	....
217	Whole No. of Electors	183	34	183	22	5	4	3
	Majority..................109							

James Monroe took the oath of office, as President, and entered upon his duties March 4, 1817.

Daniel D. Tompkins, elected Vice-President, took the oath of office, and attended in the Senate, March 4, 1817.

The Seminole and a few of the Creek Indians commenced depredations on the frontiers of Georgia and Alabama towards the close of 1817, for which they were severely chastised by a force under General Jackson, and gladly sued for peace.

In February, 1819, a treaty was negotiated at Washington, by which Spain ceded to the United States East and West Florida and the adjacent Islands. In the same year the southern portion of Missouri Territory was set off under the name of Arkansas, for which a territorial government was formed; and Alabama was constituted a State, and admitted into the Union.

Early in 1820 the province of Maine, which had been connected with Massachusetts since 1652, was separated from it, and was admitted into the Union as an independent State.

Election for the Ninth Term, commencing March 4, 1821, and terminating March 3, 1825.

No. of Electors from each State.	STATES.	PRESID'T.		VICE PRESIDENT.				
		James Monroe, of Virginia.	John Quincy Adams, of Massachusetts.	Daniel D. Tompkins, of New York.	Richard Stockton, of New Jersey.	Robert C. Harper, of Maryland.	Richard Rush, of Pennsylvania.	Daniel Rodney, of Delaware.
8	New Hampshire...............	7	1	7	....	....	1	....
15	Massachusetts................	15	....	7	8	....	....	....
4	Rhode Island..................	4	....	4	....	....	....	....
9	Connecticut...................	9	....	9	....	....	....	....
8	Vermont.......................	8	....	8	....	....	....	....
29	New York.....................	29	....	29	....	....	....	....
9	New Jersey....................	8	....	8	....	....	....	....
25	Pennsylvania..................	24	....	24	....	....	....	....
4	Delaware......................	4	....	....	....	....	....	4
11	Maryland.....................	11	....	10	....	1	....	....
25	Virginia.......................	25	....	25	....	....	....	....
15	North Carolina................	15	....	15	....	....	....	....
11	South Carolina................	11	....	11	....	....	....	....
8	Georgia.......................	8	....	8	....	....	....	....
12	Kentucky.....................	12	....	12	....	....	....	....
8	Tennessee.....................	7	....	7	....	....	....	....
8	Ohio..........................	8	....	8	....	....	....	....
3	Louisiana.....................	3	....	3	....	....	....	....
3	Indiana.......................	3	....	3	....	....	....	....
3	Mississippi....................	2	....	2	....	....	....	....
3	Illinois........................	3	....	3	....	....	....	....
3	Alabama......................	3	....	3	....	....	....	....
9	Maine.........................	9	....	9	....	....	....	....
3	Missouri......................	3	....	3	....	....	....	....
235	No. of Electors...............	231	1	218	8	1	1	4
	Majority..................... 118							

James Monroe was re-elected President, but there is no notice on the Journals of Congress that he again took the oath of office.

Daniel D. Tompkins was re-elected Vice President, but there is no record of his having taken the oath of office.

Public attention was much occupied in 1824–5 by a visit from the venerable General Lafayette, who, after the lapse of nearly half a century from the period of his military career, was again welcomed with every token of respect that could be devised for honoring the "Nation's Guest." He landed in New York in August, 1824, and after remaining there a short time, set out on a tour through all the States. Upwards of a year was taken up in accomplishing this gratifying object; and in September, 1825, he sailed from Washington in the frigate Brandywine for his native home.

ELECTORAL VOTES

Election for the Tenth Term, commencing March 4, 1825, and terminating March 3, 1829.

No. of Electors from each State.	STATES.	PRESIDENT.				VICE PRESIDENT.				
		Andrew Jackson, of Tennessee.	John Quincy Adams, of Massachusetts.	Wm. H. Crawford, of Georgia.	Henry Clay, of Kentucky.	John C. Calhoun, of South Carolina.	Nathan Sanford, of New York.	Nathaniel Macon, of North Carolina.	Andrew Jackson, of Tennessee.	Henry Clay, of Kentucky.	Martin Van Buren, of New York.
8	New Hampshire	....	8	....	....	7	.	....	1	....	....
15	Massachusetts	....	15	....	....	15	....	....	....	....	....
4	Rhode Island	....	4	....	....	3	....	....	....	....	....
8	Connecticut	....	8	....	....	...	....	....	8	....	....
7	Vermont	....	7	....	....	7	....	....	....	....	....
36	New York	1	26	5	4	29	7	....	....	....	....
8	New Jersey	8	....	....	....	8	....	....	....	....	....
28	Pennsylvania	28	....	....	....	28	....	....	....	....	....
3	Delaware	....	1	2	....	1	....	....	....	....	2
11	Maryland	7	3	1	....	10	....	....	1	....	....
24	Virginia	....	....	24	....	....	....	24	....	....	....
15	North Carolina	15	....	....	....	15	....	....	....	....	....
11	South Carolina	11	....	....	....	11	....	....	....	....	....
9	Georgia	....	....	9	....	....	....	....	....	9	....
14	Kentucky	....	....	....	14	7	7	....	....	....	....
11	Tennessee	11	....	....	....	11	....	....	....	....	....
16	Ohio	....	....	....	16	....	16	....	....	....	....
5	Louisiana	3	2	....	....	5	....	....	....	....	....
5	Indiana	5	....	....	....	5	....	....	....	....	....
3	Mississippi	3	....	....	....	3	....	....	....	....	....
3	Illinois	2	1	....	....	3	....	....	....	....	....
5	Alabama	5	....	....	....	5	....	....	....	....	....
9	Maine	....	9	....	....	9	....	....	....	....	....
3	Missouri	....	....	....	3	....	....	....	3	....	....
261	Whole No. of Electors...	99	84	41	37	182	30	24	13	9	2
	Majority............ 131										

Neither candidate for the Presidency having received a majority of the electoral votes, it devolved upon the House of Representatives to choose a President from the three highest on the list of those voted for, which three were Andrew Jackson, John Quincy Adams, and William H. Crawford. Twenty-four tellers (one member from each State) were appointed, who, after examining the ballots, announced that the votes of thirteen States had been given for John Quincy Adams; the votes of seven States for Andrew Jackson; and the votes of four States for William H. Crawford. The Speaker then declared that John Quincy Adams, having received a majority of the votes of all the States, was duly elected President of the United States for four years, commencing on the 4th of March, 1825; on which day Mr. Adams took the oath of office, and entered upon his duties.

John C. Calhoun, having been elected Vice President, took the oath of office, and attended in the Senate, March 4, 1825.

Election for the Eleventh Term, commencing March 4, 1829, and terminating March 3, 1833.

No. of Electors from each State.	STATES.	Andrew Jackson, of Tennessee.	John Quincy Adams, of Massachusetts.	John C. Calhoun, of South Carolina.	Richard Rush, of Pennsylvania.	William Smith, of South Carolina.
9	Maine...........................	1	8	1	8	...
8	New Hampshire................	...	8	...	8	....
15	Massachusetts..................	....	15	....	15	....
4	Rhode Island....................	....	4	....	4	....
8	Connecticut.....................	....	8	....	8	....
7	Vermont........................	....	7	....	7	...
36	New York.......................	20	16	20	16	....
8	New Jersey.....................	....	8	....	8	....
28	Pennsylvania...................	28	....	28	....	....
3	Delaware........................	....	3	....	3	....
11	Maryland........................	5	6	5	6	....
24	Virginia.........................	24	....	24	....	....
15	North Carolina..................	15	....	15	....	....
11	South Carolina..................	11	....	11	....	....
9	Georgia.........................	9	....	2	....	7
14	Kentucky........................	14	....	14	....	....
11	Tennessee.......................	11	....	11	....	....
16	Ohio............................	16	....	16	....	....
5	Louisiana........................	5	....	5	....	....
3	Mississippi......................	3	....	3	....	....
5	Indiana..........................	5	....	5	....	....
3	Illinois..........................	3	....	3	....	....
5	Alabama.........................	5	....	5	....	....
3	Missouri.........................	3	....	3	....	....
261	Whole No. of Electors...........	178	83	171	83	7
	Majority........................	131				

Andrew Jackson took the oath of office, as President, and entered upon his duties March 4, 1829.

John C. Calhoun took the oath of office, as Vice President, and presided in the Senate March 4, 1829.

A series of unfortunate political and social occurrences soon led to a rupture of that cordiality which had formerly existed between these two distinguished individuals, the consequences of which were peculiarly disastrous to the political aspirations of Mr. Calhoun, who was never afterwards regarded with much favor beyond the immediate limits of his own State.

NOTE.—It was during this administration that the doctrine of State's rights was so strongly urged by Calhoun, and to this period may be dated the origin of the great rebellion of 1861.

Election for the Twelfth Term, commencing March 4, 1833, and terminating March 3, 1837.

No. of Electors from each State.	STATES.	PRESIDENT.					VICE PRESIDENT.				
		Andrew Jackson, of Tennessee.	Henry Clay, of Kentucky.	John Floyd, of Virginia.	William Wirt, of Maryland.	Martin Van Buren of New York.	John Sergeant, of Pennsylvania.	William Wilkins, of Pennsylvania.	Henry Lee, of Massachusetts.	Amos Ellmaker, of Pennsylvania.
10	Maine..........................	10				10				
7	New Hampshire.................	7				7				
14	Massachusetts..................		14				14			
4	Rhode Island...................		4				4			
8	Connecticut....................		8				8			
7	Vermont.......................				7					7
42	New York......................	42				42				
8	New Jersey....................	8				8				
30	Pennsylvania...................	30						30		
3	Delaware.......................		3				3			
10	Maryland.......................	3	5			3	5			
23	Virginia........................	23				23				
15	North Carolina..................	15				15				
11	South Carolina..................			11					11	
11	Georgia........................	11				11				
15	Kentucky......................		15				15			
15	Tennessee.....................	15				15				
21	Ohio...........................	21				21				
5	Louisiana......................	5				5				
4	Mississippi.....................	4				4				
9	Indiana........................	9				9				
5	Illinois.........................	5				5				
7	Alabama.......................	7				7				
4	Missouri.......................	4				4				
288	Whole No. of Electors........	219	49	11	7	189	49	30	11	7
	Majority....................115									

Andrew Jackson, re-elected President, took the oath of office, and continued his duties, March 4, 1833.

Martin Van Buren, having been elected Vice President, took the oath of office, and attended in the Senate, March 4, 1833.

Early in June, 1833, the President left Washington on a tour through the Northern States, and was everywhere received with an enthusiasm that evinced the cordial approval of his administration by the people. One of his first measures, on returning to the seat of government, was the removal of the public moneys from the United States Bank, for which act he encountered the most virulent hostility of a small majority of the Senate, who passed resolutions censuring his course. But this injustice has not been perpetuated; for on the 16th of January, 1837, these partisan resolutions were expunged from the records by order of a handsome majority.

Election for the Thirteenth Term, commencing March 4, 1837, and terminating March 3, 1841.

No. of Electors from each State.	STATES.	PRESIDENT.					VICE PRESIDENT.			
		Martin Van Buren of New York.	Wm. H. Harrison, of Ohio.	Hugh L. White, of Tennessee.	Daniel Webster, of Massachusetts.	Willie P. Mangum of North Carolina.	R. M. Johnson, of Kentucky.	Francis Granger, of New York.	John Tyler, of Virginia.	William Smith, of Alabama.
10	Maine............	10					10			
7	New Hampshire.....	7					7			
14	Massachusetts.....				14			14		
4	Rhode Island.......	4					4			
8	Connecticut.......	8					8			
7	Vermont..........		7					7		
42	New York.........	42					42			
8	New Jersey........		8					8		
30	Pennsylvania......	30					30			
3	Delaware.........		3					3		
10	Maryland.........		10					10		
23	Virginia..........	23								23
15	North Carolina.....	15					15			
11	South Carolina.....					11			11	
11	Georgia...........			11					11	
15	Kentucky.........		15					15		
15	Tennessee........			15					15	
21	Ohio..............		21					21		
5	Louisiana.........	5					5			
4	Mississippi........	4					4			
9	Indiana...........		9					9		
5	Illinois...........	5					5			
7	Alabama..........	7					7			
4	Missouri..........	4					4			
3	Arkansas..........	3					3			
3	Michigan..........	3					3			
294	Whole No. of Electors...	170	73	26	14	11	147*	77	47	23
	Majority............148									

Martin Van Buren, elected President, took the oath of office, and entered upon his duties, March 4, 1837.

Richard M. Johnson, elected Vice President, took the oath of office, and attended in the Senate, March 4, 1837.

Urged by the unprecedented financial embarrassments which were experienced in every branch of industry, and especially by the mercantile class, Mr. Van Buren's first measure was to convene a special meeting of Congress early in September, '37, which continued in session forty days, but accomplished very little. A bill authorizing the issue of $10,000,000 in treasury notes was passed; but the Independent Treasury bill (the great financial measure of the administration) was then rejected, although afterwards (in 1840) adopted.

*Elected by the Senate.

ELECTORAL VOTES.

Election for the Fourteenth Term, commencing March 4, 1841, and terminating March 3, 1845.

No. of Electors from each State.	STATES.	PRESID'T.		VICE PRESIDENT.			
		Wm. H. Harrison, of Ohio.	Martin Van Buren of New York.	John Tyler, of Virginia.	Rich'd M. Johnson of Kentucky.	L. W. Tazewell, of Virginia.	James K. Polk, of Tennessee.
10	Maine............................	10	....	10	....	....	....
7	New Hampshire...............	....	7	....	7	....	....
14	Massachusetts.................	14	....	14	....	....	....
4	Rhode Island...................	4	....	4	....	....	....
8	Connecticut.....................	8	....	8	....	....	....
7	Vermont.........................	7	....	7	....	....	....
42	New York.......................	42	....	42	....	....	....
8	New Jersey.....................	8	....	8	....	....	....
30	Pennsylvania...................	30	....	30	....	....	....
3	Delaware.........................	3	....	3	....	....	....
10	Maryland........................	10	....	10	....	....	....
23	Virginia..........................	....	23	....	22	....	1
15	North Carolina................	15	....	15	....	....	....
11	South Carolina................	....	11	....	....	....	....
11	Georgia..........................	11	....	11	....	11	....
15	Kentucky........................	15	....	15	....	....	....
15	Tennessee.......................	15	....	15	....	....	....
21	Ohio..............................	21	....	21	....	....	....
5	Louisiana........................	5	....	5	....	....	....
4	Mississippi......................	4	....	4	....	....	....
9	Indiana...........................	9	....	9	....	....	....
5	Illinois...........................	....	5	....	5	....	....
7	Alabama.........................	....	7	....	7	....	....
4	Missouri.........................	....	4	....	4	....	....
3	Arkansas.........................	....	3	....	3	....	....
3	Michigan........................	3	....	3	....	....	....
294	No. of Electors...............	234	60	234	48	11	1
	Majority....................148						

William H. Harrison, elected President, took the oath of office, and entered upon his duties, March 4, 1841.

John Tyler, elected Vice President, took the oath of office, and attended in the Senate, March 4, 1841.

Soon after his inauguration, President Harrison issued a proclamation, convening Congress for an extra session on the 31st of May, to consider "sundry weighty and important matters, chiefly growing out of the state of the revenue and finances of the country." But he did not live to submit his remedial plans—dying, after a very brief illness, on the 4th of April, exactly one month after coming into office. He was the first President who had died during his official term, and a messenger was immediately dispatched with a letter, signed by all the members of the Cabinet, conveying the melancholy intelligence to the

Vice President, then at Williamsburg, Va. By extraordinary means he reached Washington at five o'clock on the morning of the 6th, and at twelve o'clock the Heads of Departments waited upon him, to pay their official and personal respects. After signifying his deep feeling of the public calamity sustained by the death of President Harrison, and expressing his profound sensibility of the heavy responsibilities so suddenly devolved upon himself, he made known his wishes that the several Heads of Departments would continue to fill the places which they then respectively occupied, and his confidence that they would afford all the aid in their power to enable him to carry on the administration of the government successfully. Mr. Tyler afterwards took and subscribed the following oath of office:

"I do solemnly swear, that I will faithfully execute the office of President of the United States, and will, to the best of my ability, preserve, protect, and defend the Constitution of the United States. JOHN TYLER.
"APRIL 6, 1841."

Pursuant to the proclamation of President Harrison, Congress met on the 31st of May, and continued in session until the 13th of September. On the 27th of July a bill for the establishment of "The Fiscal Bank of the United States," passed the Senate by a vote of 26 to 23, and was concurred in by the House of Representatives on the 6th of August—128 to 91. President Tyler, however, returned the bill on the 16th, with his objections, and it was lost for lack of a constitutional majority. But the friends of a national bank were not to be deterred from their purpose by a single repulse: another bill (about the same in substance) was immediately hurried through both Houses, under the title of "The Fiscal Corporation of the United States," but this shared the fate of its predecessor.

A Senate bill for the establishment of a uniform system of bankruptcy throughout the United States, was concurred in by the House on the 18th of August, and became a law; but, meeting with very general condemnation, it was soon after repealed.

A bill was also passed at this extra session for the distribution of the proceeds of the sales of the public lands among the several States, in proportion to population.

In 1842 an important treaty, adjusting the north-eastern boundary of the United States, was negotiated at Washington between Mr. Webster, on the part of this country, and Lord Ashburton, on the part of Great Britain.

During the last year of Mr. Tyler's administration much excitement prevailed on the proposed annexation of Texas to the Union, which was strongly resisted at the North, on the ground that the South and southern institutions would thereby gain increased power in the national councils. A treaty of annexation, signed by the President, was rejected by the Senate, but measures were taken by which Texas was admitted the year following.

ELECTORAL VOTES.

Election for the Fifteenth Term, commencing March 4, 1845, and terminating March 3, 1849.

No. of Electors from each State.	STATES.	PRES'T. James K. Polk, of Tennessee.	PRES'T. Henry Clay, of Kentucky.	V. PRES'T George M. Dallas, of Pennsylvania.	V. PRES'T L. Frelinghuysen, of New Jersey.
9	Maine	9	....	9	....
6	New Hampshire	6	....	6	....
12	Massachusetts	....	12	....	12
4	Rhode Island	....	4	....	4
6	Connecticut	....	6	....	6
6	Vermont	....	6	....	6
36	New York	36	....	36	....
7	New Jersey	....	7	....	7
26	Pennsylvania	26	....	26	....
3	Delaware	....	3	....	3
8	Maryland	....	8	....	8
17	Virginia	17	....	17	....
11	North Carolina	....	11	....	11
9	South Carolina	9	....	9	....
10	Georgia	10	....	10	....
12	Kentucky	....	12	....	12
13	Tennessee	....	13	....	13
23	Ohio	....	23	....	22
6	Louisiana	6	....	6	....
6	Mississippi	6	....	6	....
12	Indiana	12	....	12	....
9	Illinois	9	....	9	....
9	Alabama	9	....	9	....
7	Missouri	7	....	7	....
3	Arkansas	3	....	3	....
5	Michigan	5	....	5	....
275	Whole No. of Electors	170	105	170	105
	Majority	13			

James K. Polk took the oath of office, as President, and entered upon his duties March 4, 1845.

George M. Dallas took the oath of office, as Vice President, and attended in the Senate, March 4, 1845.

The most important incidents of Mr. Polk's administration were the admission of Texas and the consequent war with Mexico, the latter of which resulted in extending our territorial boundaries to the Pacific Ocean, embracing regions of incalculable value.

Election for the Sixteenth Term, commencing March 4, 1849, and terminating March 3, 1851.

No. of Electors from each State.	STATES.	PRES'T. Zachary Taylor, of Louisiana.	Lewis Cass, of Michigan.	V. PRES'T Millard Fillmore, of New York.	William O. Butler, of Kentucky.
9	Maine...	....	9	....	9
6	New Hampshire.................................	....	6	....	6
12	Massachusetts..................................	12	....	12	....
4	Rhode Island...................................	4	....	4	....
6	Connecticut....................................	6	....	6	....
6	Vermont..	6	....	6	....
36	New York......................................	36	....	36	....
7	New Jersey....................................	7	....	7	....
26	Pennsylvania...................................	26	....	26	....
3	Delaware.......................................	3	....	3	....
8	Maryland.......................................	8	....	8	....
17	Virginia..	....	17	....	17
11	North Carolina..................................	11	....	11	....
9	South Carolina.................................	....	9	....	9
10	Georgia..	10	....	10	....
12	Kentucky.......................................	12	....	12	....
13	Tennessee......................................	13	....	13	....
23	Ohio...	....	23	....	23
6	Louisiana......................................	6	....	6	....
6	Mississippi.....................................	....	6	....	6
12	Indiana..	....	12	....	12
9	Illinois...	....	9	....	9
9	Alabama.......................................	....	9	....	9
7	Missouri.......................................	....	7	....	7
3	Arkansas......................................	....	3	....	3
5	Michigan......................................	....	5	....	5
3	Florida..	3	....	3	....
4	Texas..	....	4	....	4
4	Iowa...	....	4	....	4
4	Wisconsin......................................	....	4	....	4
290	Whole No. of Electors.........................	163	127	163	127
	Majority......................................	146			

Zachary Taylor took the oath of office, as President, and entered upon his duties March 4, 1849. He did not, however, long enjoy his honors—death suddenly closing his earthly career, July 9, 1850.

Millard Fillmore took the oath of office, as Vice President, and entered upon his duties March 4, 1849. Congress being in session at the time President Taylor died, the Vice President sent a message to both houses on the 10th of July, in which he feelingly announced the melancholy event. On the same day he took the requisite oath, and entered on the execution of the office of President.

Willie P. Mangum, of N. C., President *pro tem* of the Senate, acted as Vice President,*ex officio*,during the remainder of the term.

Election for the Seventeenth Term, commencing March 4, 1853, and terminating March 3, 1857.

No. of Electors from each State.	STATES.	PRES'T. Franklin Pierce, of New Hampshire.	PRES'T. Winfield Scott, of New Jersey.	V. PRES'T William R. King, of Alabama.	V. PRES'T Wm. A. Graham, of North Carolina.
8	Maine	8	....	8	....
5	New Hampshire	5	....	5	....
13	Massachusetts	....	13	....	13
4	Rhode Island	4	....	4	....
6	Connecticut	6	....	6	....
5	Vermont	....	5	....	5
35	New York	35	....	35	....
7	New Jersey	7	....	7	....
27	Pennsylvania	27	....	27	....
3	Delaware	3	....	3	....
8	Maryland	8	....	8	....
15	Virginia	15	....	15	....
10	North Carolina	10	....	10	....
8	South Carolina	8	....	8	....
10	Georgia	10	....	10	....
12	Kentucky	....	12	....	12
12	Tennessee	....	12	....	12
23	Ohio	23	....	23	....
6	Louisiana	6	....	6	....
7	Mississippi	7	....	7	....
13	Indiana	13	....	13	....
11	Illinois	11	....	11	....
9	Alabama	9	....	9	....
9	Missouri	9	....	9	....
4	Arkansas	4	....	4	....
6	Michigan	6	....	6	....
3	Florida	3	....	3	....
4	Texas	4	....	4	....
4	Iowa	4	....	4	....
5	Wisconsin	5	....	5	....
4	California	4	....	4	....
296	Whole No. of Electors	254	42	254	42
	Majority	149			

Franklin Pierce took the oath of office, as President, and entered upon his duties March 4, 1853.

The oath of office was administered to William R. King by a commission while he was on a visit to Cuba for the benefit of his health; but he died soon after his return home, and Jesse D. Bright, of Indiana, then President of the Senate, acted as Vice President, *ex officio,* during the remainder of the term.

John P. Hale, of N. H., and George W. Julian, of Ind., were nominated by the "Free Democracy" for President and Vice Presidents, but they did not receive a single electoral vote.

Election for the Eighteenth Term, commencing March 4, 1857, and terminating March 3, 1861.

No. of Electors from each State.	STATES.	James Buchanan, of Pennsylvania.	John C. Fremont, of New York.	Millard Fillmore, of New York.	John C. Breckenridge, of Kentucky.	William L. Dayton, of New Jersey.	Andrew J. Donelson, of Tennessee.
8	Maine................		8			8	
5	New Hampshire........		5			5	
13	Massachusetts.........		13			13	
4	Rhode Island..........		4			4	
6	Connecticut...........		6			6	
5	Vermont..............		5			5	
35	New York.............		35			35	
7	New Jersey...........	7			7		
27	Pennsylvania..........	27			27		
3	Delaware.............	3			3		
8	Maryland.............			8			8
15	Virginia..............	15			15		
10	North Carolina........	10			10		
8	South Carolina........	8			8		
10	Georgia...............	10			10		
12	Kentucky.............	12			12		
12	Tennessee............	12			12		
23	Ohio..................		23			23	
6	Louisiana.............	6			6		
7	Mississippi............	7			7		
13	Indiana...............	13			13		
11	Illinois...............	11			11		
9	Alabama..............	9			9		
9	Missouri..............	9			9		
4	Arkansas..............	4			4		
6	Michigan..............		6			6	
3	Florida...............	3			3		
4	Texas.................	4			4		
4	Iowa..................		4			4	
5	Wisconsin*............		5			5	
4	California.............	4			4		
296	No. of Electors.......	174	114	8	174	111	8
	Majority.............149						

James Buchanan took the oath of office, as President, and entered upon his duties, March 4, 1857.

John C. Breckenridge took the oath of office, as Vice-President, and entered upon his duties, March 4, 1857.

*When the Electoral votes were being counted, in Joint Convention of the Senate and House of Representatives, objections were made to including the votes of Wisconsin, because the electors did not meet until the day after that prescribed by law. The President of the Convention stated that he merely announced that James Buchanan had been elected President of the United States, without any reference to the contested votes, and declined expressing an opinion on the subject.

ELECTORAL VOTES.

Election for the Nineteenth Term, commencing March 4, 1861, and terminating March 3, 1865.

No. of Electors from each State.	STATES.	PRESIDENT. Abraham Lincoln, of Illinois.	Jno. C. Breckenridge of Kentucky.	John Bell, of Tennessee.	Stephen A. Douglas, of Illinois.	VICE PRESIDENT. Hannibal Hamlin, of Maine.	Joseph Lane, of Texas.	Edward Everett, of Massachusetts.	Herschel V. Johnson of Georgia.
8	Maine...............	8				8			
5	New Hampshire......	5				5			
13	Massachusetts.......	13				13			
4	Rhode Island........	4				4			
6	Connecticut..........	6				6			
5	Vermont.............	5				5			
35	New York............	35				35			
7	New Jersey..........	4			3	4			3
27	Pennsylvania........	27				27			
3	Delaware............		3				3		
8	Maryland............		8				8		
15	Virginia.............			15				15	
10	North Carolina......		10				10		
8	South Carolina......		8				8		
10	Georgia.............		10				10		
12	Kentucky............			12				12	
12	Tennessee...........			12				12	
23	Ohio................	23				23			
6	Louisiana...........		6				6		
7	Mississippi..........		7				7		
13	Indiana.............	13				13			
11	Illinois..............	11				11			
9	Alabama.............		9				9		
9	Missouri............				9				9
4	Arkansas............		4				4		
6	Michigan............	6				6			
3	Florida..............		3				3		
4	Texas...............		4				4		
4	Iowa................	4				4			
5	Wisconsin...........	5				5			
4	California...........	4				4			
4	Minnesota...........	4				4			
3	Oregon..............	3				3			
315	Whole No. of Electors...... 180	180	72	39	12	180	72	39	12
	Majority................157								

Abraham Lincoln took the oath of office as President, and entered upon his duties, March 4th, 1861. Hannibal Hamlin took the oath of office as Vice-President, and attended in the Senate as its President, on the 4th of March, 1861. The accession of Mr. Lincoln to the Presidency was made the pretext for the great rebellion of 1861.

GENERAL REMARKS.

The propriety of holding our national elections so often as once every four years has been questioned by some of the ablest minds in the country; the frequent occurrence of those exciting political campaigns which precede the choice of the President being regarded as threatening to the peace and well being of the nation. The circumstances of the past ten years would seem to indicate that the plan has not been a good one. It may be doubted, however, whether those bitter partizan jealousies which culminated, in 1861, in the great evil of rebellion, resulted so much from mere party contention as from the sectional character of the two parties most conspicuous in the contest. And it may be said with a considerable degree of safety that so long as parties are promiscuously distributed over the country no serious evils need be appprehended from the frequency of presidential campaigns.

The people of the United States were always remarkable for the readiness with which they returned to a state of perfect equanimity immediately after the most exciting political contests until the year 1860; and this political flexibility is no doubt attributable to that thorough training in the great school of liberty which, not only the present generation of Americans, but their ancestors enjoyed.

GEORGE WASHINGTON,
THE FIRST PRESIDENT OF THE UNITED STATES,

The most exemplary character, perhaps, that ever adorned any era in history, and who received in his life-time the noble appellations of "the Founder of a Republic," and "the Father of his Country," was born in the county of Westmoreland, Virginia, on the 22d of February, 1732. His early instruction was domestic and scanty, but full of good discipline and sound principles; and as his father died when he was only ten years old, he had no subsequent opportunities for acquiring a thorough literary or scientific education. However as his mind was naturally mathematical and philosophical, he prepared himself to be useful to his fellow-citizens as a civil engineer; and as the country was wild, and much of it then unsurveyed, he occasionally found agreeable and profitable employment in surveying different parts of his native State. He also directed much of his attention to the science of arms, in the use of which every young man was instructed, in order to repel the incursions of the Indians, who were often led on by skillful Frenchmen. At the age of nineteen he was appointed one of the Adjutant Generals of Virginia, which gave him the rank of major, and soon after he was advanced to a colonelcy, and sent by Gov. Dinwiddie to the Ohio with dispatches to the French commander, who was erecting fortifications from Canada to New Orleans, in violation of existing treaties. The Governor was so much pleased with the faithful discharge of this duty, that he ordered his journal, which extended to only eighty days, to be printed; but, small as it was, it afforded evidence of great sagacity, fortitude, and a sound judgment, and firmly laid the foundation of his future fame.

In the spring of 1755, Washington was persuaded to accompany Gen. Braddock as an aid, with the rank of colonel, in his disastrous expedition against Fort DuQuesne; and had his advice been followed on that occasion, the result would have been different.

Three years afterwards (1758) Washington commanded the Virginians in another expedition against the fort, which terminated successfully. At the close of this campaign he left the army, and was soon after married to Mrs. Martha Custis, (the widow of Col. Daniel Parke Custis,) whose maiden name was Dandridge, and whose intelligent and patriotic conduct, as wife and widow, will ever be gratefully remembered in American annals.

In 1759 he was elected to the House of Burgesses, and continued to be returned to that body, with the exception of occasional intervals, until 1774, when he was sent to represent Virginia in the Continental Congress. His well-tempered zeal and military skill, which enabled him to suggest the most proper means for national defence, if the country were urged to extremities, soon fixed all eyes upon him, as one well qualified to direct in the hour of peril; and accordingly, after the first scene of the revolutionary drama was opened at Lexington and Concord, and an army had concentrated at Cambridge, he was, on the 15th of June, 1775, unanimously appointed commander-in-chief of the American forces.' The self-sacrificing spirit which governed his future course is too well known to require any elucidation.

After bringing the war to a successful termination, he hastened to Annapolis, where Congress was then in session, and on the 23d of December, 1783, formally resigned his commission.

In May, 1787, he was elected to the Convention which met at Philadelphia for the purpose of forming a Constitution, and was at once called upon to preside over its deliberations. After that admirable instrument was adopted by the people, he was unanimously elected the first President of the United States for four years; at the expiration of which, he was unanimously re-elected for a second term.

On the 12th of December, 1799, he was seized with an inflammation in the throat, which grew worse the next day, and terminated his life on the 14th, in the 68th year of his age.

JOHN ADAMS,
THE SECOND PRESIDENT OF THE UNITED STATES,

And whose fame as a patriot and statesman is imperishable, was born at Braintree, Massachusetts, October 19, 1735. He early displayed superior capacity for learning, and graduated at Cambridge college with great credit. After qualifying himself for the legal profession, he was admitted to practice in 1761, and soon attained that distinction to which his talents were entitled. From the commencement of the troubles with Great Britain, in 1769, he was among the most active in securing the freedom of his country. Being elected to the first Continental Congress, he took a prominent part in all the war measures that were then originated; and subsequently suggested the appointment of Washington as commander-in-chief of the army. He was one of the committee which reported the Declaration of Independence in 1776, and the next year visited France as commissioner to form a treaty of alliance and commerce with that country. Although the object had been accomplished before his arrival, his visit had otherwise a favorable effect on the existing position of affairs; and he was afterwards appointed to negotiate a treaty of peace with Great Britain, which, after many laborious and fruitless efforts, was finally accomplished in 1783. In 1785, he was sent to England as the first minister from this country, and on his return was elected first Vice-President, in which office he served two terms, and was then, in 1797, elected to succeed Washington as President. Many occurrences tended to embarrass his administration, and to render it unpopular; but it is now generally admitted to have been characterized by patriotism and vigor equal to the emergencies which then existed. His political opponents, however, managed to defeat his re-election, and he was succeeded in the Presidency by Mr. Jefferson, in 1801; after which, he retired to his farm at Quincy, where his declining years were passed in the gratification of his unabated love for reading and contemplation, and where he was constantly cheered by an interesting circle of friendship and affection. The semi-centennial anniversary of American Independence, (July 4, 1826,) was remarkable, not merely for the event which it commemorated, but for the decease of two of the most active participants in the measures by which independence was achieved. On that day, Adams and Jefferson were both gathered to their fathers, within about four hours of each other, "cheered by the benediction of their country, to whom they left the inheritance of their fame, and the memory of their bright example."

As has been noticed elsewhere, Mr. Adams deemed it prudent, in the early part of his administration, when impending difficulties with France seemed to render war inevitable, to offer Washington the commission of Lieutenant-General and Commander-in-Chief of the army, which he accepted as a matter of duty, and held until his death, but fortunately never found it necessary to take the field.

THOMAS JEFFERSON,

THE THIRD PRESIDENT OF THE UNITED STATES,

Was born at Shadwell, Albemarle county, Va., (near Monticello, the seat where he died,) April 13, 1743. He was educated at William and Mary's college, and graduated with distinction when quite young. He was a great lover of learning, and particularly of natural philosophy. With the celebrated George Wythe he commenced the study of the law, and became a favorite pupil. Mr. Jefferson was never distinguished as an advocate, but was considered a good lawyer. Soon after he came to the bar, he was elected a member of the House of Burgesses, and in that body was duly appreciated for his learning and aptitude for business. He at once took fire at British oppression; and in 1774, he employed his pen in discussing the whole course of the British ministry. The work was admired, and made a text-book by his countrymen. In June, 1775, he took his seat in the Continental Congress, from Virginia. In that body he soon became conspicuous, and was considered a firm friend of American liberty. In 1776, he was chosen chairman of the committee that drafted the Declaration of Independence. This instrument is nearly all his own, and was sanctioned by his coadjutors with few alterations. In 1778, Mr. Jefferson was appointed ambassador to France, to form a treaty with that government, but ill-health prevented his accepting this office. He succeeded Patrick Henry, in 1779, as Governor of Virginia, and continued in that station two years. In 1781 he composed his notes on Virginia. In 1783, he was sent to France, to join the ministers of our country, Mr. Adams and Dr. Franklin. In 1785, he succeeded Dr. Franklin as ambassador, and continued performing the duties of that office for two years, when he retired and returned home. In 1789, he was made Secretary of State, under Washington, in which situation he was highly distinguished for his talents. This station he resigned in 1793, and retired to private life. In 1797, he was elected Vice President of the United States, and took his seat as President of the Senate, on the following 4th of March. In 1801, he was elected President of the United States, which office he held for eight years. After completing his second term, he retired to private life, in which he spent his days in philosophical pursuits, until the 4th of July, 1826, when he expired, just fifty years after penning the Declaration of Independence. His course was one of his own. Never lived there a politician, who did more than Thomas Jefferson, to bring his fellow-citizens to his own opinions.

JAMES MADISON,

THE FOURTH PRESIDENT OF THE UNITED STATES,

Was born in Orange county, Va., March 16, 1751. His studies, preparatory to entering Princeton College, were pursued under the most favorable circumstances, he being provided with the most accomplished instructors, and he graduated with high honor in 1771. On returning to Virginia, he zealously commenced the study of the law, which he subsequently abandoned for political life.

In 1776, he was elected to the General Assembly of Virginia; and from this period, for more than forty years, he was continually in office, serving his State and his country in various capacities, from that of a State Legislator to that of President.

In 1778, he was elected by the Legislature to the executive council of the State, where he rendered important aid to Henry and Jefferson, governors of Virginia, during the time he held a seat in the council; and by his probity of character, faithfulness in the discharge of duty, and amiableness of deportment, he won the approbation of these great men. In the winter of 1779–80, he took his seat in the Continental Congress, and became immediately an active and leading member, as the journal of that body abundantly testifies.

In 1784, '5, 6, he was a member of the Legislature of Virginia. In 1787, he became a member of the Convention held in Philadelphia, for the purpose of preparing a Constitution for the government of the United States. Perhaps no member of that body had more to do with the formation of that noble instrument, the "Constitution of the United States of America," than Mr. Madison.

It was during the recess between the proposition of the Constitution by the Convention of 1787, and its adoption by the States, that that celebrated work, "The Federalist," made its appearance. This is known to be the joint production of Alexander Hamilton, John Jay, and James Madison. This same year he was elected to Congress, and held his seat until the Continental Congress passed away among the things that were. He was a member of the State Convention of Virginia which met to adopt the Constitution, and on the establishment of the new Congress under the Constitution, he was chosen a member, retaining his seat until the close of Washington's administration.

In 1801, as one of the presidential electors, he had the gratification of voting for his illustrious friend Jefferson, who immediately offered him a place in his cabinet, which was accepted. Accordingly he entered on the discharge of his duties as Secretary of State, which duties he continued to perform during the whole of Mr. Jefferson's administration, and on the retirement of that great statesman, in 1809, he succeeded to the Presidency, in which office he served two terms.

Mr. Madison then retired to his peaceful home in Virginia, where he passed the remainder of his days in favorite pastimes, loved by the many and respected by all, until the 28th day of June, 1826, when the last surviver of the framers of our Constitution was gathered to his fathers, full of years and glory.

JAMES MONROE,
THE FIFTH PRESIDENT OF THE UNITED STATES,

One of he few exalted characters that served his country in both a civil and military capacity, was born in Westmoreland county, Va., April 26, 1758, and was educated at William and Mary's college, whence he graduated in 1776, and commenced the study of the law. Anxious to aid in the struggle for independence, which had then just began, he abandoned his studies, and entered the army as a cadet—joining a corps under the gallant General Mercer. He soon distinguished himself in several well-fought battles, and rapid promotion followed, until he reached the rank of captain. He was at Harlem Heights and White Plains, and shared the perils and fatigues of the distressing retreat of Washington through New Jersey, as well as the glory of the victory over the Hessians at Trenton, where he received a musket ball in the shoulder; notwithstanding which, he valiantly "fought out the fight." He subsequently accepted the post of an aid to Lord Stirling, with the rank of Major, in which position he saw much hard service—being engaged in almost every conflict for the two succeeding campaigns, and displaying great courage and coolness at the bloody battles of Brandywine, Germantown, and Monmouth.

Aspiring to a separate command, he obtained permission to raise a regiment in his native State; for which purpose he left the army, and returned to Virginia, where he encountered so many unexpected and discouraging obstacles, that he finally relinquished the enterprise, and resumed his law studies in the office of Mr. Jefferson.

In 1780 he was elected to the Virginia Legislature, and in the following year was made one of Governor Jefferson's council, in which he continued until 1783, when, at the age of twenty four years, he became a member of the Continental Congress. After serving three years in that body, he was again returned to the State Legislature.

In 1788, while a member of the Convention to decide upon the adoption of the new Constitution, he voted in the minority against that instrument; but this vote did not at all affect his popularity. Two years afterwards he was elected United States' Senator, and in 1794 he was sent envoy extraordinary and minister plenipotentiary to the court of Versailles. After settling the cession of Louisiana to the United States, he went to England to succeed Mr. King as minister at the court of St. James. The affair of the frigate Chesapeake placing him in an uncomfortable situation, he returned to the United States, and, in 1810, was once more elected to the Virginia Legislature. He was soon after chosen Governor of that State, in which office he remained until Mr. Madison called him to assume the duties of Secretary of State in his cabinet. In 1817, he was elected President of the United States, and in 1821 was unanimously re-elected, with the exception of a single vote in New Hampshire. His administration was a prosperous and quiet one.

_{He united with Jefferson and Madison in founding the University of Virginia; and when the convention was formed for the revision of the Constitution of his State, he was called to preside over its action. Not long after this, he went to reside with a beloved daughter (the wife of Samuel L. Gouverneur, Esq.) in New York City, where he lived until the anniversary of Independence in 1831, when, "amidst the pealing joy and congratulations of that proud day, he passed quietly and in glory away."}

JOHN QUINCY ADAMS,

THE SIXTH PRESIDENT OF THE UNITED STATES,

Was born at Quincy, Massachusetts, July 11, 1767, and received the advantages of a pretty thorough education before entering Harvard College, which was not until the year 1786. After graduating with marked credit, he commenced the study of law at Newburyport, in the office of the Hon. Theophilus Parsons, for many years Chief Justice of Massachusetts. While pursuing his studies he found leisure to write several newspaper essays, which attracted much attention, and displayed a maturity of taste and judgment seldom attained so early in life. In 1794 Washington appointed him minister to the Netherlands, and subsequently transferred him to Portugal. He was afterwards, at different periods, minister to Prussia, Russia, and England; and was one of the commissioners who negotiated the treaty of peace with Great Britain, at Ghent, in 1815. In 1817 he was appointed Secretary of State, in which office he continued during Mr. Monroe's administration, eight years; when he was elected by the House of Representatives President of the United States—the people having failed in making a choice. Like his father, he encountered strong opposition, and only served one term in this office, being defeated in a re-election by General Jackson. He then retired to his farm at Quincy, but did not long remain in private life; for two years afterwards, he was chosen Representative in Congress, and continued to be re-elected until his death, which occurred in the capitol at Washington, February 23, 1848. Two days previous to this sad event, while engaged in his duties in the House of Representatives, he received a paralytic stroke, which apparently deprived him of all consciousness. He was borne to the Speaker's room, where he received every attention that could be bestowed by anxious and devoted friends, but all in vain—his hour was come. The last words he was heard to utter were, "This is the last of earth."

Mr. Adams was a man of rare gifts and rich acquisitions. A diligent student, and economical of his time, he found opportunity, amidst all his public cares, to cultivate his tastes for literature and the sciences. He was one of the finest classical and belles-lettres scholars of his time, and filled the chair of Professor of Rhetoric and Belles-Lettres in Harvard College for several years. Even in his old age, he often astonished his hearers with the elegant classical allusions and rhetorical tropes with which he enriched and embellished his own productions.

ANDREW JACKSON,

THE SEVENTH PRESIDENT OF THE UNITED STATES,

A statesman of rare integrity, and a general of invincible skill and courage, was born at Waxhaw, Lancaster county, S. C., in 1767, and while yet a mere lad, did something towards achieving the independence of his country. It is said that he commenced his military career at the age of fourteen years, and was soon after taken prisoner, together with an elder brother. During his captivity, he was ordered by a British officer to perform some menial service, which he promptly refused, and for this refusal was "severely wounded with the sword which the Englishman disgraced." He was educated for the bar, and commenced practice at Nashville, Tenn., but relinquished his legal pursuits to "gain a name in arms." In the early part of the war of 1812, Congress having voted to accept fifty thousand volunteers, General Jackson appealed to the militia of Tennessee, when twenty-five hundred enrolled their names, and presented themselves to Congress, with Jackson at their head. They were accepted, and ordered to Natchez, to watch the operations of the British in lower Mississippi. Not long after, he received orders from headquarters to disband his men, and send them to their homes. To obey, he foresaw, would be an act of great injustice to his command, and reflect disgrace on the country, and he resolved to disobey. He accordingly broke up his camp, and returned to Nashville, bringing all his sick with him, whose wants on the way he relieved with his private means, and there disbanded his troops in the midst of their homes.

He was soon called to the field once more, and his commission marked out his course of duty on the field of Indian warfare. Here for years he labored, and fought, and diplomatized, with the most consummate wisdom and undaunted courage. It was about this time that the treaty of the "Hickory Ground" occurred, which gave him the familiar sobriquet of "Old Hickory."

The crowning glory of his whole military career was the battle of New Orleans; which will ever occupy one of the brightest pages in American history.

At the close of the war he returned to his home in Nashville; but in 1818 was again called on by his country to render his military services in the expulsion of the Seminoles. His conduct during this campaign has been both bitterly condemned and highly applauded. An attempt in the House of Representatives to inflict a censure on the old hero for the irregularities of this campaign, after a long and bitter debate, was defeated by a large majority.

In 1828, and again in 1832, General Jackson was elected to fill the presidential chair; thus occupying that elevated position for eight successive years. He then retired to his hospitable mansion ("the Hermitage") near Nashville, "loaded with wealth and honors, bravely won," where he continued to realize all the enjoyments that are inseparable from a well-spent life, until death translated him to those higher rewards, which "earth can neither give nor take away." He died June 8, 1845, and his last hours were soothed by a trustful reliance on the Savior of the world for salvation.

MARTIN VAN BUREN. 127

MARTIN VAN BUREN,
THE EIGHTH PRESIDENT OF THE UNITED STATES,

Was born in the flourishing town of Kinderhook, New York, September 5, 1782, and early received the best education that could then be obtained in the schools in his immediate vicinity.

Having sufficiently prepared himself for the study of law, he entered the office of Francis Sylvester, in his native town, where he remained about six years. But law did not engross his whole time: he found leisure occasionally to peer into the mysteries of political economy, and finally arrived at the conclusion that his chances for fame and fortune were at least equal in the arena of politics to anything he might accomplish by a strict adherence to legal pursuits. Fully impressed with this idea, he early set about cultivating what little popularity could be gained in his limited sphere, and so won upon the confidence of his neighbors and friends as to be appointed, while yet in his *teens*, a delegate to a convention in his native county, in which important political measures were to be acted upon.

In 1808 he was appointed Surrogate of Columbia county, the first public office he ever held; and in 1812 and 1816 he was elected to the State Senate, in which body he became a distinguished leader of the Madison party, and one of its most eloquent supporters.

In 1821 he was elected to the United States Senate, in which he held his seat for nearly eight years, and became remarkable not only for his close attention to business, but also for his devotion to the great principles of the Democratic party.

In 1828 he was elected Governor of his native State, and entered upon the duties of that office on the first of January, 1829; but he filled the gubernatorial chair for only a few weeks. In March following, when General Jackson was elevated to the Presidency, he tendered Mr. Van Buren the post of Secretary of State, which was accepted. At the expiration of two years he resigned his seat in the Cabinet, and was immediately appointed minister to England; but when his nomination was submitted to the Senate, (June 25, 1831,) it was rejected by the casting vote of the Vice President, (Mr. Calhoun) and of course he was recalled. As his friends attributed his rejection entirely to personal and political rancor, it only served to raise Mr. Van Buren in the estimation of his political adherents; and the result was, that in May following he was nominated with great unanimity for the Vice-Presidency by the Democratic Convention at Baltimore. His triumphant election was regarded not merely as a high compliment to himself, but as a wholesome rebuke to his opponents.

In 1836 he was put in nomination for the chief magistracy, to which he was elected by a large majority over Gen. Harrison; but at the next Presidential election the tables were turned, and he only received sixty votes out of two hundred and ninety-four.

After his defeat, he returned to Kinderhook, where he remained some time, and then visited Europe, with one of his sons, whose restoration to health was the principal object of his journey. Not long after his return, he consented to become once more a candidate for the Presidency, and in 1848 received the nomination of the Free-Soil party; but did not secure a single electoral vote.

WILLIAM HENRY HARRISON,

THE NINTH PRESIDENT OF THE UNITED STATES,

Was born in Charles City county, Va., February 9, 1773, and was educated for the medical profession at Hampden Sydney College. He graduated at a time when our north-western frontier was suffering much from the neighboring Indians; and believing that he could be of greater service in repelling the savage invaders than in pursuing his studies, he accepted an ensign's commission from President Washington, and joined the army. He was promoted to a lieutenancy in 1792, and his skill and bravery were highly commended by General Wayne, under whose command he was engaged in several actions. After the bloody battle of Miami Rapids, he was rewarded with the rank of captain, and immediately placed in command of Fort Washington. In 1797 he resigned his commission, for the purpose of accepting the office of Secretary of the North-West Territory, from which he was elected a delegate to Congress in 1799.

When a territorial government was formed for Indiana, he was appointed the first Governor, and continued in that office till 1813. To his civil and military duties he added those of commissioner and superintendent of Indian affairs; and, in the course of his administration, he concluded thirteen important treaties with the different tribes. On the 7th of November, 1811, he gained the celebrated battle of Tippecanoe, the news of which was received throughout the country with a burst of enthusiasm. During the war of 1812 he was made commander of the north-western army of the United States, and he bore a conspicuous part in the leading events in the campaign of 1812, '13—the defence of Fort Meigs, and the victory of the Thames. In 1814, he was appointed, in conjunction with his companions in arms, Governor Shelby and General Cass, to treat with the Indians in the north-west, at Greenville; and, in the following year, he was placed at the head of a commission to treat with various other important tribes.

In 1816, he was elected a member of Congress from Ohio; and, in 1828, he was sent minister plenipotentiary to the republic of Colombia. On his return, he took up his residence at North Bend, on the Ohio, where he lived upon his farm, in comparative retirement, till 1836, when he became a candidate for the Presidency; and although defeated on the first trial, four years afterwards he was elected by a large majority, and inaugurated in 1841. But he did not long survive this crowning honor, as he died on the 4th of April, just one month after entering upon his duties. His funeral obsequies were performed on the 7th, and an immense concourse assembled to pay their testimony of respect. Funeral services and processions also took place in most of the principal cities throughout the country. As General Harrison was the first President who died while in office, his successor, Mr. Tyler, recommended that the 14th of May be observed as a day of fasting and prayer, and accordingly it was so observed.

JOHN TYLER,

THE SUCCESSOR OF GEN. HARRISON, AS PRESIDENT,

Was born at Williamsburg, Virginia, March 29, 1790, and at the age of twelve years entered William and Mary's College, where he graduated with distinguished merit five years afterwards. Few have commenced life at so early a period as Mr. Tyler—he having been admitted to the bar when only nineteen, and elected to the Virginia Legislature before attaining his twenty-second year. In 1816 he was sent to Congress; in 1825, elected Governor of Virginia, and in 1827 became United States Senator; in which capacity he firmly supported the administration of General Jackson—voting against the tariff bill of 1828, and against re-chartering the United States Bank. Notwithstanding this last vote, the friends of the bank, presuming upon his well-known conservatism, at the special session of Congress called by his predecessor, introduced a bill for the establishment of the "Fiscal Bank of the United States," which passed both houses by small majorities, and which Mr. Tyler felt bound to veto. But this did not dishearten the friends of the measure, who modified and rechristened their financial plan, which, under the name of "Fiscal Corporation of the United States," again passed both houses of Congress, and was again vetoed by the President. Of course, a large portion of the party that elected him were greatly dissatisfied with his course, and their denunciation of his alleged faithlessness were "loud and deep." To add to the embarrassments which were accumulating around him, all the members of his Cabinet, with the exception of Mr. Webster, resigned their places; but even this implied rebuke did not shake his integrity of purpose. An equally efficient phalanx of talent was called to his aid, and he had the satisfaction of seeing that his views were endorsed by a large number of leading statesmen. It has often been asserted that Mr. T. had pledged himself to sustain the financial schemes of the bank and its friends; but this has always been denied, and circumstances certainly warrant the conclusion that the assertion is unfounded. So gross and bitter were the assaults made upon him, that he felt called upon to defend himself from their violence; and, after declaring his determination to do his duty, regardless of party ties, he said: "I appeal from the vituperation of the present day to the pen of impartial history, in confidence that neither my motives nor my acts will bear the interpretation which, for sinister motives, has been placed upon them." On the expiration of his official term, he retired to his estate at Williamsburg.

JAMES KNOX POLK,

THE TENTH PRESIDENT OF THE UNITED STATES,

Was born at Mecklenberg, N. C., November 2, 1795, and there received the rudiments of his early education. In 1806 his father removed to Nashville, Tennessee, taking his family with him, and here it was that Mr. Polk pursued those preliminary studies which were requisite to qualify him for the legal profession. After due preparation, he entered the office of Hon. Felix Grundy, under whose able instruction he made such rapid progress, that he was admitted to practice in 1820. His duties at the bar did not prevent him from taking part in the political affairs of the day; and in this sphere his comprehensive views and zealous devotion to democracy soon secured him a widely-extended popularity, which resulted in his election to the Legislature of Tennessee in 1823. In 1825, while yet in his thirtieth year, he was chosen a member of Congress, in which body be remained fourteen years—being honored with the Speakership for several sessions. So well satisfied were his constituents with his congressional course, that he was elected Governor by a large majority, but some questions of local policy subsequently defeated his re-election.

In 1844 he was unexpectedly nominated for the office of President of the United States by the Democratic Convention at Baltimore; and, having received sixty-five electoral votes more than his rival candidate, Mr. Clay, he was inaugurated on the 4th of March, 1845.

Soon after Mr. Polk assumed the reins of government, the country became involved in a war with Mexico, which was little more than a series of victories wherever the American banner was displayed, and which resulted in important territorial acquisitions. The ostensible ground for this war, on the part of Mexico, was the admission of Texas into the Union, which was one of the first acts of Mr. Polk's administration. The Mexicans, however, paid dearly for asserting their frivolous claim to Texas as a revolted province, and the prompt and energetic course pursued by Mr. Polk was sanctioned and sustained by a large majority of the people.

But notwithstanding the advantageous issue of the war, the acquisition of Texas, and the satisfactory settlement of several vexed questions of long standing, Mr. Polk was not nominated for a second term—various extraneous matters leading to the selection of another candidate. Perhaps it was fortunate for the country and for himself that he was permitted to retire to the more congenial enjoyment of private life; for his health had become very much impaired, and he did not long survive after reaching his home in Nashville. He died June 15, 1849.

ZACHARY TAYLOR,

THE ELEVENTH PRESIDENT OF THE UNITED STATES,

Was born in Orange county, Virginia, November 24, 1790, and, after receiving an indifferent education, passed a considerable portion of his boyhood amid the stirring scenes which were being enacted at that time on our western border. In 1808 he was appointed a lieutenant in the United States infantry, and subsequently was promoted to a captaincy for his efficient services against the Indians. Soon after the declaration of war in 1812 he was placed in command of Fort Harrison, which he so gallantly defended with a handful of men against the attack of a large body of savages, as to win the brevet rank of major. So familiar did he become with the Indian character, and with the mode of warfare of that wily foe, that his services at the West and South were deemed indispensable in the subjugation and removal of several hostile tribes. While effecting these desirable objects, he was occasionally rewarded for his toils and sacrifices by gradual promotion, and in 1840 attained the rank of brigadier general. At the commencement of the troubles with Mexico, in 1845, he was ordered to occupy a position on the American side of the Rio Grande, but not to cross that river unless attacked by the Mexicans. He was not, however, allowed to remain long in repose: the enemy, by attacking Fort Brown, which he had built on the Rio Grande, opposite Matamoras, soon afforded him an opportunity to display his skill and valor, and gloriously did he improve it. The brilliant battles of Palo Alto and Resaca de la Palma, where he contended successfully against fearful odds, were precursors to a series of victories which have few parallels in military annals. The attack on Matamoras, the storming of Monterey, the sanguinary contest at Buena Vista, and the numerous skirmishes in which he was engaged, excited universal admiration; and on his return home, after so signally aiding to "conquer a peace" with Mexico, he was everywhere received with the most gratifying demonstrations of respect and affection. In 1848 General Taylor received the nomination of the Whig party for the office of President of the United States, and, being elected, was inaugurated the year following. But the cares and responsibilities of this position were greater than his constitution could endure, hardened as it had been both in Indian and civilized warfare. After the lapse of little more than a year from the time he entered upon his new career, he sunk under its complicated trials, and his noble spirit sought refuge in a more congenial sphere, July 9, 1850.

MILLARD FILLMORE,

THE SUCCESSOR OF GEN. TAYLOR, AS PRESIDENT,

Was born at Summer Hill, Cayuga county, New York, January 7, 1800, and did not enjoy the advantages of any other education than what he derived from the then inefficient common schools of the county. At an early age he was sent into the wilds of Livingston county to learn a trade, and here he soon attracted the attention of a friend, who placed him in a lawyer's office—thus opening a new, and what was destined to be a most honorable and distinguished career. In 1827 he was admitted as an attorney, and two years afterwards as counselor in the Supreme Court. Soon attracting attention, he established himself at Buffalo, where his talents and business habits secured him an extended practice.

His first entrance into public life was in January, 1829, when he took his seat as a member of the Assembly from Erie county At this time he distinguished himself for his untiring opposition to imprisonment for debt, and to this are the people indebted in a great degree for the expunging of this relic of barbarism from the statute book. Having gained a high reputation for legislative capacity, in 1833 he was elected a member of the National House of Representatives; and on the assembling of the Twenty-Seventh Congress, to which he was re-elected by a larger majority than was ever given to any person in his district, he was placed in the arduous position of Chairman of the Committee of Ways and Means. The measures which he brought forward and sustained with matchless ability, speedily relieved the government from its existing pecuniary embarrassments. In 1847 he was elected Comptroller of the State of New York by a larger majority than had ever been given to any State office for many years. In 1848 he was selected as a candidate for Vice President, General Taylor heading the ticket. On his election to that high office, he resigned his position as Comptroller, and entered upon his duties as President of the United States Senate. The courtesy, ability, and dignity exhibited by him, while presiding over the deliberations of that body, received general commendation. Upon the sudden death of Gen. Taylor, he became President, and promptly selected a cabinet, distinguished for its ability, patriotism, and devotion to the Union, and possessing in an eminent degree the confidence of the country.

After serving out the constitutional term, Mr. Fillmore returns to Buffalo, and again resumed those pursuits which had prepared the way to the elevated position from which he had just retired. He was welcomed home by troops of friends, with whom he still continues to enjoy an unabated popularity.

It should be borne in mind by every aspiring young man, that Mr. Fillmore is entirely indebted to his own exertions for his success in life. From a very humble origin, he attained the highest office in the world, climbing the rugged steep of fame step by step, with indefatigable industry and untiring perseverance, until he at length gained the summit, where he is long likely to enjoy his well-earned position.

FRANKLIN PIERCE,
THE TWELFTH PRESIDENT OF THE UNITED STATES,

Was born at Hillsborough, N. H., November 23, 1804, and early received the advantage of a liberal education. After going through a regular collegiate course at Bowdoin college, which he entered at the age of sixteen, he became a law student in the office of Judge Woodbury, at Portsmouth, whence he was transferred to the law school at Northampton, where he remained two years, and then finished his studies with Judge Parker at Amherst. Although his rise at the bar was not rapid, by degrees he attained the highest rank as a lawyer and advocate.

In 1829 he was elected to represent his native town in the State Legislature, where he served four years, during the two last of which he held the speakership, and discharged the duties of the office with universal satisfaction.

From 1833 to 1837 he represented his State in Congress, and was then elected to the United States Senate, having barely reached the requisite age to qualify him for a seat in that body.

In 1834 he married Miss Jane Means, daughter of the Rev. Dr. Appleton, formerly President of Bowdoin college—soon after which, he removed to Concord, where he still holds a residence. He was re-elected at the expiration of his Senatorial term, but resigned his seat the year following, for the purpose of devoting himself exclusively to his legal business, which had become so extensive as to require all his attention.

In 1846 he declined the office of Attorney-General, tendered him by President Polk; but when the war with Mexico broke out, he was active in raising the New England regiment of volunteers; and afterwards accepted the commission of Brigadier General, with which he at once repaired to the field of operations, where he distinguished himself in several hard-fought battles. At Cerro-Gordo and Chapultapec he displayed an ardor in his country's cause which extorted praise from his most inveterate political opponents; and on his return home he was everywhere received with gratifying evidences that his services were held in grateful remembrance by the people.

At the Democratic Convention held in Baltimore in 1852, after trying in vain to concentrate their votes on a more prominent candidate, that body unexpectedly nominated General Pierce for the office of President of the United States, to which he was elected by an unprecedented majority over his rival, General Scott—receiving 254 votes out of 296. He was duly inaugurated on the 4th of March, 1853, and his administration was more remarkable for its futile attempts to reconcile conflicting interests, than for the achievement of any particular measure of great public utility. However, it will better become his future than his present biographer to "speak of him as he is; nor aught extenuate, nor aught set down in malice."

JAMES BUCHANAN,
THIRTEENTH PRESIDENT OF THE UNITED STATES.

For the high position he so long maintained in the political affairs of this country, Mr. Buchanan is not alone indebted to his early and thorough education, but his entire devotion to whatever he undertook, and his perseverance in surmounting obstacles which would have intimidated less determined minds, had a large share in promoting his advancement. He is of Irish parentage, and was born at Stony Batter, Franklin county, Pa., April 23, 1791. At the age of seven years he removed with his father's family to Mercersburg, and there received an education that fitted him for entering Dickinson college in 1805, where he graduated two years afterwards with the highest honors. He then studied law with James Hopkins, of Lancaster, and in 1812 was admitted to the bar, at which he attained a high rank and commanded an extensive practice.

In 1814 he commenced political life as a member of the Pennsylvania State Legislature, and in 1820 was sent as a representative to Congress, where he remained for ten years—at the expiration of which, he declined a re-nomination.

In 1831 he was appointed minister to Russia by President Jackson, of whom he was always the consistent friend and supporter, and he negotiated a commercial treaty which proved of great advantage to American commerce.

In December, 1834, having been elected to the United States Senate, he took his seat in that body, and continued one of its most efficient members until 1845, when he accepted the office of Secretary of State under Mr. Polk. He held this responsible place until the expiration of Mr. Polk's term of service, when he returned home to repose awhile. But he did not by any means become an idle spectator in passing events: his letters and speeches show that he was no less vigilant as a private citizen, than as a counselor in the Cabinet, or a representative and senator in Congress.

On the accession of Mr. Pierce to the Presidency, in 1853, Mr. Buchanan was appointed minister to England, with which country questions were then pending that required great prudence and discrimination for their satisfactory adjustment. In his intercourse with the British diplomatists he was not only discreet, but displayed sound sense, courtly forbearance, a just assertion of our rights, and the true dignity of the American character. So entirely unexceptionable was his whole course while abroad, that on his return to this country, in April, 1856 —he landed in New York on the sixty-fifth anniversary of his birth-day—he was received with an enthusiasm, seldom accorded to political men.

In June, 1856, Mr. Buchanan was nominated by the Democratic Convention at Cincinnati as a candidate for the Presidency; and although there were powerful political elements arrayed against him in the succeeding campaign, he was triumphantly elected to that responsible and honorable office.

His administration was attended with unusual difficulties— difficulties which it would seem he was not fully able to meet.

The troubles in Kansas, arising from the repeal of the Missouri Compromise, and the opposition made to his views touching the admission of Kansas with the Lecompton Constitution, by the Douglas wing of the Democratic party, were matters of sore vexation to him, and tended greatly to unpopularize the latter part of his public life. But these were considerations of small moment as compared to the embarrassment which the Government suffered in consequence of the treacherous intrigues of some of the members of his Cabinet. His Secretary of War and Secretary of the Treasury, afterwards so conspicuous in the great Rebellion, were particularly instrumental in crippling the pecuniary and military resources of the country, and turning them to the benefit of the South. When treason began to assume a threatening attitude Buchanan declared against the right of secession, but at the same time denied the right of coercion by the Government. This, perhaps, is the most inconsistent, inexplicable position ever taken by any of the Nation's chief rulers. On the 4th of March, 1861, Mr. Buchanan retired from the Presidency, leaving to his successor the highly perplexing task of setting to rights the machinery of a government crippled and weakened in all its parts, and fully ripe for the most gigantic civil war known to history.

It was, at one time, presumed by many that Mr. Buchanan was not only encouraging the rebellion by his weak, indecisive policy towards armed traitors, and by winking at the thieving proceedings of some of his Cabinet officers, but that he was himself leagued with the leaders of the secession movement, and secretly acted in unison with them.

While it is true that the unhindered appropriation of millions of treasure to the furtherance of rebellious schemes, and the large deposit of choice arms made in Southern arsenals, would indicate an affiliation of the President with the chief rebels of the South, yet there has never been adduced any direct proof of such affiliation; and nothing said or done by Mr. Buchanan since his retirement shows active sympathy with the rebellion There is, however, evidence on every hand of weakness—an element of character he never manifested prior to his Executive career—of that negative disposition which will, under circumstances such as surrounded him during the latter part of his administration, wholly unfit a man for the performance of his duties.

The subject of the present sketch would, doubtless, have been a very good Executive at a period when the country was undisturbed by sectional agitation; at a time when there were no conflicting local interests to stir up and embitter South against North. But the exigencies of the period during which he sat at the helm of state demanded a man who could take hold with a strong hand; a man of Jacksonian character, who, with the loftiest political integrity and most devoted loyalty, combined a Napoleonic will; a man who, foreseeing the certain results of the pursuit of a conciliatory course with rebellion, would have given it a decisive blow in its very infancy.

But it seems that Mr. Buchanan proposed to deal with secessionists as an over-fond, weak-minded mother deals with a spoiled child—scolding and coaxing alternately, satisfied to exhibit her authority by the former, and confident that she can reform her fondling by the latter. Perhaps he may be partially excused by some in consideration of the debt of gratitude he felt he owed to the Southern States, for the valuable services they had rendered him in his election. But a truly great executive never allows his feelings to interfere with the performance of duty. The life of the nation was in jeopardy; that grand superstructure, the American Government, whose foundation stones had been cemented by the sacred blood of the Revolutionary sires, whose columns had been reared by the wisest, purest statesmen the world ever saw, and about whose lofty dome the brightest seraphs of Heaven chanted their sweetest lays—that great temple around which clustered the hopes of the liberty loving world, was threatened with destruction, and there can hardly be any excuse for him who, having the power to save, refused to adopt such decisive measures as were essential to salvation.

It is true that the Southern people had acted a very important part in the election of Mr. Buchanan, but it is very far from being true that a majority of these people were in favor of secession. The great Democratic party was not a party of traitors, either South or North. The masses of the people of the Southern States were by no means desirous of severing their connection with the Government of the United States, as was amply testified in the overwhelming Union majorities given in North Carolina, Tennessee, and other Southern States, even after South Carolina had sloughed off, and all the preliminary steps had been taken by the leading secessionists toward the formation of a Southern Confederacy. And there is no doubt that had Mr. Buchanan taken hold of the rebellion, while it was in the larva, with that determination to crush it which the great Jackson exhibited when South Carolina proposed her scheme of nullification, it had never seen its winged existence.

Buchanan's administration, in one respect, may possibly yet be productive of good, in that it may serve to impress the people with the importance of selecting a man for the chief magistracy who loves the right and dares to do it.

ABRAHAM LINCOLN,

FOURTEENTH PRESIDENT OF THE UNITED STATES,

Was born in Hardin county, Kentucky, February 12th, 1809. The record of his boyhood and youth, so far as we have been able to trace it, is not distinguished by anything more remarkable than the usual experience of children of pioneers in a new country. In 1816 he removed with his parents to what is now Spencer county, Indiana. Here he enjoyed the advantages of a

10

little schooling—less than a year, however, in all. Whatever else he afterward learned from books was without the aid of the schoolmaster—the result of his own energy and indomitable perseverence.

In 1832 he served in the Blackhawk war, and on his return from that service, was nominated for the Illinois Legislature from the connty of Macon. In 1834 he was elected to the Legislature, and re-elected in 1836, 1838, and 1840. While in the Legislature he placed himself on record against slavery, and it is but just to say that the principles which actuated him then are the moving principles of the great party he to-day represents, as the Executive of the Nation.

For many years Mr. Lincoln was a prominent leader of the Whig party in Illinois, and was on the electoral ticket in several Presidential campaigns. In 1844 he canvassed the entire State for Henry Clay, of whom he was a sincere and enthusiastic friend, and exerted himself powerfully for the favorite of his party. In 1846 he was elected to Congress, and took his seat on the first Monday in December, 1847, the only Whig representative from his State.

In November, 1860, he was elected President of the United States by the party known as Republicans.

On the 11th of February, 1861, he left his home in Springfield, Illinois, and proceeded to Washington, passing en route the cities of Toledo, Indianapolis, Cincinnati, Columbus, Steubenville, Pittsburg, Cleveland, Buffalo, Albany, Poughkeepsie, New York, Trenton, Philadelphia, Harrisburg, and Baltimore, at all of which places, except the last, he was received with great cordiality, and addressed the people. At Baltimore a plot had been formed to assassinate him; and in this affair it seems that some of the most prominent citizens of that place were implicated. But Mr. Lincoln, by prompt, shrewd management, reached Washington uninjured, and on the 4th of March, 1861, was duly inaugurated; and proceeded upon the duties of his office, notwithstanding the threats of Baltimoreans that he never should be installed. In his inaugural address, in view of the threatening attitude assumed by some of the Southern States, in consequence of the accession of a Republican administration, after declaring that there never had been any just cause for the apprehension that such an administration would encroach upon the constitutional rights of any State, he said that he had "no purpose, directly or indirectly, to interfere with the institution of slavery in the States where it existed; that he, as well as every member of Congress, was sworn to support the whole Constitution, one of the provisions of which is, that "no person held to service or labor in one State, under the laws thereof, escaping into another, shall, in consequence of any law or regulation therein, be discharged from such service or labor, but shall be delivered up on claim of the party to whom such service or labor may be due;" that he took his oath to support the Constitution without any mental reservation; that while he did not then choose to specify particular acts of Congress as proper to be enforced, he did suggest that it would be much safer for all, both in official and private stations, to conform to and abide by all those acts which stand unrepealed, than to violate any of them, trusting to find impunity in having them held to be unconstitutional; that he held that in the contemplation of universal law and of the Constitution, the union of the States is perpetual; that no State could, upon its own mere motion, get out of the Union; that acts of violence within any State or States against the authority of the United States are insurrectionary or revolutionary, and that he should, as the Constitution expressly enjoined upon him, take care that the laws of the Union should be executed in all the States; that while he should perform this duty perfectly, so far as practicable, unless restrained by his rightful masters, the American people, he trusted the declaration so to do would not be regarded as a menace, but only as the express purpose of the Union to maintain itself.

The inaugural address, while considered as clear and explicit by many, was regarded as very obscure and unsatisfactory by others, (the people of the South,) and on the 13th of April, 1861, Messrs. Preston, Stuart and Randolph, appointed by the Virginia Convention, were formally received by the President, and presented resolutions requesting that, inasmuch as "great uncertainty prevailed in the public mind as to the policy" to be pursued by the Federal Executive, he should communicate to the Convention the course he intended to take in regard to the "Confederate States."

To this request, the President replied that, while he was sorry that dangerous uncertainty should exist respecting his mode of procedure with the seceded States, he could give no clearer exposition of his policy than was given in his inaugural address, a careful consideration of which he recommended to the Virginia Convention.

Two days after this, Fort Sumpter having been reduced by the Confederate Government, and other demonstrations of a revolutionary character having been made, the President issued a proclamation calling for 75,000 volunteers, for three months, to suppress the rebellion, and summoned Congress to assemble in extraordinary session. The call was heartily responded to, and in a few days a vastly greater number than had been requested, offered themselves to their country. Meantime Washington was placed in a state of defence. Shortly after the commencement of hostilities a blockade of all the Southern ports was declared. This was directly followed by a blockade of Virginia and North Carolina. On the 3d of May, 1861, the President issued a call for 42,034 additional volunteers, for the term of three years. Congress having assembled, he addressed a message to that body, asking that at least 400,000 men and $400,000,000 be placed at his control, that the work of crushing the rebellion might be expedited. Congress readily complied, granting more men and money than had been asked.

On the 16th of August, 1861, the President issued a proclamation prohibiting all commercial intercourse between the loyal and seceded States. In the latter part of August, he modified a proclamation issued by Gen. Fremont, which declared martial law in the State of Missouri, ordering the confiscation of the property of disloyal persons, and declaring their slaves free. The two latter of these measures Mr. Lincoln declared void. For this act he was blamed by many of his own party at the time.

Passing some other acts of less importance, we next notice the message addressed to Congress on the 6th of March, 1862, by the President, recommending that the Government co-operate with any State desiring a gradual emancipition of the slaves, by affording it such pecuniary aid as would enable it to "compensate for the inconveniences, public and private, produced by such change of system." This message was hailed by the radical anti-slavery party of the country as the initiatory step toward a final and total abolition of slavery; by conservative Union men, with indifference, and by the secessionists as a hostile encroachment upon State rights.

On the 11th of March, 1862, Mr. Lincoln assumed command of the Army and Navy of the United States, ordering a general movement of both, and confining General McClellan to the command of the Department of the Potomac.

April 16th, 1862, he approved and signed an act of Congress, abolishing the institution of slavery in the District of Columbia, which act "recognized and practically applied" the principles of compensation and colonization.

During the month of May, the President issued two proclamations, the one declaring the ports of Port Royal, Beaufort, and New Orleans open for trade, the other repudiating an order issued by Gen. Hunter, emancipating all the slaves in Georgia, Florida and South Carolina. This act also produced some dissatisfaction. During the years 1862-1863, Mr. Lincoln was actively employed in calling out and furnishing troops, and making important changes in the organization of the army. It was also during this period that he issued his general emancition proclamations, the first on the 22d day of September, 1862, declaring that all slaves held in any State, or part of a State, found in actual rebellion against the authority of the United States on the 1st day of January, 1863, should then and forever thereafter be free; the second, on the 1st of January, 1863, declaring that, in accordance with the first proclamation, slavery is abolished in all the States and counties then in armed rebellion against the Government.

These measures, while they greatly unpopularized the President with certain parties in the Northern and Southern Border States, were regared as the exponents of the true policy by the radicals. His suspension of the writ of *habeas corpus*, in certain cases, September 15th, 1863, also produced considerable stir in political circles.

At the Republican Convention which met at Baltimore in January, 1864, Mr. Lincoln was re-nominated for the Presidency of the United States.

We have occupied more space in this than in any of the foregoing biographical sketches for the reason that the circumstances surrounding Mr. Lincoln's administration are, to the people, of more importance than those of any preceding administration, and not from any desire to render peculiarly conspicuous the subject of the present sketch.

THE PRESIDENT'S DEDICATORY ADDRESS AT GETTYSBURG.

On the 19th of November, 1863, the President participated in the solemn and imposing ceremonies incident to the consecration of the National Cemetery at Gettysburg. Arriving in the town on the previous evening, he was the recipient of a delightful serenade, which he acknowledged in a brief speech. On the next day he delivered the following beautiful dedicatory address, which may be regarded as a fair specimen of his eloquence:

"Four-score and seven years ago our fathers brought forth upon this continent a new nation, conceived in liberty, and dedicated to the proposition that all men are created equal. Now we are engaged in a great civil war, testing whether that nation, or any nation so conceived and so dedicated, can long endure. We are met on a great battle field of that war. We are met to dedicate a portion of it as a last resting-place of those who here gave their lives that that nation might live. It is altogether fitting and proper that we should do this.

" But in a larger sense we can not dedicate, we can not consecrate, we can not hallow this ground. The brave men, living and dead, who struggled here, have consecrated it far above our power to add or detract. The world will little note, nor long remember what we say here, but it can never forget what they did here. It is for us, the living, rather to be dedicated here to the unfinished work that they have thus far so nobly carried on. It is rather for us to be here dedicated to the great task remaining before us—that from these honored dead we take increased devotion to the cause for which they here gave the last full measure of devotion,—that we here highly resolve that the dead shall not have died in vain, that the nation shall, under God, have a new birth of freedom, and that the government of the people, by the people, and for the people, shall not perish from the earth."

JOHN CHARLES FREMONT,

THE REPUBLICAN CANDIDATE FOR PRESIDENT.

Several biographies of this accomplished mathematician and indomitable explorer have been issued since he was nominated for the Presidency by the "National People's Convention" at Philadelphia. From these we learn that he is the son of a French gentleman of the same name, who, not long after his arrival in this country, married Mrs. Ann Beverly Whiting, of Gloucester county, Va. The "first fruit" of this union was the subject of this sketch, who was born at Savannah, Ga., January 21, 1813. Five years after this event, when Mr. Fremont was making arrangements to return to France with his family, he suddenly died, leaving his widow, with two sons and a daughter, but ill provided for in a pecuniary view. "Bowed down, but not discouraged," she gathered her scanty resources together, and settled in Charleston, S. C., where, at the age of thirteen, Charles was taken into the office of John W. Mitchell, Esq., who, actuated by benevolent motives, afterwards had him qualified for the legal profession; but his tastes did not lie in that channel: a thorough knowledge of mathematics seemed to be the all-absorbing object of his ambition, and his devoted application to this science was unquestionably the means of his success in after-life.

He entered the naval service in 1833 as a professor of mathematics; but not long afterwards was transferred to the corps of topographical engineers, with the rank of second lieutenant. In conjunction with the late Captain Williams, he was engaged in several important national surveys, which led to his being afterwards associated with Mr. Nicholet, of St. Louis, in the exploration and survey of the vast region north of the Missouri and west of the Mississippi.

After returning to Washington city, and while engaged in preparing his report and maps of this last survey, he became acquainted with Miss Jessie Benton, daughter of the distinguished Senator, to whom he was married in 1841.

In May, 1842, he set out on the first of his three great exploring expeditions, the developments of which have been of incalculable importance, not only to this country, but to the whole civilized world. This resulted in a thorough exploration of the famous South Pass across the Rocky Mountains, on the highest peak of which the American flag was planted for the first time; the second, in 1843, furnished accurate information regarding the Great Salt Lake, the great interior basin of Utah, the mountain range of the Sierra Nevada, and the golden regions of California; and the third, in 1845, among other advantages, secured the possession of the last named territory, of which Col. Fremont became, in 1846, the first governor and military commander, and in which was subsequently elected the first United States Senator after its admission as a State.

In 1848, a court-martial having found him technically guilty of some frivolous charges preferred by Gen. Kearney, he persisted in relinquishing his military position, notwithstanding President Polk offered him a new commission of the same grade. But this did not dampen his spirit of adventure: relying upon his own means and the aid of friends, he has since been as zealously engaged as ever in bringing to light the hidden resources of our comparatively inaccessible regions.

At the commencement of the great Rebellion, Fremont stood out boldly for the Union, and his high qualifications as a commander, and his thorough knowledge of the West, secured to him the command of the Western Department of the land and naval forces of the United States. This office was assigned him July 9, 1861. Inspired by that ardor and propelled by that energy which have ever marked his career, he proceeded at once to the organization of his department, and projected a campaign, which, if he had been allowed to carry forward, would doubtless have reflected additional lustre upon his already brilliant reputation. But, unfortunately for him, perhaps for the country, he was, upon charges of mismanagement which were never well sustained, removed from his command, Nov. 2, 1861. On the 31st of May, 1864, he was again nominated for the Presidency by a convention of Radical Republicans opposed to the administration of Mr. Lincoln. This nomination he accepted with the understanding that if the Republican convention at Baltimore should repudiate Mr. Lincoln, he should withdraw from the canvass. Whether Fremont's motive in taking this step was patriotic, or whether it was personal, we, of course, have no accurate means of determining; but certain we are that his acceptance of the Cleveland nomination was regarded by many of his old political friends as a very unfortunate affair.

The platform of principles upon which he was nominated is given on another page of this work.

The following passage from Fremont's letter of acceptance, after his nomination for the Presidency in 1856, is a good example of his style in composition:

NEW YORK, July 8, 1856.

GENTLEMEN:—You call me to a high responsibility by placing me in the van of a great movement of the people of the United States, who, without regard to past differences, are united in a common effort to bring back the action of the Federal Government to the principles of Washington and Jefferson. Comprehending the magnitude of the trust which they have declared themselves willing to place in my hands, and deeply sensible of the honor which their unreserved confidence, in this threatening position of the public affairs implies, I feel that I can not better respond than by a sincere declaration that, in the event of my election to the Presidency, I should enter upon the execution of its duties with a single determination to promote the good of the whole country, and to direct solely to this end all the powers of the Government, irrespective of party issues and regardless

of sectional strifes. The declaration of principles embodied in
the resolves of your Convention expresses the sentiments in
which I have been educated, and which have been ripened into
convictions by personal observation and experience. With this
declaration and avowal, 1 think it necessary to revert to only
two of the subjects embraced in those resolutions, and to these
only, because events have surrounded them with grave and critical circumstances, and given to them especial importance.

MAJOR GENERAL GEORGE B. McCLELLAN,

Was born in the city of Philadelphia, December 3, 1826. His father, Dr. George McClellan, for many years one of the professors of Jefferson Medical College, was a distinguished physician and surgeon. The son was, for a short season, a student at the University of Pennsylvania. At the age of sixteen he left this institution and entered West Point.

In 1846 he graduated at the latter place, second in his class, and entered the army as Brevet Second Lieutenant of Engineers. He was immediately afterwards ordered to Mexico as Lieutenant of Sappers, Miners, and Pontooniers. During the

Mexican war he distinguished himself on several occasions as a gallant and efficient officer, and was, in May, 1848, made Brevet Captain.

After peace was made with Mexico he was ordered to West Point, where he assumed the supervision of field labors and became instructor of the bayonet exercise. While thus employed he translated a "Manual of Bayonet Exercise" from the French. In 1851 he was sent to superintend the construction of Fort Delaware, and in the year following accompanied Capt. R. B. Marcy (now his father-in-law) on an expedition to explore the Red river.

He was appointed to accompany Gen. Persifer F. Smith, as Senior Engineer, to Texas, to survey the rivers and harbors of that State, in September of the same year.

In the spring following he was placed in charge of the survey of a northern route for a railroad to the Pacific, and was subsequently detailed for the examination of the western part of the proposed line. This duty was performed in a superior manner, for which a high compliment was bestowed upon him by the Secretary of War. Soon after this he was detailed to visit the principal railway lines in the United States, and to thoroughly investigate the railroad system of the country, with a view of obtaining such information as would be of service in the successful operation of the Pacific railroad. A full report of his proceedings was published in November, 1854.

The next public service required of him was the performance of a secret mission to the West Indies, which resulted in the collection of a vast amount of information valuable to the government.

In July, 1853, he was promoted to a First Lieutenancy in the army, and in March, 1855, was commissioned as Captain in the First Cavalry. One year later he was sent, with Majors Danlafield and Mordecai, to gather military information in the Crimea.

The report of his investigations in this great field of strife, published by order of Congress, is regarded by military men as replete with valuable instruction.

On the 16th of January, 1857, he resigned his commission, and removing to Chicago, filled for three years the responsible position of Vice President and Engineer of the Illinois Central railroad. At the end of this time he resigned and was made General Superintendent of the Ohio and Mississippi railroad, and two months later became President of the eastern division of the same road, having his residence at Cincinnati, and receiving a salary of $10,000 per annum, which position and income he enjoyed until the breaking out of the rebellion.

At this time he offered his services to the country and soon after received a commission as Major General from the Governor of Ohio.

In May, 1861, he was placed in command of the Department of the Ohio—a department formed of the States of Ohio, Indiana and Illinois—with headquarters at Cincinnati. Four days later he was commissioned as Major General in the regular army. Shortly after this he took the field in Western Virginia, and conducted a very successful campaign, during which the battles of Phillipi and Rich Mountain were fought.

At the termination of this campaign he was ordered to turn his command over to General Rosecrans and report to Washington, upon doing which, he was appointed commander of the Army of the Potomac. This command he retained with varying success until the 7th of November, 1862, when he was superceded by Gen. Burnside.

During the several campaigns he conducted while in command of this department he won two of the most brilliant victories of the war—those of Malvern Hill and Antietam, and was universally beloved by the soldiers. The modesty with which he received the order to retire, and the utter disregard of all personal claims he manifested in taking leave of his army contrast widely with the spirit exhibited by others under similar circumstantes, as his farewell address to his army, which we here present, will amply testify:

"HEADQUARTERS, ARMY OF THE POTOMAC,
"Camp near Rectortown, Nov. 7, 1862.

"*Officers and Soldiers of the Army of the Potomac:*

"An order of the President devolves upon Major General Burnside the command of this army. In parting with you, I can not express the love and gratitude I bear you. As an army you have grown up under my care. In you I have never found doubt or coldness. The battles you have fought under my command will proubly live in our nation's history. The glory you have achieved, our mutual perils and fatigues, the graves of our comrades fallen in battle and by disease, the broken forms of those whom wounds and sickness have disabled—the strongest associations which can exist among men—unite us still by an indissoluble tie. We shall ever be comrades in supporting the constitution of our country and the nationality of its people.

"GEORGE B. McCLELLAN,
"Major General U. S. A."

On the Sunday evening previous to his departure, the officers assembled at his tent for the purpose of bidding adieu to their gallant leader, and from the eyes of many of their number dropped scalding tears of sorrow and regret. The following day he reviewed the army of heroes who had followed him through many months and many scenes, and as he rode along their lines, pronouncing the last farewell, wild and unrestrained huzzas rent the air; and they rushed from the ranks and in every conceivable manner gave evidence of their devotion and confidence, and of their annoyance and regret at the separation. On the tenth he took the railroad cars at Warrenton, and upon reaching Warrenton Junction was again received with the most gratifying manifestations. In answer to the unanimous request for a parting speech, General McClellan said: "I wish you to stand by General Burnside as you have stood by me, and all will be well. Good-bye."

At other stations on the road he was also greeted with enthusiastic cheering. Reaching Washington, he quietly went to the Philadelphia depot, and then pushing through the city of his nativity without tarrying, much to the disappointment of hosts of admirers, he proceeded to Trenton.

LIEUTENANT-GENERAL ULYSSES S. GRANT,

Was born at Mount Pleasant, Clermont county, Ohio. It seems that the only marked traits of character he exhibited in early boyhood were energy, industry, will. His educational advantages, at this period, were those of the common, country school —no more.

In the year 1839, at the age of seventeen, he entered the United States Military Academy at West Point, from which he graduated on the 30th day of January, 1843. During his stay at this Institution he manifested that untiring industry, close application and unconquerable will which distinguished his boyhood, and which have constituted so conspicuous an element of his military character. It appears, however, that he was never regarded as a genius; and the grade he sustained on the day of graduation—that of 21 in a class of about 42—would not indicate extraordinary advancement in the studies assigned him. But it was remarked by those who conducted him through his Academic course, as it has been by those who have observed his military career, that he never lost an inch of the ground gained at each successive step in his progress. At his graduation it is said he possessed a "practical knowledge of the use of the rifled musket, the field piece, mortar, siege, and sea-coast guns, small sword and bayonet, as well as the construction of field works, and the fabrication of all munitions and *materiel* of war."

At the close of his Academic course, he entered the United States regular army as a Brevet Second-Lieutenant of infantry. At this time, the United States being at peace with all nations, Grant was attached as a Supernumerary Lieutenant to the fourth infantry, then stationed on the frontier in Missouri and Missouri Territory, and engaged in keeping down the Indian tribes that at that time were very troublesome to the early settlers of that region. Here Grant had not been many months when he was ordered, with his regiment, to join the army of General Taylor, in Texas. Soon after this, Corpus Christi, an important port on the Texan shore, was taken possession of by the American army as a base of operations against the Mexicans, between whom and the United States disputes respecting certain imaginary boundary lines were fast ripening into a war; and it was here that Grant received his commission as full Second Lieutenant of Infantry. This commission dated from the 30th day of September, 1845. On the 8th day of May, 1846, he participated in the battle of Palo Alto, and although not noticed in the official reports, was spoken of by his comrades as having displayed great gallantry. He was likewise engaged in the subsequent brilliant operations of General Taylor along the banks of the Rio Grande. On the 23d of September, 1846, he took part, with great credit to himself, in the splendid affair at Monterey. It is a noteworthy fact that, although Grant's conduct in every one of these engagements was highly meritorious, he remained in the back ground, claiming no honors or promotions, but quietly biding his time.

After the formal declaration of war by the United States, against Mexico, he was transferred to the command of General Scott, and subsequently (March 29, 1847,) participated in the siege of Vera Cruz. Immediately after this affair, he was appointed the Quartermaster of his regiment, which office he retained throughout the Mexican campaign. He was, however, honored with the appointment, on the field, of First Lieutenant, to date from the 8th of September, 1847, for gallant and distinguished voluntary services rendered on that day in the famous battle of Molino del Ray. Congress afterwards wished to confirm the appointment as a mere brevet, but Grant refused to accept it under such circumstances.

On the 13th of September, 1847, he was made Brevet Captain of the regular army for gallant conduct in the battle of Chepultepec, which battle occurred on the preceding day. On the 16th of November, 1847, he was commissioned a First Lieutenant in the fourth regiment of regular infantry, still retaining his brevet rank of Captain.

At the close of the Mexican war, Grant, upon the distribution of his regiment in companies and sections among the various Northern frontier defences, along the borders of the States of Michigan and New York, took command of his company in one of these defences. His regiment having been afterwards consolidated and ordered to the Department of the Pacific, Grant, with his own and some other companies, was sent into Oregon to Fort Dallas. He received his full promotion to Captain of infantry, in August, 1853, and was, shortly afterwards, attached to the Department of the West; but, not regarding military so favorable to progress as civil life, he resigned his connection with the United States army on the 31st day of July, 1854, after which he resided near the city of St. Louis, Missouri, until the year 1859. Here he resided on a small farm, occupying himself in winter by hauling wood to the Carondelet market, and during the summer in the collection of debts, for which latter business, it is said, he had little capacity.

In the year 1859, he embarked in the leather trade with his father, the firm opening business in the city of Galena, Illinois. Grant continued in the leather business, driving a prosperous trade, up to the breaking out of the Rebellion in 1861, when he offered his services to his country, upon the first call for volunteers, and was appointed by Governor Yates as Commander-in-Chief of the Illinois forces and mustering officer of Illinois volunteers. Desiring active service in the field, he resigned his appointment as mustering officer, and accepted the Colonelcy of the 21st regiment of Illinois volunteers, with a commission dating from June 15, 1861. In August, 1861, Colonel Grant was promoted to the rank of Brigadier General of volunteers, his commission dating from May 17, 1861.

Shortly after this he was appointed commandant of the post at Cairo—which post included the Missouri shore of the Mississippi river, from Cape Girardeau to New Madrid, and the opposite shore, to the point of land on which Cairo stands. This position Grant filled with great ability, checkmating, by his adroit maneuvering, the efforts of the rebels to occupy, permanently, southern Kentucky, and conducting those successful expeditions against Forts Henry and Donelson, which opened the way to the occupation of Western Tennessee.

On the 16th of February, 1862, the day after the surrender of Fort Donelson, he was appointed Major General of volunteers, and was placed in command of an expedition up the Tennessee river against the rebels in and about Corinth, under command of Johnston and Beauregard. This expedition terminated in the great battle of Shiloh or Pittsburg Landing—which battle, occupying two days, (April 6th and 7th, 1862,) was one of the bloodiest of the war, and resulted in the defeat of the rebels and their retreat upon Corinth.

For the immense slaughter which attended this battle, General Grant was very severely censured by the people, generally, throughout the Western States.

Soon after this, General Halleck having assumed command of the army before Corinth, and that place having fallen into the hands of the United States forces by evacuation, an important change took place in the army, which resulted in the assignment of General Grant to the District of West Tennessee, and the promotion of General Halleck to the office of General-in-Chief. The former soon after formed the plan of opening the Mississippi river to its mouth. Memphis having been given up to our troops, the chief obstacle in the way of the prosecution of the design were Vicksburg and Port Hudson.

After a series of expeditions and battles, land and naval, in which the courage and fortitude of the Union troops were no less prominently exhibited than the superior engineering powers and unyielding stubbornness of General Grant, Vicksburg was reduced by siege, and was occupied by Grant on the 4th of July, 1863; and directly after this (July 8, 1863) followed the surrender of Port Hudson to General N. P. Banks.

On the 16th of October, 1863, the Departments of the Ohio, of the Cumberland, and of the Tennessee were formed into the Military Division of the Mississippi, under the command of General Grant. The General, however, was not long in this position until, the grade of Lieutenant General having been revived, he was promoted to that office—which office gave him control of the entire forces of the United States. This appointment was made in February, 1864, and was immediately followed by the most active, thorough preparations for a movement upon Richmond by the Army of the Potomac under the personal command of General Grant, and an expedition against Atlanta under command of General Sherman. The battles of the Wilderness, of Spottsylvania Court House, and the siege of Petersburg have been thus far the chief results of Grant's movements. What may be the ultimate fruits it is not the province of the biographer to anticipate.

ANDREW JOHNSON,

Was born at Raleigh, North Carolina, December 29th, 1808, and is now fifty-five years old. He lost his father when only four years old. At the age of ten he was apprenticed to a tailor in Raleigh, and served with him an apprenticeship of seven years. His mother was poor, and had been unable to give him any educational advantages, but young Andy, whose unconquerable spirit was not to be restrained by any disadvantages, became stimulated with a desire for knowledge. He acquired the alphabet with no other instructions than those obtained from the journeymen with whom he worked. He learned to read from an old volume of speeches, loaned him by a friend, and thenceforward, after ten hours' work with his goose, needle and scissors, applied himself with vigor to study for three or four hours each evening. In 1824, having completed his apprenticeship, he went to Laurens Court House, South Carolina, where he worked as journeyman for two years. In 1826 he set out for the West, taking his mother, whom already, at his early age and with his scanty wages, he was supporting. He made his home at Greenville, Tennessee, where he remained and commenced business, and where he became a thriving and popular man. With the indefatigable thirst for knowledge which had characterized his early career, he still pursued his studies, and in the evenings which followed a day of labor, with his wife as instructress, pushed on in the road to knowledge.

He entered early into political life, being elected to the first office which he ever held—that of Alderman of the village of Greenville—in 1828. He was re-elected to the same office in 1829. In 1830 he was elected Mayor, and retained that position for three years. In 1835 he was sent to the Legislature, where he chiefly distinguished himself by taking strong grounds against a scheme of internal improvements, which he argued was extravagant and useless. The measure was popular, however, and he was defeated in 1837. In 1838 he was a candidate again, and was this time successful. In 1840 he served as Presidential Elector for the State at large on the Democratic ticket, and during the campaign rendered efficient service to the party as a stump speaker. In 1841 he was elected to the State Senate, and in 1843, at the age of thirty-five, he was elected to Congress, where he held his seat; being four times re-elected, until 1853. During this time he was thoroughly identified with the old Democratic party, and supported all the party measures. In 1853 he was elected Governor, after a very exciting contest, over Gustavus A. Henry. He was re-elected in 1855 over Meredith P. Gentry, the Whig candidate. At the expiration of his Gubernatorial term, in 1857, he was chosen United States Senator by a Democratic majority in the Legislature of Tennessee. In that body he commanded the respect of all his compeers, as an able, eloquent, and patriotic statesman. At the breaking out of the rebellion, Senator Andrew Johnson still proclaimed his allegiance to the United States, and continued to hold his seat in the Senate, though his course subjected him to much unpopularity and even danger.

When, in the spring of 1862, our army had penetrated Tennessee to Nashville, and the northern and central portions of the States were wrested from rebel control, the President desired the services of a wise and sagacious man, of unquestionable loyalty, to act as Military Governor of that State, and he did not have long to look—Andrew Johnson was at once recognized as the man for the place, and being commissioned a Brigadier General, he repaired to Nashville, where he has for two years discharged the delicate and responsible duty of his charge with a degree of wisdom and efficiency, which has challenged general admiration. Under his administration, the rebellion has steadily been losing its hold in Tennessee, and loyalty as constantly cultivated and developed.

He was nominated for the Vice Presidency by the Union Convention, at Baltimore, June 8, 1864.

PROPOSED CRITTENDEN COMPROMISE.

At the commencement of the Congressional session of 1860, the portentious clouds of civil war, gathering and blackening in the Southern horizon of our national sky, filled the hearts of the stoutest patriots with the most gloomy apprehensions, and cast a melancholy shadow over every Union-loving soul throughout the country, somewhat akin to that which hovers over an affectionate son or daughter, upon the approaching dissolution of a cherished, devoted mother. The following compromise, offered by Senator Crittenden, December 19, 1860, is one of the many measures proposed in Congress for adjusting the difficulties of that period:

Resolved, By the Senate and House of Representatives, That the following articles be proposed and submitted as an amendment to the Constitution, which shall be valid as a part of the Constitution, when ratified by the conventions of three-fourths of the people of the States:

1st. In all the territory now or hereafter acquired, north of 36° 30′, slavery, or involuntary servitude, except for the punishment of crime, is prohibited; while in all the territory south of that, slavery is hereby recognized as existing, and shall not be interfered with by Congress, but shall be protected as property by all the departments of the territorial government during its continuance. All the territory north or south of said line, within such boundaries as Congress may prescribe, when it contains a population necessary for a member of Congress, with a republican form of government, shall be admitted into the Union on an equality with the original States, with or without slavery, as the Constitution of the State shall prescribe.

2nd. Congress shall have no power to abolish slavery in the State permitting it.

3rd. Congress shall have no power to abolish slavery in the District of Columbia while it exists in Virginia and Maryland, or either; nor shall Congress at any time prohibit the officers of Government, or Members of Congress, whose duties require them to live in the District of Columbia, bringing slaves there and using them as such.

4th. Congress shall have no power to hinder the transportation of slaves from one State to another, whether by land, navigable river, or sea.

5*th.* Congress shall have the power by law, to pay any owner the full value of any fugitive slave, in all cases where the marshal is prevented from discharging his duty by force or rescue, made after arrest. In all such cases the owner shall have the power to sue the county in which the rescue or violence was made; and the county shall have the right to sue the individuals who committed the wrong, in the same manner as the owner could sue.

6*th.* No future amendment or amendments shall effect the preceding article, and Congress shall never have power to interfere with slavery within the States where it is permitted.

EMANCIPATION PROCLAMATION.

Whereas, on the twenty-second day of September, in the year of our Lord one thousand eight hundred and sixty-two, a proclamation was issued by the President of the United States containing among other things the following, to-wit:

That on the first day of January, in the year of our Lord one thousand eight hundred and sixty-three, all persons held as slaves within any State, or designated part of a State, the people whereof shall then be in rebellion against the United States, shall be then, thenceforth and forever free, and the Executive Government of the United States, including the military and naval authorities thereof, will recognize and maintain the freedom of such persons, or any of them, in any efforts they may make for their actual freedom.

That the Executive will, on the first day of January aforesaid, by proclamation, designate the States and parts of States, if any, in which the people therein respectively shall then be in rebellion against the United States, and the fact that any State, or the people thereof, shall on that day be in good faith represented in the Congress of the United States by members chosen thereto, at elections wherein a majority of the qualified voters of such States shall have participated, shall, in the absence of strong countervailing testimony, be deemed conclusive evidence that such State and the people thereof are not then in rebellion against the United States.

Now, therefore, I, Abraham Lincoln, President of the United States, by virtue of the power in me vested as Commander-in-chief of the Army and Navy of the United States in time of actual armed rebellion against the authority and Government of the United States, and as a fit and necessary war measure for suppressing said rebellion, do, on this first day of January, in the year of our Lord one thousand eight hundred and sixty-three, and in accordance with my purpose so to do, publicly proclaimed for the full period of one hundred days from the day of the first above-mentioned order, and designate, as the States and parts of States wherein the people thereof respectively are this day in rebellion against the United States, the following to-wit: Arkansas, Texas, Louisiana, except the parishes of St. Bernard, Plaquemines, Jefferson, St. John, St.

Charles, St. James, Ascension, Assumption, Terre Bonne, La fourche, St. Mary, St Martin and Orleans, including the city of New Orleans. Mississippi, Alabama, Florida, Georgia, South Carolina, North Carolina, and Virginia, except the forty-eight counties designated as West Virginia, and also the counties of Berkeley, Accomac, Northampton, Elizabeth City, York, Princess Ann, and Norfolk, including the cities of Norfolk and Portsmouth, and which excepted parts are, for the present, left precisely as if this proclamation were not issued.

And by virtue of the power and for the purpose aforesaid, I do order and declare that all persons held as slaves within said designated States and parts of States are, and henceforward shall be free; and that the Executive Government of the United States, including the military and naval authorities thereof, will recognize and maintain the freedom of said persons.

And I hereby enjoin upon the people so declared to be free, to abstain from all violence, unless in necessary self-defence, and I recommend to them, that in all cases, when allowed, they labor faithfully for reasonable wages.

And I further declare and make known that such persons of suitable condition will be received into the armed service of the United States to garrison forts, positions, stations, and other places, and to man vessels of all sorts in said service.

And upon this, sincerely believed to be an act of justice, warranted by the Constitution, upon military necessity, I invoke the considerate judgment of mankind and the gracious favor of Almighty God.

In witness whereof I have hereunto set my hand and caused the seal of the United States to be affixed.

[L. S.] Done at the City of Washington, this first day of January, in the year of our Lord one thousand eight hundred and sixty-three, and of the Independence of the United States of America the eighty-seventh.

By the President: ABRAHAM LINCOLN.
WILLIAM H. SEWARD, *Secretary of State.*

LETTER FROM THE PRESIDENT EXPLAINING THE EMANCIPATION PROCLAMATION.

The following letter, written in August, 1863, in answer to an invitation to attend a meeting of unconditional Union men held in Illinois, gives at length the President's views at that time on his Emancipation proclamation:

"EXECUTIVE MANSION, WASHINGTON, *August 26th*, 1863.

"MY DEAR SIR: Your letter inviting me to attend a mass meeting of unconditional Union men, to be held at the capitol of Illinois on the third day of September, has been received. It would be very agreeable to me to thus meet my old friends at my own home; but I can not just now be absent from this city so long as a visit there would require. The meeting is to be of all those who maintain unconditional devotion to the Union, and I am sure my old political friends will thank me for tendering, as I do, the nation's gratitude to those other noble men whom no partisan malice or partisan hope can make false to the nation's life. There are those who are dissatisfied with me. To such I would say:—You desire peace, and you blame me that you do not have it. But how can we attain it? There are but three conceivable ways:—First, to suppress the rebellion by force of arms. This I am trying to do. Are you for it? If you are, so far we are agreed. If you are not for it, a second way is to give up the Union. I am against this. If you are, you should say so, plainly. If you are not for force, nor yet for dissolution, there only remains some imaginable compromise. I do not believe that any compromise embracing the maintenance of the Union is now possible. All that I learn leads to a directly opposite belief. The strength of the rebellion is its military—its army. The army dominates all the country and all the people within its range. Any offer of any terms made by any man or men within that range in opposition to that army is simply nothing for the present, because such man or men have no power whatever to enforce their side of a compromise, if one were made with them. To illustrate: Suppose refugees from the South and peace men of the North get together in convention, and frame and proclaim a compromise embracing a restoration of the Union. In what way can that compromise be used to keep General Lee's army out of Pennsylvania? General Meade's army can keep Lee's army out of Pennsylvania, and I think can ultimately drive it out of existence. But no paper compromise to which the controllers of General Lee's army are not agreed, can at all effect that army. In an effort at such compromise we would waste time which the enemy would improve to our disadvantage, and that would be all. A compromise, to be effective, must be made either with those who control the rebel army, or with the people, first liberated from the domination of that army by the success of our army. Now, allow me to assure you that no word or intimation from the rebel army, or from any of the men controlling it, in relation to any peace compromise, has ever come to my knowledge or belief. All charges and intimations to the contrary are deceptive and groundless. And I promise you that if any such proposition shall hereafter come, it shall not be rejected and kept secret from you. I freely acknowledge myself to be the servant of the people, according to the bond of service, the

United States constitution; and that, as such, I am responsible to them. But, to be plain. You are dissatisfied with me about the negro. Quite likely there is a difference of opinion between you and myself upon that subject. I certainly wish that all men could be free, while you, I suppose, do not. Yet I have neither adopted nor proposed any measure which is not consistent with even your view, provided you are for the Union. I suggested compensated emancipation, to which you replied that you wished not to be taxed to buy negroes. But I have not asked you to be taxed to buy negroes, except in such way as to save you from greater taxation, to save the Union exclusively by other means.

"You dislike the emancipation proclamation, and perhaps would have it retracted. You say it is unconstitutional. I think differently. I think that the constitution invests the commander-in-chief with the law of war in time of war. The most that can be said, if so much, is, that the slaves are property. Is there, has there ever been, any question that by the law of war, property both of enemies and friends, may be taken when needed? And is it not needed whenever taking it helps us or hurts the enemy? Armies, the world over, destroy enemies' property when they can not use it; and even destroy their own to keep it from the enemy. Civilized beligerents do all in their power to help themselves or hurt the enemy, except a few things regarded as barbarous or cruel. Among the exceptions are the massacre of vanquished foes and non-combatants, male and female. But the proclamation, as law, is valid or is not valid. If it is not valid it needs no retraction. If it is valid it can not be retracted, any more than the dead can be brought to life. Some of you profess to think that its retraction would operate favorably for the Union. Why better after the retraction than before the issue? There was more than a year and a half of trial to suppress the rebellion before the proclamation was issued, the last one hundred days of which passed under an explicit notice, that it was coming unless averted by those in revolt returning to their allegiance. The war has certainly progressed as favorably for us since the issue of the proclamation as before. I know as fully as one can know the opinion of others, that some of the commanders of our armies in the field, who have given us our most important victories, believe the emancipation policy and the aid of colored troops to be the heaviest blows yet dealt to the rebellion, and that at least one of these important successes could not have been achieved when it was but for the aid of black soldiers. Among the commanders holding these views are some who have never had any affinity with what is called abolitionism or with 'republican party politics.'—But who hold them purely as military opinions.

I submit their opinions as being entitled to some weight against the objections often urged that emancipation and arming the blacks are unwise as military measures, and were not adopted as such in good faith. You say that you will not fight to free negroes. Some of them seem to be willing to fight for you—but no matter. Fight you, then, exclusively to save the Union. I issued the proclamation on purpose to aid you in saving the Union. Whenever you shall have conquered all resistance to the Union, if I shall urge you to continue fighting, it will be an apt time then for you to declare that you will not fight to free negroes. I thought that in your struggle for the Union, to whatever extent the negroes should cease helping the enemy, to that extent it weakened the enemy in his resistance to you. Do you think differently? I thought that whatever negroes can be got to do as soldiers, leaves just so much less for white soldiers to do in saving the Union. Does it appear otherwise to you? But negroes, like other people, act upon motives. Why should they do any thing for us if we will do nothing for them? If they stake their lives for us they must be prompted by the strongest motive, even the promise of freedom. And the promise being made, must be kept. The signs look better. The Father of Waters again goes unvexed to the sea. Thanks to the great North-west for it. Not yet wholly to them. Three hundred miles up they met New England, Empire, Keystone and Jersey, hewing their way right and left. The Sunny South, too, in more colors than one, also lent a hand. On the spot their part of the history was jotted down in black and white. The job was a great national one, and let none be blamed who bore an honorable part in it; and, while those who have cleared the great river may well be proud, even that is not all. It is hard to say that anything has been more bravely or better done than at Antietam, Murfreesboro, Gettysburg, and on many fields of less note. Nor must Uncle Sam's webfleet be forgotten. At all the waters' margins they have been present:—not only on the deep sea, the broad bay and the rapid river, but also up the narrow, muddy bayou; and wherever the ground was a little damp they have been and made their tracks. Thanks to all. For the great republic—for the principles by which it lives and keeps alive—for man's vast future—thanks to all. Peace does not appear so far distant as it did. I hope it will come soon, and come to stay: and so come as to be worth the keeping in all future time. It will then have proved that among freeman there can be no successful appeal from the ballot to the bullet, and that they who take such appeal are sure to lose their case and pay the cost. And then there will be some black men who can remember that, with silent tongue, and clenched teeth, and steady eye, and well poised bayonet, they have helped mankind

on to this great consummation: while I fear that there will be
some white men unable to forget that with malignant heart and
deceitful speech they have striven to hinder it. Still let us
not be over sanguine of a speedy final triumph. Let us be
quite sober. Let us diligently apply the means, never doubting
that a just God, in His own good time, will give us the rightful
result.   Yours very truly,   A. LINCOLN."

PROCLAMATION OF ANDREW JACKSON.

The President of the United States to the nullifiers of South Carolina:

WHEREAS, A convention assembled in the State of South Carolina have passed an ordinance, by which they declare, "that the several acts and parts of acts of the Congress of the United States, purporting to be laws for the imposing of duties and imposts on the importation of foreign commodities, and now having actual operation and effect within the United States, and more especially," two acts for the same purposes passed on the 29th of May, 1828, and on the 14th of July, 1832, "are unauthorized by the Constitution of the United States, and violate the true meaning and intent thereof, and are null and void, and no law," nor binding on the citizens of that State or its officers: and by the said ordinance, it is further declared to be unlawful for any of the constituted authorities of the State or of the United States to enforce the payment of the duties imposed by the said acts with the same State, and that it is the duty of the Legislature to pass such laws as may be necessary to give full effect to the said ordinance:

AND WHEREAS, By the said ordinance, it is further ordained that in no case of law or equity decided in the courts of said State, wherein shall be drawn in question the validity of the said ordinance, or of the acts of the Legislature that may be passed to give it effect, or of the said laws of the United States, no appeal shall be allowed to the Supreme Court of the United States, nor shall any copy of the record be permitted or allowed for that purpose; and that any person attempting to take such appeal shall be punished as for a contempt of court:

And, finally, the said ordinance declares that the people of South Carolina will maintain the said ordinance at every hazard; and that they will consider the passage of any act, by Congress, abolishing or closing the ports of the said State, or otherwise obstructing the free ingress or egress of vessels to and from the said ports, or any other act of the Federal Government to coerce the State, shut up her ports, destroy or harrass her commerce, or to enforce the said act otherwise than through the civil tribunals of the country, as inconsistant with the longer continuance of South Carolina in the Union, and that the people of the said State will thenceforth hold themselves absolved from all further obligation to maintain or preserve their political connection with the people of the other States, and will forthwith proceed to organize a separate government, and do all other acts and things which sovereign and independent States may of right do.

AND WHEREAS, The said ordinance prescribes to the people of South Carolina a course of conduct in direct violation of their duty as citizens of the United States, contrary to the laws of their country, subversive of its Constitution, and having for its object the destruction of the Union,—that Union, which, coeval with our political existence, led our fathers, without any other ties to unite them than those of patriotism and a common cause, through a sanguinary struggle to a glorious independence,—that sacred Union, hitherto inviolate, which, perfected by our happy Constitution, has brought us, by the favor of Heaven, to a state of prosperity at home, and high consideration abroad, rarely, if ever, equalled in the history of nations. To preserve this bond of our political existence from destruction, to maintain inviolate this state of national honor and prosperity, and to justify the confidence my fellow citizens have reposed in me, I, ANDREW JACKSON, President of the United States, have thought proper to issue this, my PROCLAMATION, stating my views of the Constitution and laws applicable to the measures adopted by the Convention of South Carolina, and to the reasons they have put forth to sustain them, declaring the course which duty will require me to pursue, and, appealing to the understanding and patriotism of the people, warn them of the consequences that must inevitably result from an observance of the dictates of the convention.

Strict duty would require of me nothing more than the exercise of those powers with which I am now, or may hereafter be invested, for preserving the peace of the Union, and for the execution of the laws. But the imposing aspect which opposition has assumed in this case, by clothing itself with State authority, and the deep interest which the people of the United States must all feel in preventing a resort to stronger measures, while there is a hope that anything will be yielded to reasoning and remonstrance, perhaps demand, and will certainly justify, a full exposition to South Carolina and the nation of the views I entertain of this important question, as well as a distinct enunciation of the course which my sense of duty will require me to pursue.

The ordinance is founded, not on the indefeasible right of resisting acts which are plainly unconstitutional, and too oppressive to be endured; but on the strange position that any one

State may not only declare an act void, but prohibit its execution—that they may do this consisiently with the Constitution—that the true construction of that instrument permits a State to retain its place in the Union, and yet be bound by no other of its laws than those it may choose to consider as constitutional. It is true, they add, that to justify this abrogation of law, it must be palpably contrary to the Constitution; but it is evident, that to give the right of resisting laws of that description, coupled with the uncontrolled right to decide what laws deserve that character, is to give the power of resisting all laws. For, as by the theory, there is no appeal, the reasons alleged by the State, good or bad, must prevail. If it should be said that public opinion is a sufficient check against the abuse of this power, it may be asked why it is not deemed a sufficient guard against an unconstitutional act of Congress? There is, however, a restraint in this last case, which makes the assumed power of a State more indefensible, and which does not exist in the other. There are two appeals from an unconstitutional act passed by Congress—one to the judiciary, the other to the people and the States. There is no appeal from the State decision in theory, and the practical illustration shows that the courts are closed against an application to review it, both judges and jurors being sworn to decide in its favor. But reasoning on this subject is superfluous, when our social compact, in express terms, declares that the laws of the United States, its Constitution, and treaties made under it, are the supreme law of the land; and, for the greater caution, adds "that the judges in every State shall be bound thereby, anything in the Constitution or laws of any State to the contrary notwithstanding." And it may be asserted without fear of refutation, that .no Federal Government could exist without a similar provision. Look for a moment to the consequence. If South Carolina considers the revenues unconstitutional, and has a right to prevent their execution in the port of Charleston, there would be a clear constitutional objection to their collection in every other port, and no revenue could be collected anywhere; for all imposts must be equal. It is no answer to repeat, that an unconstitutional law is no law, so long as the question of its legality is to be decided by the State itself; for every law operating injuriously upon any local interest will be perhaps thought, and certainly represented, as unconstitutional, and, as has been shown, there is no appeal.

If this doctrine had been established at an earlier day, the Union would have been dissolved in its infancy. The excise law in Pennsylvania, the embargo and non-intercourse law in the eastern States, the carriage tax in Virginia, were all deemed unconstitutional, and were more unequal in their operation than any of the laws now complained of; but fortunately none of those States discovered that they had the right now claimed by South Carolina. The war into which we were forced to support the dignity of the nation and the rights of our citizens, might have ended in defeat and disgrace instead of victory and honor, if the States who supposed it a ruinous and unconstitutional measure, had thought they possessed the right of nullifying the act by which it was declared, and denying supplies for its prosecution. Hardly and unequally as those measures bore upon several members of the Union, to the legislatures of none did this efficient and peaceable remedy, as it is called, suggest itself. The discovery of this important feature in our Constitution was reserved to the present day. To the statesmen of South Carolina belongs the invention, and upon the citizens of that State will unfortunately fall the evils of reducing it to practice.

If the doctrine of a State veto upon the laws of the Union carries with it internal evidence of its impracticable absurdity, our Constitutional history will also afford abundant proof that it would have been repudiated with indignation, had it been proposed to form a feature in our Government.

In our colonial state, although dependent on another power, we very early considered ourselves as connected by common interest with each other. Leagues were formed for common defence, and, before the Declaration of Independence, we were known in our aggregate character as the United Colonies of America. That decisive and important step was taken jointly. We declared ourselves a nation by a joint, not by several acts; and when the terms of our Confederation were reduced to form, it was that of a solemn league of several States, by which they agreed that they would collectively form one nation for the purpose of conducting some certain domestic concerns and all foreign relations. In the instrument forming that Union is found an article which declares that "every State shall abide by the determination of Congress on all questions which, by that Confederation, should be submitted to them."

Under the Confederation, then, no State could legally annul a decision of the Congress, or refuse to submit to its execution; but no provision was made to enforce these decisions. Congress made requisitions, but they were not complied with. The Government could not operate on individuals. They had no judiciary, no means of collecting revenue.

But the defects of the Confederation need not be detailed. Under its operation we could scarcely be called a nation. We had neither prosperity at home nor consideration abroad. This state of things could not be endured, and our present happy Constitution was formed, but formed in vain, if this fatal doctrine prevails. It was formed for important objects that are announced in the preamble made in the name and by the authority of the people of the United States, whose delegates framed, and whose conventions approved it. The most important among these objects, that which is placed first in rank, on which all others rest, is, "to form a more perfect Union." Now, is it possible that even if there were no express provision giving supremacy to the Constitution and laws of the United States—can it be conceived, that an instrument made for the purpose of "forming a more perfect Union" than that of the Confederation, could be so constructed by the assembled wisdom of our country as to substitute for that Confederation a form of government dependent for its existence on the local interest, the party spirit of a State, or of a prevailing faction in a State? Every man of plain, unsophisticated understanding, who hears the question, will give such an answer as will preserve the Union. Metaphysical subtlety, in pursuit of an impracticable theory, could alone have devised one that is calculated to destroy it.

I consider, then, the power to annul a law of the United States, assumed by one State, incompatible with the existence of the Union, contradicted expressly by the letter of the Constitution, unauthorized by its spirit, inconsistent with every principle on which it was founded, and destructive of the great object for which it was formed.

After this general view of the leading principle, we must examine the particular application of it which is made in the ordinance.

The preamble rests its justification on these grounds: It assumes, as a fact, that the obnoxious laws, although they purport to be laws for raising revenue, were in reality intended for the protection of manufacturers, which purpose it asserts to be unconstitutional; that the operation of these laws is unequal; that the amount raised by them is greater than is required by the wants of the Government; and, finally, that the proceeds are to be applied to objects unauthorized by the Constitution. These are the only causes alleged to justify an open opposition to the laws of the country, and a threat of seceding from the Union, if any attempt should be made to enforce them. The first virtually acknowledges that the law in question was passed under a power expressly given by the Constitution to lay and collect imposts; but its constitutionality is drawn in question from the motives of those who passed it. However apparent this purpose may be in the present case, nothing can be more dangerous than to admit the position that an unconstitutional purpose, entertained by the members who assent to a law enacted under constitutional power, shall make the law void: for how is that purpose to be ascertained? How often may bad purposes be falsely imputed,—in how many cases are they concealed by false professions,—in how many is no declaration of motive made? Admit this doctrine, and you give to the States an uncontrolled right to decide, and every law may be annulled under this pretext. If, therefore, the absurb and dangerous doctrine should be admitted, that a State may annul an unconstitutional law, or one that it deems such, it will not apply to the present case.

The next objection is, that the laws in question operate unequally. This objection may be made with truth to every law that has been or may be passed. The wisdom of man never yet contrived a system of taxation that would operate with perfect equality. If the unequal operation of a law makes it unconstitutional, and if all laws of that description may be abrogated by any State for that cause, then indeed is the Federal Constitution unworthy the slightest effort for its preservation. We have hitherto relied on it as the perpetual bond of our Union. We have received it as the work of the assembled wisdom of the nation. We have trusted to it as the sheet anchor of our safety in the stormy times of conflict with a foreign or domestic foe. We have looked to it with sacred awe as the palladium of our liberties, and with all the solemnities of religion have pledged to each other our lives and fortunes here, and our hopes of happiness hereafter, in its defence and support. Were we mistaken, my countrymen, in attaching this importance to the Constitution of our country? Was our devotion paid to the wretched, inefficient, clumsy, contrivance which this new doctrine would make it? Did we pledge ourselves to the support of an airy nothing,—a bubble that must be blown away by the first breath of dissatisfaction? Was this self-destroying, visionary theory, the work of the profound statesmen, the exalted patriots, to whom the task of constitutional reform was entrusted? Did the name of Washington sanction, did the States deliberately ratify such an anamoly in the history of fundamental legislation? No. We were not mistaken. The letter of this great instrument is free from this radical fault; its language directly contradicts the imputation; its spirit,—its evident intent, contradicts it. No, we did not err! Our Constitution does not contain the absurdity of giving power to make laws, and another power to resist them. The sages whose memory will always be reverenced, have given us a practical, and, as they hoped, a permanent constitutional compact. The Father of his Country did not affix his revered name to so palpable an absurdity. Nor did the States, when they severally ratified it, do so under the impression that a veto on the laws of the United States, was reserved to them, or that they could exercise it by implication. Search the debates in all their conventions, examine the speeches of the most zealous opposers of federal authority, look at the amendments that were proposed,—they are all silent,—not a syllable uttered, not a vote given, not a motion made, to correct the explicit supremacy given to the laws of the Union over those of the States, or to show that implication, as is now contended, could defeat it. No, we have not erred! The Constitution is still the object of our reverence, the bond of our Union, our defence in danger, the source of our prosperity in peace; it shall descend as we have received it, uncorrupted by sophistical construction, to our posterity, and the sacrifices of local interest, of State prejudices, of personal animosities, that were made to bring it into existence, will again be patriotically offered for its support.

The two remaining objections made by the ordinance to these laws, are that the sums intended to be raised by them are greater than are required, and that the proceeds will be unconstitutionally employed.

The Constitution has given, expressly, to Congress the right of raising revenue, and of determinining the sum the public exigencies will require. The States have no control over the exercise of this right, other than that which results from the power of changing the representatives who abuse it, and thus procure redress. Congress may, undoubtedly, abuse this discretionary power; but the same may be said of others with which they are vested. Yet this discretion must exist somewhere. The Constitution has given it to the representatives of all the people, checked by the representatives of the States and by the executive power. The South Carolina construction gives it to the legislature or the convention of a single State, where neither the people of the different States, nor the States in their separate capacity, nor the chief magistrate elected by the people, have any representation. Which is the most discreet disposition of the power? I do not ask you, fellow-citizens, which is the constitutional disposition—that instrument speaks a language not to be misunderstood. But if you were assembled in general convention, which would you think the safest depository of this discretionary power in the last resort? Would you add a clause giving it to each of the States, or would you sanction the wise provisions already made by your Constitution? If this should be the result of your deliberations when providing for the future, are you, can you be ready to risk all that we hold dear to establish, for a temporary and a local purpose, that which you must acknowledge to be destructive, and even absurd, as a general provision? Carry out the consequences of this right vested in the different States, and you must perceive that the crisis your conduct presents at this day would recur whenever any law of the United States displeased any of the States, and that we should soon cease to be a nation.

The ordinance, with the same knowledge of the future that

characterizes a former objection, tells you that the proceeds of the tax will be unconstitutionally applied. If this could be ascertained with certainty, the objection would, with more propriety, be reserved for the law so applying the proceeds, but surely can not be urged against the laws levying the duty.

These are the allegations contained in the ordinance. Examine them seriously, my fellow-citizens; judge for yourselves. I appeal to you to determine whether they are so clear, so convincing, as to leave no doubt of their correctness; and even if you should come to this conclusion, how far they justify the reckless, destructive course which you are directed to pursue. Review these objections, and the conclusions drawn from them, once more. What are they? Every law, then, for raising revenue, according to the South Carolina ordinance, may be rightfully annulled, unless it be so framed as no law ever will or can be framed. Congress have a right to pass laws for raising a revenue, and each State has a right to oppose their execution — two rights directly opposed to each other; and yet is this absurdity supposed to be contained in an instrument drawn for the express purpose of avoiding collisions between the States and the General government, by an assembly of the most enlightened statesmen and purest patriots ever embodied for a similar purpose.

In vain have these sages declared that Congress shall have power to lay and collect taxes, duties, imposts, and excises; in vain have they provided that they shall have power to pass laws which shall be necessary and proper to carry those powers into execution; that those laws and that Constitution shall be the "supreme law of the land, and that the judges in every State shall be bound thereby, anything in the Constitution or laws of any State to the contrary notwithstanding." In vain have the people of the several States solemnly sanctified these provisions, made them their paramount law, and individually sworn to support them whenever they were called on to execute any office. Vain provision! ineffectual restrictions! vile profanation of oaths! miserable mockery of legislation! if the bare majority of the voters in any one State may, on a real or supposed knowledge of the intent with which a law has been passed, declare themselves free from its operation — say here it gives too little, there too much, and operates unequally — here it suffers articles to be free that ought to be taxed — there it taxes those that ought to be free — in this case the proceeds are intended to be applied to purposes which we do not approve — in that the amount raised is more than is wanted. Congress, it is true, are invested by the Constitution with the right of deciding these questions according to their sound discretion; Congress is composed of the representatives of all the States, and of all the people of all the States; but we, part of the people of one State, to whom the Constitution has given no power on the subject, from whom it has expressly taken it away — we, who have solemnly agreed that this Constitution shall be our law — we, most of whom have sworn to support it — we now abrogate this law, and swear, and force others to swear that it shall not be obeyed; and we do this, not because Congress have no right to pass such laws — this we do not alledge — but because they have passed them with improper views. They are unconstitutional from the motives of those who passed them, which we can never with certainty know; from their unequal operation, although it is impossible, from the nature of things, that they should be equal; and from the disposition which we presume may be made of their proceeds, although that disposition has not been declared. This is the plain meaning of the ordinance, in relation to laws which it abrogates for alleged unconstitutionality. But it does not stop there. It repeals, in express terms, an important part of the Constitution itself, and of laws passed to give it effect, which have never been alleged to be unconstitutional. The Constitution declares that the judicial powers of the United States extend to cases arising under the laws of the United States; and that such laws, the Constitution and treaties, shall be paramount to the State Constitutions and laws. The judiciary act prescribes the mode by which the case may be brought before a court of the United States by appeal, when a State tribunal shall decide against this provision of the Constitution. The ordinance declares that there shall be no appeal, makes the State law paramount to the Constitution and laws of the United States, forces judges and jurors to swear that they will disregard their provisions, and even makes it penal in a suit to attempt relief by appeal. It further declares that it shall not be lawful for the authorities of the United States, or of that State, to enforce the payment of duties imposed by the revenue laws within its limits.

Here is a law of the United States, not even pretended to be unconstitutional, repealed by the authority of a small majority of the voters of a single State. Here is a provision of the Constitution, which is solemnly abrogated by the same authority.

On such expositions and reasonings, the ordinance grounds not only an assertion of the right to annul the laws, of which it complains, but to enforce it by a threat of seceding from the Union, if any attempt is made to execute them.

This right to secede is deduced from the nature of the Constitution, which they say is a compact between sovereign States, who have preserved their whole sovereignty, and therefore are subject to no superior; that because they made the compact, they can break it, when, in their opinion, it has been departed from by the other States. Fallacious as this course of reasoning is, it enlists State pride, and finds advocates in the honest prejudices of those who have not studied the nature of our government sufficiently to see the radical error on which it rests.

The people of the United States formed the Constitution, acting through the State Legislatures in forming the compact, to meet and discuss its provisions, and acting in separate conventions when they ratified those provisions; but the terms used in its construction show it to be a government in which the people of all the States collectively are represented. We are *one people* in the choice of President and Vice President. Here the States have no other agency than to direct the mode in which the votes shall be given. The candidates having a majority of all the votes are chosen. The electors of a majority of States may have given their votes for one candidate, and yet another may be chosen. The people, then, and not the States, are represented in the executive branch.

In the House of Representatives there is this difference, that the people of one State do not, as in the case of President and Vice President, all vote for the same officers. The people of all the States do not vote for all the members, each State electing only its own representatives. But this creates no national distinction. When chosen, they are all representatives of the United States, not representatives of the particular State from whence they come. They are paid by the United States, not by the State; nor are they accountable to it for any act done in the performance of their legislative functions; and however they may in practice, as it is their duty to do, consult and prefer the interests of their particular constituents, when they come in conflict with any other partial or local interest, yet it is the first and highest duty, of a representative of the United States to promote the general good.

The Constitution of the United States, then, forms a *government*, not a league; and whether it be formed by compact between the States, or in any other manner, its character is the same. It is a government in which all the people are represented, which operates directly on the people individually, not upon the States; they retained all the power they did not grant. But each State having expressly parted with so many powers, as to constitute jointly with the other States a single nation, can not from that period possess any right to secede, because such secession does not break a league, but destroys the unity of a nation; and any injury to that unity is not only a breach, which would result from the contravention of a compact, but it is an offense against the whole Union. To say that any State may at pleasure secede from the Union, is to say that the United States are not a nation; because it would be a solecism to contend, that any part of a nation might dissolve its connection with the other parts, to their injury or ruin, without committing any offense. Secession, like any other revolutionary act, may be morally justified by the extremity of oppression; but to call it a constitutional right, is confounding the meaning of the terms; and can only be done through gross error, or to deceive those who are willing to assert a right, but would pause before they made a revolution, or incur the penalties consequent on a failure.

Because the Union was formed by compact, it is said the parties to that compact may, when they feel themselves aggrieved, depart from it; but it is precisely because it is a compact, that they can not. A compact is an agreement, or binding obligation. It may, by its terms, have a sanction or penalty for its breach, or it may not. If it contains no sanction, it may be broken with no other consequence than moral guilt; if it have a sanction, then the breach incurs the designated or implied penalty. A league between independent nations generally has no sanction, other than a moral one; or, if it should contain a penalty, as there is no common superior, it can not be enforced. A government, on the contrary, always has a sanction, express or implied; and in our case, it is both necessarily implied, and expressly given. An attempt by force of arms to destroy a government, is an offense, by whatever means the constitutional compact may have been formed; and such government has the right, by the law of self defense, to pass acts for punishing the offender, unless that right is modified, restrained or resumed by the constitutional act. In our system, although it is modified, in the case of treason, yet authority is expressly given to pass all laws necessary to carry its powers into effect, and under this grant provision has been made for punishing acts, which obstruct the due administration of the laws.

It would seem superfluous to add anything to show the nature of that Union, which connects us; but as erroneous opinions on this subject are the foundation of doctrines the most destructive to our peace, I must give further development to my views on this subject. No one, fellow-citizens, has a higher reverence for the reserved rights of the States, than the magistrate who now addresses you. No one would make greater personal sacrifices or official exertion to defend them from violation; but equal care must be taken to prevent, on their part, an improper interference with, or resumption of the rights they have vested in the nation. The line has not been so distinctly drawn, as to avoid doubts in some cases of the exercise of power. Men of the best intentions and soundest views may differ in their construction of some parts of the Constitution; but there are others on which dispassionate reflection can leave no dougt. Of this nature appears to be the assumed right of secession. It rests, as we have seen, on the alleged undivided sovereignty of the States, and on their having formed, in this sovereign capacity, a compact, which is called the Constitution, from which, because they made it, they have the right to secede. Both of these positions are erroneous, and some of the arguments to prove them so have been anticipated.

The States severally have not retained their entire sovereignty. It has been shown that, in becoming parts of a nation, not members of a league, they surrendered many of their essential parts of sovereignty. The right to make treaties, declare war, levy taxes, exercise exclusive judicial and legislative powers, were all of them functions of sovereign power. The States, then, for all these purposes, were no longer sovereign. The allegiance of their citizens was transferred, in the first instance, to the government of the United States; they became American citizens, and owed obedience to the Constitution of the United States, and to laws made in conformity with the powers it vested in Congress. This last position has not been, and can not be denied. How, then, can that State be said to be sovereign and independent whose citizens owe obedience to laws not made by it, and whose magistrates are sworn to disregard those laws when they come in conflict with those passed by another? What shows conclusively that the States can not be said to have reserved an undivided sovereignty, is, that they expressly ceded the right to punish treason, not treason against their separate power, but treason against the United States. Treason is an offense against sovereignty, and sovereignty must reside with the power to punish it. But the reserved rights of the States are not less sacred because they have, for their common interest, made the General Government the depository of these powers.

The unity of our political character (as has been shown for another purpose) commenced with its very existence. Under the royal government we had no separate character: our opposition to its oppressions began as *united colonies*. We were the United States under the Confederation, and the name was perpetuated, and the Union rendered more perfect by the Federal Constitution. In none of these stages did we consider ourselves in any other light than as forming one nation. Treaties and alliances were made in the name of all. Troops were raised for the joint defence. How, then, with all these proofs, that under all changes of our position we had, for designated purposes and with defined powers, created national governments; how is it, that the most perfect of those several modes of union should now be considered as a mere league, that may be dissolved at pleasure? It is from an abuse of terms. "Compact" is used as synonymous with "league," although the true term is not employed, because it would at once show the fallacy of the reasoning. It would not do to say that our Constitution was only a league; but it is labored to prove it a compact (which in one sense it is,) and then to argue that, as a league is a compact, every compact between nations must of course be a league, and that from such an engagement every sovereign power has a right to recede. But it has been shown, that in this sense the States are not sovereign, and that even if they were, and the national Constitution had been formed by compact, there would be no right in any one State to exonerate itself from its obligations.

So obvious are the reasons which forbid this secession, that it is necessary only to allude to them. The Union was formed for the benefit of all. It was produced by mutual sacrifices of interests and opinions. Can those sacrifices be recalled? Can the States, who magnanimously surrender their title to the territories in the West, recall the grant? Will the inhabitants of the inland States agree to pay the duties, that may be imposed without their assent, by those on the Atlantic or the Gulf, for their own benefit? Shall there be a free port in one State, and onerous duties in another? No one believes that any right exists, in a single State, to involve the others in these and countless other evils, contrary to the engagements solemnly made. Every one must see that the other States, in self-defence, must oppose it at all hazards.

These are the alternatives that are presented by the convention: A repeal of all the acts for raising revenue, leaving the Government without the means of support, or an acquiescence in the dissolution of our Union by the secession of one of its members. When the first was proposed, it was known that it could not be listened to for a moment. It was known, if force was applied to oppose the execution of the laws, that it must be repelled by force; that Congress could not, without involving itself in disgrace, and the country in ruin, accede to the proposition; and yet, if this is not done on a given day, or if any attempt is made to execute the laws, the State is, by the ordinance, declared to be out of the Union. The majority of a convention assembled for the purpose have dictated these terms, or rather this rejection of all terms, in the name of the people of South Carolina. It is true that the Governor of the State speaks of the submission of their grievances to a convention of all the States, which, he says, they "sincerely and anxiously seek and desire." Yet this obvious and constitutional mode of obtaining the sense of the other States, on the construction of the Federal compact, and amending it if necessary, has never been attempted by those who have urged the State on to this destructive measure. The State might have proposed to call for a general convention of the other States; and Congress, if a sufficient number of them concurred, must have called it. But the first magistrate of South Carolina, when he expressed a hope that, "on a review by Congress and the functionaries of the general government of the merits of the controversy," such a convention will be accorded to them, must have known that neither Congress, nor any functionary of the general government, has authority to call such a convention, unless it be demanded by two-thirds of the States. This suggestion, then, is another instance of the reckless inattention to the provisions of the Constitution, with which this crisis has been madly hurried on; or of the attempt to persuade the people that a constitutional remedy has been sought and refused. If the Legislature of South Carolina "anxiously desire" a general convention to consider their complaints, why have they not made application for it, in the way the Constitution points out? The assertion that they "earnestly seek" it, is completely negatived by the omission.

This, then, is the position in which we stand. A small majority of the citizens of one State in the Union have elected delegates to a State convention; that convention has ordained that all the revenue laws of the United States must be repealed, or that they are no longer a member of this Union. The Governor of that State has recommended to the Legislature the raising of an army to carry the secession into effect, and that he may be empowered to give clearances to vessels in the name of the State. No act of violent opposition to the laws has yet been committed, but such a state of things is hourly apprehended; and it is the intent of this instrument to proclaim, not only that the duty imposed on me by the Constitution "to take care that the laws be faithfully executed," shall be performed to the extent of the powers already vested in me by law, or of such others as the wisdom of Congress shall devise and entrust to me for that purpose, but to warn the citizens of South Carolina who have been deluded into an opposition to the laws, of the danger they will incur by obedience to the illegal and disorganizing ordinance of the convention; to exhort those who have refused to support it to persevere in their determination to uphold the Constitution and laws of their country; and to point out to all the perilous situation into which the good people of that State have been led, and that the course they are urged to pursue is one of ruin and disgrace to the very State whose rights they affect to support.

Fellow-citizens of my native State, let me not only admonish you, as the First Magistrate of our common country, not to incur the penalty of its laws, but use the influence that a father would over his children whom he saw rushing to certain ruin. In that paternal language, with that paternal feeling, let me tell you, my countrymen, that you are deluded by men who are either deceived themselves, or wish to deceive you. Mark under what pretences you have been led on to the brink of insurrection and treason, and on which you stand! First, a diminution of the value of your staple commodity, lowered by over-production in other quarters, and the consequent diminution in the value of your lands, were the sole effect of the tariff laws.

The effect of those laws was confessedly injurious, but the evil was greatly exaggerated by the unfounded theory you were taught to believe, that its burthens were in proportion to your exports, not to your consumption of imported articles. Your pride was roused by the assertion that a submission to those laws was a state of vassalage, and that resistence to them was equal, in patriotic merit, to the opposition our fathers offered to the oppressive laws of Great Britain. You were told that this opposition might be peaceably—might be constitutionally made; that you might enjoy all the advantages of the Union, and bear none of its burthens. Eloquent appeals to your passions, to your State pride, to your native courage, to your sense of real injury, were used, to prepare you for the period when the mask, which concealed the hideous features of disunion, should be taken off. It fell, and you were made to look with complacency on objects which, not long since, you would have regarded with horror. Look back to the arts which have brought you to this state—look forward to the consequences to which it must inevitably lead! Look back to what was first told you as an inducement to enter into this dangerous course. The great political truth was repeated to you, that you had the revolutionary right of resisting all laws that were palpably unconstitutional and intolerably oppressive; it was added that the right to nullify a law rested on the same principle, but that it was a peaceable remedy! This character which was given to it, made you receive, with too much confidence, the assertions that were made of the unconstitutionality of the law and its oppressive effects. Mark, my fellow-citizens, that, by the admission of your leaders, the unconstitutionality must be *palpable*, or it will not justify either resistance or nullification! What is the meaning of the word *palpable*, in the sense in which it is here used? that which is apparent to every one; that which no man of ordinary intellect will fail to perceive. Is the unconstitutionality of these laws of that description? Let those among your leaders who once approved and advocated the principle of protective duties, answer the question; and let them choose whether they will be considered as incapable, then, of perceiving that which must have been apparent to every man of common understanding, or as imposing on your confidence, and endeavoring to mislead you now. In either case, they are unsafe guides in the perilous path they urge you to tread. Ponder well on this circumstance, and you will know how to appreciate the exaggerated language they address to you. They are not champions of liberty, emulating the fame of our revolutionaty fathers; nor are you an oppressed people, contending, as they repeat to you, against worse than colonial vassalage.

You are free members of a flourishing and happy Union. There is no settled design to oppress you. You have indeed felt the unequal operation of laws which may have been unwisely, not unconstitutionally passed; but that inequality must necessarily be removed. At the very moment when you were madly urged on to the unfortunate course you have begun, a change in public opinion had commenced. The nearly approaching payment of the public debt, and the consequent necessity of a diminution of duties, had already produced a considerable reduction, and that, too, on some articles of general consumption in your State. The importance of this change was underrated, and you are authoritatively told that no further alleviation of your burthens were to be expected at the very time when the condition of the country imperiously demanded such a modification of the duties as should reduce them to a just and equitable scale. But, as if apprehensive of the effect of this change in allaying your discontents, you were precipitated into the fearful state in which you now find yourselves.

I have urged you to look back to the means that were used to hurry you on to the position you have now assumed, and forward to the consequences it will produce. Something more is necessary. Contemplate the condition of that country of which you still form an important part. Consider its Government, uniting in one bond of common interest and general protection so many different States,—giving to all their inhabitants the proud title of American citizens, protecting their commerce, securing their literature and their arts; facilitating their intercommunication; defending their frontiers, and making their names respected in the remotest parts of the earth. Consider the extent of its territory; its increasing and happy population; its advance in arts, which render life agreeable; and the sciences, which elevate the mind! See education spreading the lights of religion, morality, and general information into every cottage in this wide extent of our Territories and States! Behold it as the asylum where the wretched and the oppressed find a refuge and support! Look on this picture of happiness and honor, and say: "*We, too, are citizens of America!* Carolina is one of these proud States,—her arms have defended,—her best blood has cemented this happy Union!" And then add, if you can, without horror and remorse, "this happy Union we will dissolve; this picture of peace and prosperity we will deface; this free intercourse we will interrupt;

these fertile fields we will deluge with blood; the protection of that glorious flag we renounce; the very name of Americans we discard." And for what, mistaken men,—for what do you throw away these inestimable blessings? for what would you exchange your share in the advantages and honor of the Union? For the dream of separate independence,—a dream interrupted by bloody conflicts with your neighbors, and a vile dependence on a foreign power. If your leaders could succeed in establishing a separation, what would be your situation? Are you united at home,—are you free from the apprehension of civil discord, with all its fearful consequences? Do our neighboring republics, every day suffering some new revolution, or contending with some new insurrection,—do they excite your envy? But the dictates of a high duty obliges me solemnly to announce that you can not succeed. The laws of the United States must be executed. I have no discretionary power on the subject,—my duty is emphatically pronounced in the Constitution. Those who told you that you might peaceably prevent their execution, deceived you,—they could not have been deceived themselves. They know that a forcible opposition could alone prevent the execution of the laws, and they know that such opposition must be repelled. Their object is disunion; but be not deceived by names; disunion, by armed force, is *treason*. Are you really ready to incur its guilt? If you are, on the heads of the instigators of the act be the dreadful consequences,—on their heads be the dishonor, but on yours may fall the punishment; on your unhappy State will inevitably fall all the evils of the conflict you force upon the government of your country. It can not accede to the mad project of disunion, of which you would be the first victims,—its First Magistrate can not, if he would, avoid the performance of his duty; the consequences must be fearful to you, distressing to your fellow-citizens here, and to the friends of good government throughout the world. Its enemies have beheld our prosperity with a vexation they could not conceal,—it was a standing refutation of their slavish doctrines, and they will point to our discord with the triumph of malignant joy. It is yet in your power to disappoint them. There is yet time to show that the descendants of the Pinckneys, the Sumters, the Rutledges, and of the thousand other names, which adorn the pages of your revolutionary history, will not abandon that Union, to support which so many of them fought, and bled, and died.

I adjure you, as you honor their memory—as you love the cause of freedom, to which they dedicated their lives—as you prize the peace of your country, the lives of its best citizens, and your own fair fame, to retrace your steps. Snatch from the archives of your State, the disorganizing edict of its convention

—bid its members to re-assemble, and promulgate the decided expressions of your will to remain in the path which alone can conduct you to safety, prosperity and honor. Tell them that, compared to disunion, all other evils are light, because that brings with it an accumulation of all. Declare that you will never take the field unless the star spangled banner of your country shall float over you; that you will not be stigmatized when dead, and dishonored and scorned while you live, as the authors of the first attack on the Constitution of your country. Its destroyers you can not be. You may disturb its peace—you may interrupt the course of its prosperity—you may cloud its reputation for stability; but its tranquility will be restored, its prosperity will return, and the stain upon its national character will be transferred, and remain an eternal blot on the memory of those who caused the disorder.

Fellow-citizens of the United States! The threat of unhallowed disunion—the names of those once respected, by whom it is uttered—the array of military force to support it—denote the approach of a crisis in our affairs, on which the continuance of our unexampled prosperity, our political existence, and perhaps that of all free governments, may depend. The conjuncture demanded a free, a full, and explicit enunciation, not only of my intentions, but of my principles of action; and as the claim was asserted of a right by a State to annul the laws of the Union, and even to secede from it at pleasure, a frank exposition of my opinions in relation to the origin and form of our government, and the construction I give to the instrument by which it was created, seemed to be proper. Having the fullest confidence in the justness of the legal and constitutional opinion of my duties, which has been expressed, I rely, with equal confidence, on your undivided support in my determination to execute the laws—to preserve the Union by all constitutional means—to arrest, if possible, by moderate but firm measures, the necessity of a recourse to force; and, if it be the will of Heaven, that the recurrence of its primeval curse on man for the shedding of a brother's blood should fall upon our land, that it be not called down by any offensive act on the part of the United States.

Fellow citizens! the momentous case is before you. On your undivided support of your Government depends the decision of the great question it involves, whether your sacred Union will be preserved, and the blessings it secures to us as one people, shall be perpetuated. No one can doubt that the unanimity with which that decision will be expressed, will be such as to inspire new confidence in republican institutions, and that the prudence, the wisdom, and the courage which it will bring to their defence, will transmit them unimpaired and invigorated to our children.

May the Great Ruler of Nations grant that the signal blessings with which He has favored ours, may not, by the madness of party or personal ambition, be disregarded and lost; and may His wise providence bring those who have produced this crisis to see their folly, before they feel the misery of civil strife, and inspire a returning veneration for that Union, which, if we may dare to penetrate His designs, He has chosen as the only means of attaining the high destinies to which we may reasonably aspire.

In testimony whereof, I have caused the seal of the United States to be hereunto affixed, having signed the same with my hand.

Done at the city of Washington, this 10th day of December, in the year of our Lord one thousand eight hundred and thirty-two, and of the independence of the United States the fifty-seventh.

By the President:

ANDREW JACKSON.

EDWD. LIVINGSTON, *Secretary of State.*

PLATFORMS OF 1860-1864.

PLATFORM OF THE BRECKINRIDGE PARTY OF 1860.

Resolved, That the platform adopted by the Democratic party at Cincinnati be affirmed, with the following explanatory resolutions :

1. That the government of a territory organized by an act of Congress is provisional and temporary, and during its existence all citizens of the United States have an equal right to settle with their property in the territory, without their rights, either in person or property, being destroyed by congressional or territorial legislation.

2. That it is the duty of the Federal Government, in all its departments, to protect the rights of persons and property in the territories, and wherever else its constitutional authority extends.

3. That when the settlers in a territory, having an adequate population, form a State Constitution, the right of sovereignty commences, and being consummated by their admission into the Union, they stand on an equality with the people of other States, and a State thus organized ought to be admitted into the Federal Union, whether its constitution prohibits or recognizes the institution of slavery.

4. That the Democratic party are in favor of the acquisition of Cuba, on such terms as shall be honorable to ourselves and just to Spain, at the earliest practicable moment.

5. That the enactments of State Legislatures to defeat the faithful execution of the Fugitive Slave Law are hostile in character, subversive of the Constitution, and revolutionary in their effect.

6. That the Democracy of the United States recognize it as an imperative duty of the government to protect the naturalized citizen in all his rights, whether at home or in foreign lands, to the same extent as its native born citizens.

WHEREAS, One of the greatest necessities of the age, in a political, commercial, postal, and military point of view, is a speedy communication between the Pacific and Atlantic coasts; therefore, be it resolved,

7. That the National Democratic party do hereby pledge themselves to use every means in their power to secure the passage of some bill, to the extent of the Constitutional authority by Congress, for the construction of a railroad to the Pacific Ocean, at the earliest practicable moment.

PLATFORM OF THE DOUGLAS PARTY OF 1860.

Resolved, That we, the Democracy of the Union in Convention assembled, hereby declare our affirmation of the resolutions unanimiously adopted and declared as a platform of principles by the Democratic Convention at Cincinnati, in the year 1856, believing that Democratic principles are unchangable in their nature when applied to the same subject matter, and we recommend as our only further resolutions the following:

That inasmuch as differences of opinion exist in the Democratic party as to the nature and extent of the powers of a Territorial Legislature, and as to the powers and duties of Congress, under the Constitution of the United States, over the institution of slavery in the territories;

Resolved, That the Democratic party will abide by the decision of the Supreme Court of the United States over the institution of slavery in the territories.

Resolved, That it is the duty of the United States to afford ample and complete protection to all its citizens, at home or abroad, and whether native or foreign born.

Resolved, That one of the necessities of the age, in a military, commercial, and postal point of view, is a speedy communication between the Atlantic and Pacific States, and the Democratic party pledge such constitutional enactment as will insure the construction of a railroad to the Pacific coast at the earliest practical period.

Resolved, That the Democratic party are in favor of the acquisition of the Island of Cuba, on such terms as shall be honorable to ourselves and just to Spain.

Resolved, That the enactments of State Legislatures to defeat the faithful execution of the Fugitive Slave Law are hostile in character, subversive to the Constitution, and revolutionary in their effect.

Resolved, That it is in accordance with the Cincinnati Platform, that during the existence of Territorial Governments, the measure of restriction, whatever it may be, imposed by the Federal Constitution on the power of the Territorial Legislature over the subject of the domestic relations, as the same has been or shall hereafter be decided by the Supreme Court of the United States, should be respected by all good citizens, and enforced with promptness and fidelity by every branch of the General Government.

THE REPUBLICAN PLATFORM OF 1860.

Resolved, That we, the delegated representatives of the Republican electors of the United States, in Convention assembled, in the discharge of the duty we owe to our constituents and our country, unite in the following resolutions:

1. That the history of the nation during the last four years has fully established the propriety and necessity of the organization and perpetuation of the Republican party, and that the causes which called it into existence are permanent in their nature, and now, more than ever, demand its peaceful and constitutional triumph.

2. That the maintenance of the principles promulgated in the Declaration of Independence, and embodied in the Federal Constitution, that "all men are created equal; that they are endowed by their Creator with certain inalienable rights, among which are those of life, liberty and the pursuit of happiness, and that Governments are instituted among men to secure the enjoyment of these rights, deriving their just power from the consent of the governed"—are essential to the preservation of our republican institutions, and that the Federal Constitution, the rights of the States, and the union of the States, must and shall be preserved.

3. That to the union of the States this nation owes its unprecedented increase in population, its surprising developments of material resources; its rapid augmentation of wealth; its happiness at home and its honor abroad; and we hold in abhorrence all schemes for disunion, come from whatever source they may; and we congratulate the country that no Republican member of Congress has uttered or countenanced the threats of disunion as often made by the Democratic members of Congress, without rebuke and with applause from their political associates; and we denounce those threats of disunion in case of a popular overthrow of their ascendency, as denying the vital principles of a free Government, and as an avowal of contemplated treason which it is the imperative duty of an indignant people sternly to rebuke and forever silence.

4. That the maintenance inviolate, of the rights of the States, and especially of each State, to order and control its own domestic institutions according to its own judgment exclusively, is essential to that balance of power on which the perfection and endurance of our political fabric depends; and we denounce the lawless invasion by armed force of the soil of any State or

Territory, no matter under what pretext, as one of the gravest of crimes.

5. That the present Democratic Administration has far exceeded our worst apprehensions in the measureless subserviency to the exactions of a sectional interest, as especially evinced in its desperate exertions to force the infamous Lecompton Constitution upon the protesting people of Kansas, construing the relation between master and servant to involve an unqualified property in persons; in its attempted enforcement everywhere, on land and sea, through the intervention of Congress and of the Federal Courts, of the extreme pretensions of a purely local interest; and in its general and unvarying abuse of the power entrusted to it by a confiding people.

6. That the people justly view with alarm the reckless extravagance which pervades every department of the Federal Government. That a return to right economy and accountability is indispensible to arrest the plunder of the public treasury by favored partisans, while the recent startling developments of frauds and corruption at the Federal metropolis show that an entire change of administration is imperatively demanded.

7. That the new dogma that the Constitution of its own force carries slavery into any or all the Territories of the United States, is a dangerous political heresy, at variance with the explicit provisions of that instrument itself, with cotemporaneous exposition, and with legislative and judicial precedents, that it is revolutionary in its tendency and subversive of the peace and harmony of the country.

8. That the nominal condition of all the territory of the United States is that of freedom; that as our Republican fathers, when they had abolished slavery in all our national territory, ordained that no person should be deprived of life, liberty or property without due process of law, it becomes our duty by legislation, whenever such legislation is necessary, to maintain this provision of the Constitution against all attempts to violate it; and we deny the authority of Congress, or a Territorial Legislature, or of any individual, to give legal existence to slavery in any Territory of the United States.

9. That we brand the recent re-opening of the African Slave Trade, under the cover of our national flag, aided by perversions of judicial power, as a crime against humanity, and a burning shame to our country and age; and we call upon Congress to take prompt and efficient measures for the total and final suppression of that execrable traffic.

10. That in the recent vetoes by their Federal Governors of the acts of the Legislatures of Kansas and Nebraska, prohibiting slavery in these Territories, we find a practical illustration of the boasted Democratic principles of non-intervention and

Popular Sovereignty, embodied in the Kansas-Nebraska bill, and a demonstration of the deception and fraud involved therein.

11. That Kansas should, of right, be immediately admitted as a State under the Constitution recently formed and adopted by her people, and accepted by the House of Representatives.

12. That while providing revenue for the support of the General Government, by duties upon imports, sound policy requires such an adjustment of these imports as to encourage the development of the industrial interests of the whole country, and we commend that policy of National Exchange which secures to the working men liberal wages, agriculture remunerative prices, to merchants and manufacturers an adequate reward for their skill, labor and enterprise, and to the nation commercial prosperity and independence.

13. That we protest against any sale or alienation to others of the public lands held by actual settlers, and against any view of the free homestead policy, which regards the settlers as paupers or suppliants for public bounty, and we demand the passage by Congress of the complete and satisfactory homestead measure which has already passed the House.

14. That the National Republican party is opposed to any change in our naturalization laws, or any State Legislation, by which the rights of citizenship hitherto accorded to immigrants from foreign lands shall be abridged or impaired, and in favor of giving a full and efficient protection to the rights of all classes of citizens, whether native or naturalized, both at home and abroad.

15. That appropriations by Congress for river and harbor improvements of a national character, is required for the accommodation and security of an existing commerce, or authorized by the Constitution and justified by the obligation of the Government to protect the lives and property of its citizens.

16. That a railroad to the Pacific ocean is imperatively demanded by the interests of the whole country; and that the Federal Government ought to render immediate and efficient aid in its construction, and that preliminary thereto, a daily overland mail should be promptly established.

17. Finally, having thus set forth our distinctive principles and views, we invite the co-operation of all citizens, however differing in other questions, who substantially agree with us, in their affirmance and support.

PLATFORM OF THE NATIONAL CONSTITUTIONAL PARTY OF 1860.

The Union, the Constitution and the Laws.

UNION PLATFORM, ADOPTED AT BALTIMORE JUNE 8, 1864.

Resolved, That it is the highest duty of every American citizen to maintain against all its enemies, the integrity of the Union, and the paramount authority of the Constitution and laws of the United States, and that, laying all political opinions aside, we pledge ourselves, as Union men, animated by a common sentiment, and aiming at a common object, to do everything in our power to aid the Government in quelling, by force of arms, the rebellion now raging against its authority, and bringing to the punishment due to their crimes, the rebels and traitors arrayed against it.

Resolved, That we approve the determination of the Government of the United States not to compromise with rebels, or to offer any terms of peace, except such as may be based upon an unconditional surrender of their hostility, &c., and a return to their just allegiance to the Constitution and laws of the United States, and that we call upon the Government to maintain this position, and to prosecute the war with the utmost possible vigor to the complete suppression of the rebellion, in full reliance upon the self-sacrifices, the patriotism, the heroic valor, and the undying devotion of the American people to their country and its free institutions.

Resolved, That slavery was the cause and now constitutes the strength of the rebellion, and that as it must be always and everywhere hostile to the principles of Republican Governments, justice and the national safety demand its utter and complete extirpation from the soil of the Republic, and that we uphold and maintain the acts and proclamations, by which the Government, in its own defence, has aimed a death blow at this gigantic evil. We are in favor, furthermore, of such an amendment to the Constitution, to be made by the people in conformity with its provisions, as shall terminate and forever prohibit the existence of slavery within the limits of the jurisdiction of the United States.

Resolved, That the thanks of the American people are due to the soldiers and sailors of the army and navy, who have periled their lives in defence of their country, and in vindication of the honor of the flag; that the nation owes them some permanent recognition of their patriotism and their valor, and ample and permanent provision for those of their survivors who have received disabling and honorable wounds in the service of their country, and that the memories of those who have fallen in its defense shall be held in grateful and everlasting remembrance.

Resolved, That we approve and applaud the political wisdom, the unselfish patriotism and unswerving fidelity to the Constitution and the principles of American liberty, with which

Abraham Lincoln has discharged, under circumstances of unparalelled difficulty, the great duties and responsibilities of the Presidential office; that we approve and endorse, as demanded by the emergency and essential to the preservation of the nation, and as within the Constitution, the measures and acts which he has adopted to defend the nation against its open and secret foes; especially the Proclamation of Emancipation, and the employment, as Union soldiers, of men heretofore held in slavery, and that we have full confidence in his determination to carry these and all other Constitutional measures, essential to the salvation of the country, into full and complete effect.

Resolved, That we deem it essential to the general welfare, that harmony should prevail in the national councils, and we regard as worthy of public confidence and official trust those only who cordially endorse the principle proclaimed in these resolutions, and which should characterize the administration of the Government.

Resolved, That the Government owes to all men employed in its armies, without distinction of color, the full protection of the laws of war, and any violation of these laws and of the usages of civilized nations in the time of war, by the rebels now in arms, should be made the subject of full and prompt redress.

Resolved, That the foreign immigration, which in the past has added so much to the wealth and development of resources and increase of power to this nation, the asylum of the oppressed of all nations, should be fostered and encouraged by a liberal and just policy.

Resolved, That we are in favor of the speedy construction of the railroad to the Pacific.

Resolved, That the national faith is pledged for the redemption of the public debt and must be kept inviolate; and that for this purpose we recommend economy and rigid responsibilities in the public expenditures, and a vigorous and just system of taxation; that it is the duty of every loyal State to sustain the use of the national currency.

Resolved, That we approve the position taken by the Government, that the people of the United States can never regard with indifference the attempt of European power to overthrow by force, or to supplant by fraud, the institutions of any Republican government on the Western Continent, and that they will view with extreme jealousy, as menacing to the peace and independence of this our country, the efforts of any such power to obtain new footholds for monarchical governments sustained by a foreign military force in near proximiry to the United States.

FREMONT PLATFORM, ADOPTED AT CLEVELAND, MAY 31, 1864.

1. That the Federal Union must be preserved.
2. That the Constitution and laws of the United States must be observed and obeyed.
3. That the rebellion must be suppressed by the force of arms, and without compromise.
4. That the rights of Free Speech, Free Press, and the Habeas Corpus must be held inviolate, save in districts where martial law has been proclaimed.
5. That the rebellion has destroyed slavery, and the Federal Constitution should be amended to prohibit its re-establishment.
6. That the right for asylum, except for crime, and subject to law, is a recognized principle—a principle of American liberty; that any violation of it must not be overlooked, and must not go unrebuked.
7. That the National policy known as the Monroe doctrine has become a recognized principle, and that the establishment of an anti-republican government on this continent by a foreign power can not be tolerated.
8. That the gratitude and support of the nation is due to the faithful soldiers, and the earnest leaders of the Union army and navy, for their heroic achievements and valor in defense of our imperiled country and of civil liberty.
9. That the one term policy for the Presidency adopted by the people is strengthened by the existing crisis, and shall be maintained by constitutional amendments.
10. That the constitution shall be so amended that the President and Vice President shall be elected by a direct vote of the people.
11. That the reconstruction of the rebellious States belongs to the people through their representatives in Congress, and not to the Executive.
12. That the confiscation of the lands of the rebels and their distribution among the soldiers and actual settlers is a measure of justice; that integrity and economy are demanded at all times in the measures of the government, and that now the want of this is criminal.

SPEECH OF A. H. STEPHENS,

OF GEORGIA, IN OPPOSITION TO SECESSION, DELIVERERED NOV. 14, 1860.

FELLOW-CITIZENS: I appear before you to-night, at the request of members of the Legislature and others, to speak of matters of the deepest interest that can possibly concern us all, of an earthly character. There is nothing—no question or subject connected with this life—that concerns a free people so intimately as that of the government under which we live. We are now, indeed, surrounded by evils. Never, since I entered upon the public stage, has the country been so environed with difficulties and dangers, that threatened the public peace and the very existence of society, as now. I do not now appear before you at my own instance. It is not to gratify any desire of my own that I am here. Had I consulted my own ease and pleasure I should not be before you; but, believing that it is the duty of every good citizen to give his counsels and views whenever the country is in danger, as to the best policy to be pursued, I am here. For these reasons, and these only, do I bespeak a calm, patient, and attentive hearing.

My object is not to stir up strife, but to allay it; not to appeal to your passions, but to your reason. Good governments can never be built up or sustained by the impulse of passion. I wish to address myself to your good sense, to your good judgment, and if, after hearing, you disagree, let us agree to disagree, and part as we met, friends. We all have the same object, the same interest. That people should disagree in republican governments, upon questions of public policy, is natural. That men should disagree upon all matters connected with human investigation, whether relating to science or human conduct, is natural. Hence, in free governments, parties will arise. But a free people should express their different opinions with liberality and charity, with no acrimony toward those of their fellows, when honestly and sincerely given. These are my feelings to-night.

Let us, therefore, reason together. It is not my purpose to say aught to wound the feelings of any individual who may be

present; and if, in the ardency with which I shall express my opinions, I shall say any thing which may be deemed too strong, let it be set down to the zeal with which I advocate my own convictions. There is with me no intention to irritate or offend.
The first question that presents itself is, shall the people of the South secede from the Union in consequence of the election of Mr. Lincoln to the Presidency of the United States? My countrymen, *I tell you frankly, candidly, and earnestly, that I do not think that they ought.* In my judgment, the election of no man, constitutionally chosen to that high office, is sufficient cause for any State to separate from the Union. It ought to stand by and aid still in maintaining the Constitution of the country. To make a point of resistance to the Government, to withdraw from it because a man has been constitutionally elected, puts us in the wrong. We are pledged to maintain the Constitution. Many of us have sworn to support it. Can we, therefore, for the mere election of a man to the Presidency, and that too in accordance with the prescribed forms of the Constitution, make a point of resistance to the Government without becoming the breakers of that sacred instrument ourselves—withdraw ourselves from it? Would we not be in the wrong? Whatever fate is to befall this country, let it never be laid to the charge of the people of the South, and especially to the people of Georgia, that we were untrue to our national engagements. Let the fault and the wrong rest upon others. If all our hopes are to be blasted, if the Republic is to go down, let us be found to the last moment standing on the deck, with the Constitution of the United States waving over our heads. Let the fanatics of the North break the Constitution, if such is their fell purpose. Let the responsibility be upon them. I shall speak presently more of their acts; but let not the South—let us not be the ones to commit the aggression. We went into the election with this people. The result was different from what we wished; but the election has been constitutionally held. Were we to make a point of resistance to the Government and go out of the Union on that account, the record would be made up hereafter against us.
But it is said Mr. Lincoln's policy and principles are against the Constitution, and that if he carries them out it will be destructive of our rights. Let us not anticipate a threatened evil. If he violates the Constitution, then will come our time to act. Do not let us break it because, forsooth he may. If he does, that is the time for us to strike. I think it would be injudicious and unwise to do this sooner. I do not anticipate that Mr. Lincoln will do anything to jeopard our safety or security, whatever may be his spirit to do it; for he is bound by the constitutional checks which are thrown around him, which at this time render

him powerless to do any great mischief. This shows the wisdom of our system. The President of the United States is no emperor, no dictator—he is clothed with no absolute power. He can do nothing unless he is backed by power in Congress. The House of Representatives is largely in the majority against him.

In the Senate he will also be powerless. There will be a majority of four against him. This, after the loss of Bigler, Fitch, and others, by the unfortunate dissensions of the National Democratic party in their States. Mr. Lincoln can not appoint an officer without the consent of the Senate—he can not form a cabinet without the same consent. He will be in the condition of George III. (the embodiment of Toryism), who had to ask the Whigs to appoint his ministers, and was compelled to receive a cabinet utterly opposed to his views; and so Mr. Lincoln will be compelled to ask of the Senate to choose for him a cabinet, if the Democracy of that body choose to put him on such terms. He will be compelled to do this or let the Government stop, if the National Democratic men—for that is their name at the North—the conservative men in the Senate, should so determine. Then how can Mr. Lincoln obtain a cabinet which would aid him, or allow him to violate the Constitution?

Why, then, I say, should we disrupt the ties of this Union when his hands are tied, when he can do nothing against us? I have heard it mooted that no man in the State of Georgia, who is true to her interests, could hold office under Mr. Lincoln. But, I ask, who appoints to office? Not the President alone; the Senate has to concur. No man can be appointed without the consent of the Senate. Should any man then refuse to hold office that was given to him by a Democratic Senate? [Mr. Toombs interrupted and said if the Senate was Democratic it was for Mr. Breckinridge.] Well, then, continued Mr. S., I apprehend no man could be justly considered untrue to the interests of Georgia, or incur any disgrace, if the interests of Georgia required it, to hold an office which a Breckinridge Senate had given him, even though Mr. Lincoln should be President.

I trust, my countrymen, you will be still and silent. I am addressing your good sense. I am giving you my views in a calm and dispassionate manner, and if any of you differ with me, you can, on any other occasion, give your views as I am doing now, and let reason and true patriotism decide between us. In my judgment, I say, under such circumstances, there would be no possible disgrace for a Southern man to hold office. No man will be suffered to be appointed, I have no doubt, who is not true to the Constitution, if Southern Senators are true to their trusts, as I can not permit myself to doubt that they will be.

My honorable friend who addressed you last night (Mr. Toombs), and to whom I listened with the profoundest attention, asks if we would submit to Black Republican rule? I say to you and to him, as a Georgian, I never would submit to any Black Republican *aggression* upon our constitutional rights. I will never consent myself, as much as I admire this Union for the glories of the past, or the blessings of the present—as much as it has done for the people of all these States—as much as the hopes of the world hang upon it, I would never submit to aggression upon my rights to maintain it longer; and if they can not be maintained in the Union, standing on the Georgia platform, where I have stood from the time of its adoption, I would be in favor of disrupting every tie which binds the States together.

I will have equality for Georgia and for the citizens of Georgia in this Union, or I will look for new safeguards elsewhere. This is my position. The only question now is, can they be secured in the Union? That is what I am counseling with you to-night about. Can they be secured? In my judgment they may be, but they may not be; but let us do all we can, so that in the future, if the worst come, it may never be said we were negligent in doing our duty to the last.

My countrymen, I am not of those who believe this Union has been a curse up to this time. True men, men of integrity, entertain different views from me on this subject. I do not question their right to do so: I would not impugn their motives in so doing. Nor will I undertake to say that this Government of our fathers is perfect. There is nothing perfect in this world, of a human origin. Nothing connected with human nature, from man himself to any of his works. You may select the wisest and best men for your judges, and yet how many defects are there in the administration of justice? You may select the wisest and best men for your legislators, and yet how many defects are apparent in your laws? And it is so in our government.

But that this government of our fathers, with all its defects, comes nearer the objects of all good governments than any other on the face of the earth is my settled conviction. Contrast it now with any on the face of the earth. [England, said Mr. Toombs.]—England, my friend says. Well, that is the next best, I grant; but I think we have improved upon England. Statesmen tried their apprentice hand on the government of England, and then ours was made. Ours sprang from that, avoiding many of its defects, taking most of the good and leaving out many of its errors, and from the whole constructing and building up this model Republic—the best which the history of the world gives an account of.

Compare, my friends, this Government with that of Spain, Mexico, the South American Republics, Germany, Ireland—are there any sons of that down-trodden nation here to-night?—Prussia, or if you travel further east, to Turkey or China. Where will you go, following the sun in its circuit round our globe, to find a government that better protects the liberties of the people, and secures to them the blessings we enjoy? I think that one of the evils that beset us is a surfeit of liberty, an exuberance of the priceless blessings for which we are ungrateful. We listened to my honorable friend who addressed you last night, (Mr. Toombs,) as he recounted the evils of this Government.

The first was the fishing bounties, paid mostly to the sailors of New England. Our friend stated that forty-eight years of our Government was under the administration of Southern Presidents. Well, these fishing bounties began under the rule of a Southern President, I believe. No one of them during the whole forty-eight years ever set his Administration against the principle or policy of them. It is not for me to say whether it was a wise policy in the beginning; it probably was not, and I have nothing to say in its defense. But the reason given for it was to encourage our young men to go to sea and learn to manage ships. We had at the time but a small navy. It was thought best to encourage a class of our people to become acquainted with seafaring life, to become sailors—to man our naval ships. It requires practice to walk the deck of a ship, to pull the ropes, to furl the sails, to go aloft, to climb the mast; and it was thought, by offering this bounty, a nursery might be formed in which young men would become perfected in these arts, and it applied to one section of the country as well as to any other.

The result of this was that in the war of 1812 our sailors, many of whom came from this nursery, were equal to any that England brought against us. At any rate, no small part of the glories of that war were gained by the veteran tars of America, and the object of these bounties was to foster that branch of the national defense. My opinion is, that whatever may have been the reason at first, this bounty ought to be discontinued—the reason for it, at first, no longer exists. A bill for this object did pass the Senate the last Congress I was in, to which my honorable friend contributed greatly, but it was not reached in the House of Representatives. I trust that he will yet see that he may with honor continue his connection with the Government, and that his eloquence, unrivaled in the Senate, may hereafter, as heretofore, be displayed in having this bounty, so obnoxious to him, repealed and wiped off the statute book.

The next evil which my friend complained of was the Tariff. Well, let us look at that for a moment. About the time I commenced noticing public matters, this question was agitating the country almost as fearfully as the slave question now is. In 1832, when I was in college, South Carolina was ready to nullify or secede from the Union on this account. And what have we seen? The Tariff no longer distracts the public counsels. Reason has triumphed! The present Tariff was voted for by Massachusetts and South Carolina. The lion and lamb lay down together—every man in the Senate and House from Massachusetts and South Carolina, I think, voted for it, as did my honorable friend himself. And if it be true, to use the figure of speech of my honorable friend, that every man in the North that works in iron and brass and wood has his muscle strengthened by the protection of the Government, that stimulant was given by his vote, and I believe every other Southern man. So we ought not to complain of that.

Mr. Toombs—The Tariff assessed the duties.

Mr. Stephens—Yes, and Massachusetts with unanimity voted with the South to lessen them, and they were made just as low as Southern men asked them to be, and that is the rate they are now at. If reason and argument, with experience, produced such changes in the sentiments of Massachusetts from 1832 to 1857, on the subject of the Tariff, may not like changes be effected there by the same means—reason and argument, and appeals to patriotism on the present vexed question? And who can say that by 1875 or 1890 Massachusetts may not vote with South Carolina and Georgia upon all those questions that now distract the country, and threaten its peace and existence. I believe in the power and efficiency of truth, in the omnipotence of truth, and its ultimate triumph when properly wielded.

Another matter of grievance alluded to by my honorable friend was the Navigation Laws. This policy was also commenced under the Administration of one of these Southern Presidents who ruled so well, and has been continued through all of them since. The gentleman's views of the policy of these laws and my own do not disagree. We occupied the same ground in relation to them in Congress. It is not my purpose to defend them now. But it is proper to state some matters connected with their origin.

One of the objects was to build up a commercial American marine by giving American bottoms the exclusive carrying trade between our own ports. This is a great arm of national power. This object was accomplished. We have now an amount of shipping, not only coastwise, but to foreign countries, which puts us in the front rank of the nations of the world. England can no longer be styled the Mistress of the Seas. What American is not proud of the result? Whether those laws should be continued is another question. But one thing is certain: no

President, Northern or Southern, has ever yet recommended their repeal. And my friend's efforts to get them repealed were met with but little favor, North or South.

These, then, were the three main grievances or ground of complaint against the general system of our Government and its workings—I mean the administration of the Federal Government. As to the acts of the Federal States I shall speak presently; but these three were the main ones used against the common head. Now, suppose it be admitted that all these are evils in the system; do they overbalance and outweigh the advantages which this same government affords in a thousand ways? Have we not at the South, as well as the North, grown great, prosperous, and happy under its operations? Has any part of the world ever shown such rapid progress in the development of wealth, and all the material resources of national power and greatness, as the Southern States have under the General Government, notwithstanding all its defects?

Mr. Toombs—In spite of it.

Mr. Stephens—My honorable friend says we have, in spite of the General Government; without it, I suppose he thinks, we might have done as well, or perhaps better, than we have done in spite of it. That may be and it may not be; but the great fact that we have grown great and powerful under the Government as it exists—there is no conjecture or speculation about that; it stands out bold, high, and prominent, like your Stone Mountain, to which the gentleman alluded in illustrating home facts in his record—this great fact of our unrivaled prosperity in the Union is admitted; whether all this is in spite of the Government—whether we of the South would have been better off without the Government—is, to say the least, problematical. On the one side we can only put the fact against speculation and conjecture on the other. But even as a question of speculation I differ with my distinguished friend.

What we would have lost in border wars without the Union, or what we have gained simply by the peace it has secured, no estimate can be made of. Our foreign trade, which is the foundation of all our prosperity, has the protection of the navy, which drove the pirates from the waters near our coast, where they had been buccaneering for centuries before, and might have been still had it not been for the American Navy under the command of such spirits as Commodore Porter. Now that the coast is clear, that our commerce flows freely onward, we can not well estimate how it would have been under other circumstances. The influence of the Government on us is like that of the atmosphere around us. Its benefits are so silent and unseen that they are seldom thought of or appreciated.

We seldom think of the single element of oxygen in the air we breathe, and yet let this simple, unseen, and unfelt agent be withdrawn, this life-giving element be taken away from this all-pervading fluid around us, and what instant and appalling changes would take place in all organic creation.

It may be that we are all that we are in "spite of the General Government," but it may be that without it we would have been far different from what we are now. It is true there is no equal part of the earth with natural resources superior perhaps to ours. That portion of this country known as the Southern States, stretching from the Chesapeake to the Rio Grande, is fully equal to the picture drawn by the honorable and eloquent Senator last night, in all its natural capacities. But how many ages and centuries passed before these capacities were developed to reach this advanced age of civilization? There these same hills, rich in ore, same rivers, same valleys and plains, are as they have been since they came from the hand of the Creator; uneducated and uncivilized man roamed over them for how long no history informs us.

It was only under our institutions that they could be developed. Their development is the result of the enterprise of our people under operations of the Government and institutions under which we have lived. Even our people, without these, never would have done it. The organization of society has much to do with the development of the natural resources of any country or any land. The institutions of a people, political and moral, are the matrix in which the germ of their organic structure quickens into life—takes root and develops in form, nature, and character. Our institutions constitute the basis, the matrix, from which spring all our characteristics of development and greatness. Look at Greece. There is the same fertile soil, the same blue sky, the same inlets and harbors, the same Ægean, the same Olympus; there is the same land where Homer sung, where Pericles spoke; it is in nature the same old Greece—but it is living Greece no more.

Descendants of the same people inhabit the country; yet what is the reason of this mighty difference? In the midst of present degradation we see the glorious fragments of ancient works of arts—temples with ornaments and inscriptions that excite wonder and admiration—the remains of a once high order of civilization which have outlived the language they spoke—upon them all Ichabod is written—their glory has departed. Why is this so? I answer, their institutions have been destroyed. These were but the fruits of their forms of government, the matrix from which their' grand development sprang, and when once the institutions of a people have been destroyed, there is no earthly power that can bring back the Promethean spark to kindle them here again, any more than in that ancient land of eloquence, poetry, and song.

The same may be said of Italy. Where is Rome, once the mistress of the world? There are the same seven hills now, the same soil, the same natural resources; nature is the same, but what a ruin of human greatness meets the eye of the traveler throughout the length and breadth of that most down-trodden land! Why have not the people of that Heaven-favored clime the spirit that animated their fathers? Why this sad difference?

It is the destruction of her institutions that has caused it; and, my countrymen, if we shall in an evil hour rashly pull down and destroy those institutions which the patriotic band of our fathers labored so long and so hard to build up, and which have done so much for us and the world, who can venture the prediction that similar results will not ensue? Let us avoid it if we can. I trust the spirit is among us that will enable us to do it. Let us not rashly try the experiment, for, if it fails, as it did in Greece and Italy, and in the South American Republics, and in every other place wherever liberty is once destroyed, it may never be restored to us again.

There are defects in our government, errors in administration, and shortcomings of many kinds; but in spite of these defects and errors, Georgia has grown to be a great State. Let us pause here a moment. In 1850 there was a great crisis, but not so fearful as this; for, of all I have ever passed through, this is the most perilous, and requires to be met with the greatest calmness and deliberation.

There were many among us in 1850 zealous to go at once out of the Union, to disrupt every tie that binds us together. Now, do you believe, had that policy been carried out at that time, we would have been the same great people that we are to-day? It may be that we would, but have you any assurance of that fact? Would you have made the same advancement, improvement, and progress in all that constitutes material wealth and prosperity that we have.

I notice, in the Comptroller-General's report, that the taxable property of Georgia is $670,000,000 and upward, an amount not far from double what it was in 1850. I think I may venture to say that for the last ten years the material wealth of the people of Georgia has been nearly if not quite doubled. The same may be said of our advance in education, and everything that marks our civilization. Have we any assurance that, had we regarded the earnest but misguided patriotic advice, as I think, of some of that day, and disrupted the ties which bind us to the Union, we would have advanced as we have? I think not. Well, then, let us be careful now before we attempt any rash experiment of this sort. I know that there are friends—whose patriotism I do not intend to question—who think this Union a curse, and that we would be better off without it. I do not so think. If we can bring about a correction of those evils which threaten—and I am not without hope that this may yet be done—this appeal to go out, with all the provisions for good that accompany it, I look upon as a great, and I fear a fatal temptation.

When I look around and see our prosperity in every thing, agriculture, commerce, art, science, and every department of education, physical and mental, as well as moral advancement, I think, in the face of such an exhibition, if we can, without the loss of power, or any essential right or interest, remain in the Union, it is our duty to ourselves and to posterity to—let us not too readily yield to this temptation—do so. Our first parents, the great progenitors of the human race, were not without a like temptation when in the garden of Eden. They were led to believe that their condition would be bettered —that their eyes would be opened—and that they would become as gods. They in an evil hour yielded—instead of becoming gods, they only saw their own nakedness.

I look upon this country with our institutions as the Eden of the world, the paradise of the universe. It may be that out of it we may become greater and more prosperous, but I am candid and sincere in telling you that I fear if we rashly evince passion, and without sufficient cause shall take that step, that instead of becoming greater or more peaceful, prosperous and happy—instead of becoming gods, we will become demons, and at no distant day commence cutting one another's throats. This is my apprehension. Let us, therefore, whatever we do, meet these difficulties, great as they are, like wise and sensible men, and consider them in the light of all the consequences which may attend our action. Let us see first clearly where the path of duty leads, and then we may not fear to tread therein.

I come now to the main question put to me, and on which my counsel has been asked. That is, what the present Legislature should do in view of the dangers that threaten us, and the wrongs that have been done us by several of our Confederate States in the Union, by the acts of their legislatures nullifying the fugitive slave law, and in direct disregard of their constitutional obligations. What I shall say will not be in the spirit of dictation; it will be simply my own judgment for what it is worth. It proceeds from a strong conviction that according to it our rights, interests, and honor—our present safety and future security can be maintained without yet looking to the last resort, the "*ultima ratio regum.*" That should not be looked to until all else fails. That may come. On this point I am hopeful, but not sanguine. But let us use every patriotic effort to prevent it while there is ground for hope.

If any view that I may present, in your judgment, be inconsistent with the best interests of Georgia, I ask you, as patriots, not to regard it. After hearing me and others whom you have advised with, act in the premises according to your own conviction of duty as patriots. I speak now particularly to the members of the Legislature present. There are, as I have said, great dangers ahead. Great dangers may come from the election I have spoken of. If the policy of Mr. Lincoln and his associates shall be carried out, or attempted to be carried out, no man in Georgia will be more willing or ready than myself to defend our rights, interest, and honor at every hazard and to the last extremity.

What is this policy? It is, in the first place, to exclude us, by an act of Congress, from the Territories with our slave property. He is for using the power of the General Government against the extension of our institutions. Our position on this point is and ought to be, at all hazards, for perfect equality between all the States, and the citizens of all the States, in the Territories, under the Constitution of the United States. If Congress should exercise its power against this, then I am for standing where Georgia planted herself in 1850. These were plain propositions which were then laid down in her celebrated platform as sufficient for the disruption of the Union if the occasion should ever come; on these Georgia has declared that she will go out of the Union; and for these she would be justified by the nations of the earth in so doing.

I say the same; I said it then; I say it now, if Mr. Lincoln's policy should be carried out. I have told you that I do not think his bare election sufficient cause: but if his policy should be carried out in violation of any of the principles set forth in the Georgia platform, that would be such an act of aggression which ought to be met as therein provided for. If his policy shall be carried out in repealing or modifying the Fugitive Slave law so as to weaken its efficacy, Georgia has declared that she will, in the last resort, disrupt the ties of the Union, and I say so too. I stand upon the Georgia platform, and upon every plank, and say, if these aggressions therein provided for take place—I say to you and to the people of Georgia, keep your powder dry, and let your assailants then have lead, if need be. I would wait for an act of aggression. This is my position.

Now upon another point, and that the most difficult and deserving your most serious consideration, I will speak. That is the course which this State should pursue toward these Northern States, which by their legislative acts have attempted to nullify the Fugitive Slave law. I know that in some of these

States their acts pretend to be based upon the principles set forth in the case of Prigg against Pennsylvania; that decision did proclaim the doctrine that the State officers are not bound to carry out the provisions of a law of Congress—that the Federal Government can not impose duties upon State officials— that they must execute their own laws by their own officers. And this may be true. But still it is the duty of the States to deliver fugitive slaves, as well as the duty of the General Government to see that it is done.

Northern States, on entering into the Federal compact, pledged themselves to surrender such fugitives; and it is in disregard of their obligations that they had passed laws which even tend to hinder or obstruct the fulfillment of that obligation. They have violated their plighted faith; what ought we to do in view of this? That is the question. What is to be done? By the law of nations you would have a right to demand the carrying out of this article of agreement, and I do not see that it should be otherwise with respect to the States of this Union; and, in case it be not done, we would by these principles, have the right to commit acts of reprisal on these faithless governments, and seize upon their property, or that of their citizens, wherever found. The States of this Union stand upon the same footing with foreign nations in this respect. But, by the law of nations, we are equally bound, before proceeding to violent measures, to set forth our grievances before the offending Government, to give them an opportunity to redress the wrong. Has our State yet done this? I think not.

Suppose it was Great Britain that had violated some compact of agreement with the General Government, what would be first done? In that case our Minister would be directed, in the first instance, to bring the matter to the attention of that Government, or a Commissioner to be sent to that country to open negotiations with her, ask for redress, and it would only be when argument and reason had been exhausted, that we should take the last resort of nations. That would be the course toward a foreign government, and toward a member of this confederacy I would recommend the same course.

Let us, therefore, not act hastily in this matter. Let your Committee on the State of the Republic make out a bill of grievances; let it be sent by the Governor to those faithless States, and if reason and argument shall be tried in vain—if all shall fail to induce them to return to their constitutional obligations—I would be for retaliatory measures, such as the Governor has suggested to you. This mode of resistance in the Union is in our power. It might be effectual, and, if in the last resort, we would be justified in the eyes of nations, not only in separating from them, but by using force.

[Some one said the argument was already exhausted.]

Mr. Stephens continued—Some friend says the argument is already exhausted. No, my friend, it is not. You have never called the attention of the Legislatures of those States to this subject, that I am aware of. Nothing has ever been done before this year. The attention of our own people has been called to this subject lately.

Now, then, my recommendation to you would be this: In view of all these questions of difficulty, let a convention of the people of Georgia be called, to which they may be all referred. Let the sovereignty of the people speak. Some think that the election of Mr. Lincoln is cause sufficient to dissolve the Union. Some think those other grievances are sufficient to dissolve the same, and that the Legislature has the power thus to act, and ought thus to act. I have no hesitancy in saying that the Legislature is not the proper body to sever our Federal relations, if that necessity should arise. An honorable and distinguished gentleman, the other night (Mr. T. R. R. Cobb), advised you to take this course—not to wait to hear from the cross-roads and groceries. I say to you, you have no power so to act. You must refer this question to the people, and you must wait to hear from the men at the cross-roads and even the groceries; for the people in this country, whether at the cross-roads or the groceries, whether in cottages or palaces, are all equal, and they are the sovereigns in this country. Sovereignty is not in the Legislature. We, the people are the sovereigns. I am one of them, and have a right to be heard, and so has any other citizen of the State. You, legislators—I speak it respectfully—are but our servants. You are the servants of the people, and not their masters. Power resides with the people in this country.

The great difference between our country and all others, such as France and England and Ireland, is, that here there is popular sovereignty, while there sovereignty is exercised by kings and favored classes. This principle of popular sovereignty, however much derided lately, is the foundation of our institutions. Constitutions are but the channels through which the popular will may be expressed. Our Constitution came from the people. They made it, and they alone can rightfully unmake it.

Mr. Toombs—I am afraid of conventions.

Mr. Stephens—I am not afraid of any convention legally chosen by the people. I know no way to decide great questions affecting fundamental laws except by representatives of the people. The Constitution of the United States was made by the representatives of the people. The Constitution of the State of Georgia was made by representatives of the people chosen at the ballot-box. But do not let the question which comes before the people be put to them in the language of my honorable friend who addressed you last night. Will you submit to abolition rule or resist?

Mr. Toombs—I do not wish the people to be cheated.

Mr. Stephens—Now, my friends, how are we going to cheat the people by calling on them to elect delegates to a convention to decide all these questions without any dictation or direction? Who proposes to cheat the people by letting them speak their own untrammeled views in the choice of their ablest and best men, to determine upon all these matters involving their peace.

I think the proposition of my honorable friend had a considerable smack of unfairness, not to say cheat. He wished to have no convention, but for the Legislature to submit their vote to the people—submission to abolition rule or resistance? Now who, in Georgia, would vote "submission to abolition rule"?

Is putting such a question to the people to vote on a fair way of getting an expression of the popular will on all these questions? I think not. Now, who in Georgia is going to submit to abolition rule?

Mr. Toombs—The convention will.

Mr. Stephens—No, my friend, Georgia will never do it. The convention will never secede from the Georgia Platform. Under that there can be no abolition rule in the General Government. I am not afraid to trust the people in convention upon this and all questions. Besides, the Legislature was not elected for such a purpose. They came here to do their duty as legislators. They have sworn to support the Constitution of the United States. They did not come here to disrupt this Government. I am therefore for submitting all these questions to a convention of the people. Submit the question to the people, whether they would submit to an abolition rule or resist, and then let the Legislature act upon that vote? Such a course would be an insult to the people. They would have to eat their platform, ignore their past history, blot out their records, and take steps backward, if they should do this. I have never yet eaten my record or words, and never will.

But how will it be under this arrangement if they should vote to resist, and the Legislature should re-assemble with this vote as their instruction? Can any man tell what sort of resistance will be meant? One man would says secede; another pass retaliatory measures; these are measures of resistance against wrong—legitimate and right—and there would be as many different ideas as there are members on this floor. Resistance don't mean secession—that, in no proper sense of the term, is resistance. Believing that the times require action, I am for presenting the question fairly to the people, for calling together an untrammeled convention, and presenting all the questions to them whether they will go out of the Union, or what course of resistance in the Union they may think best, and then let the Legislature act, when the people in their majesty are heard; and I tell you now, whatever that convention does, I hope and trust our people will abide by. I advise the calling of a convention with the earnest desire to preserve the peace and harmony of the State. I should dislike, above all things, to see violent measures adopted, or a disposition to take the sword in hand, by individuals, without the authority af law.

My honorable friend said last night, "I ask you to give me the sword, for if you do not give it to me, as God lives, I will take it myself."

Mr. Toombs—I will.

Mr. Stephens—I have no doubt that my honorable friend feels as he says. It is only his excessive ardor that makes him use such an expression; but this will pass off with the excitement of the hour. When the people in their majesty shall speak, I have no doubt that he will bow to their will, whatever it may be upon the "sober second thought."

Should Georgia determine to go out of the Union—I speak for one, though my views might not agree with them—whatever the result may be, I shall bow to the will of her people. Their cause is my cause, and their destiny is my destiny; and I trust this will be the ultimate course of all. The greatest curse that can befall a free people is civil war.

But, as I said, let us call a convention of the people; let all these matters be submitted to it, and when the will of a majority of the people has been thus expressed, the whole State will present one unanimous voice in favor of whatever may be demanded; for I believe in the power of the people to govern themselves, when wisdom prevails and passion is silent.

Look at what has already been done by them for advancement in all that ennobles man. There is nothing like it in the history of the world. Look abroad from one extent of the country to the other—contemplate our greatness. We are now among the first nations of the earth. Shall it be said, then, that our institutions, founded upon principles of self-government, are a failure?

Thus far it is a noble example, worthy of imitation. The gentleman, Mr. Cobb, the other night said it had proven a failure. A failure in what? In growth? Look at our expanse in national power. Look at our population and increase in all that makes a people great. A failure? Why, we are the admiration of the civilized world, and present the brightest hopes of mankind.

Some of our public men have failed in their aspirations; that is true, and from that come a great part of our troubles.

No, there is no failure of this Government yet. We have made great advancement under the Constitution, and I can not but hope that we shall advance higher still. Let us be true to our cause.

Now, when this convention assembles, if it shall be called, as I hope it may, I would say in my judgment, without dictation, for I am conferring with you freely and frankly, and it is thus that I give my views, I should take into consideration all those questions which distract the public mind; should view all the grounds of secession so far as the election of Mr. Lincoln is concerned, and I have no doubt they would say that the constitutional election of no man is sufficient cause to break up the Union, but that the State should wait until he at least does some unconstitutional act.

Mr. Toombs—Commit some overt act.

Mr. Stephens—No, I did not say that. The word overt is a sort of technical term connected with treason, which has come to us from the mother country, and it means an open act of rebellion. I do not see how Mr. Lincoln can do this unless he should levy war upon us. I do not therefore use the word overt. I do not intend to wait for that. But I use the word unconstitutional act, which our people understand much better, and which expresses just what I mean. But as long as he conforms to the Constitution, he should be left to exercise the duties of his office.

In giving this advice I am but sustaining the Constitution of my country, and I do not thereby become a Lincoln aid man either, but a Constitutional aid man. But this matter the convention can determine.

As to the other matter, I think we have a right to pass retaliatory measures, provided they be in accordance with the Constitution of the United States, and I think they can be made such. But whether it would be wise for this Legislature to do this now is the question. To the convention, in my judgment, this matter ought to be referred. Before we commit reprisal on New England we should exhaust every means of bringing about a peaceful solution of the question.

Thus did Gen. Jackson in the case of the French. He did not recommend reprisals until he had treated with France, and got her to promise to make indemnification, and it was only on her refusal to pay the money which she had promised that he recommended reprisals. It was after negotiation had failed. I do think, therefore, that it would be best, before going to extreme measures with our Confederate States, to make a presentation of our demands, to appeal to their reason and judgment to give us our rights. Then, if reason should not triumph, it will be time enough to commit reprisals, and we should be justified in the eyes of the civilized world. At least, let the States know what your grievances are, and if they refuse, as I said, to give us our rights under the Constitution of our country, I should be willing, as a last resort, to sever the ties of this Union.

My own opinion is, that if this course be pursued, and they are informed of the consequences of refusal, these States will secede; but if they should not, then let the consequences be with them, and let the responsibility of the consequences rest upon them. Another thing I would have that convention to do. Re-affirm the Georgia platform with an additional plank in it. Let that plank be the fulfillment of the obligation on the part of those States to repeal these obnoxious laws as condition of our remaining in the Union. Give them time to consider it, and I would ask all States south to do the same thing.

I am for exhausting all that patriotism can demand before taking the last step. I would invite, therefore, South Carolina to a conference. I would ask the same of all the other Southern States, so that if the evil has got beyond our control, which God, in his mercy, grant may not be the case, let us not be divided, among ourselves, but, if possible, secure the united co-operation of all the Southern States; and then, in the face of the civilized world, we may justify our action; and, with the wrong all on the other side, we can appeal to the God of battles to aid us in our cause. But let us not do any thing in which any portion of our people may charge us with rash or hasty action. It is certainly a matter of great importance to tear this Government assunder. You were not sent here for that purpose. I would wish the whole South to be united if this is done; and I believe, if we pursue the policy which I have indicated, this can be effected.

In this way our sister Southern States can be induced to act with us, and I have but little doubt that the States of New York, and Pennsylvania, and Ohio, and the other Western States, will compel their Legislatures to recede from their hostile attitudes if the others do not. Then with these we would go on without New England if she choose to stay out.

A voice in the assembly—We will kick them out.

Mr. Stephens—I would not kick them out. But if they chose to stay out, they might. I think, moreover, that these Northern States, being principally engaged in manufactures, would find that they had as much interest in the Union under the Constitution as we, and that they would return to their constitutional duty—this would be my hope. If they should not, and if the Middle States and Western States do not join us, we should at least have an undivided South. I am, as you clearly perceive, for maintaining the Union as it is, if possible. I will exhaust every means thus to maintain it with an equality in it. My principles are these:

First, the maintenance of the honor, the rights, the equality, the security, and the glory of my native State in the Union; but if these can not be maintained in the Union, then I am for their maintenance, at all hazards, out of it. Next to the honor and glory of Georgia, the land of my birth, I hold the honor and glory of my common country. In Savannah I was made to say, by the reporters—who very often make me say things which I never did say—that I was first for the glory of the whole country, and next for that of Georgia.

I said the exact reverse of this. I am proud of her history, of her present standing. I am proud even of her motto, which I would have duly respected at the present time by all her sons —Wisdom, Justice, and Moderation. I would have her rights and that of the Southern States maintained now upon these principles. Her position now is just what it was in 1860, with respect to the Southern States. Her platform then has been adopted by most, if not all the other Southern States. Now I would add but one additional plank to that platform, which I have stated, and one which time has shown to be necessary.

If all this fails, we shall have the satisfaction of knowing that we have done our duty and all that patriotism could require.

Pay of Officers of the United States,
CIVIL AND MILITARY.

EXECUTIVE DEPARTMENT.

President	$25,000	per annum
Private Secretary	2,500	" "
Private Secretary to sign Patents	1,500	" "
Vice President	8,000	" "

HEADS OF DEPARTMENTS.

Secretary of State	$8,000	per annum
Secretary of the Treasury	8,000	" "
Secretary of War	8,000	" "
Secretary of the Navy	8,000	" "
Secretary of the Interior	8,000	" "
Postmaster General	8,000	" "
Attorney General	8,000	" "

MINISTERS AND DIPLOMATIC AGENTS OF THE UNITED STATES IN FOREIGN COUNTRIES — ENVOYS EXTRAORDINARY AND MINISTERS PLENIPOTENTIARY.

Minister to Great Britain	$17,500	per annum
Minister to Russia	12,000	" "
Minister to France	17,500	" "
Minister to Spain	12,000	" "
Minister to Prussia	12,000	" "
Minister to Austria	12,000	" "
Minister to Italy	12,000	" "
Minister to China	12,000	" "
Minister to Mexico	12,000	" "
Minister to Brazil	12,000	" "
Minister to Chili	10,000	" "
Minister to Peru	10,000	" "
Minister to Nicaragua	7,000	" "

PAY OF OFFICERS OF THE UNITED STATES.

MINISTERS RESIDENT.

Minister in Portugal................................	$7,500	per annum
Minister in Belgium.................................	7,500	" "
Minister in Netherlands............................	7,500	" "
Minister in Denmark................................	7,500	" "
Minister in Sweden and Norway................	7,500	" "
Minister in Switzerland.............................	7,500	" "
Minister in Pontif States..........................	7,500	" "
Minister in Turkey...................................	7,500	" "
Minister in Japan.....................................	7,500	" "
Minister in Costa Rica..............................	7,500	" "
Minister in Guatemala..............................	7,500	" "
Minister in Honduras................................	7,500	" "
Minister in Salvador.................................	7,500	" "
Minister in New Granada..........................	7,500	" "
Minister in Venezuela...............................	7,500	" "
Minister in Ecuador..................................	7,500	" "
Minister in Argentine Confederation...........	7,500	" "
Minister in Hawaiin Islands.......................	7,500	" "

WAR DEPARTMENT.

Secretary of War.....................................	$8,000	per annum
Assistant Secretary of War........................	3,000	" "
Second Assistant Secretary of War.............	3,000	" "
Commander-in-Chief................................	5,340	" "
Adjutant General.....................................	3,594	" "
Assistant Adjutant General.......................	2,532	" "
Second Assistant Adjutant General............	1,956	" "
Third Assistant Adjutant General...............	1,956	" "
Fourth Assistant Adjutant General..............	1,956	" "
Chief Clerk Adjutant General's Bureau.......	1,800	" "
Inspector General.....................................	2,532	" "
Judge Advocate General...........................	2,532	" "
Deputy Judge Advocate............................	1,956	" "
Quartermaster General.............................	3,594	" "
Deputy Quartermaster General..................	2,244	" "
Assistant Quartermaster...........................	2,532	" "
Chief Clerk Quartermaster's Bureau...........	1,800	" "
Chief Engineer..	3,594	" "
Assistant Engineer...................................	1,596	" "
Chief Clerk of Engineer Bureau.................	1,800	" "
Provost Marshal General...........................		
Surgeon General.....................................	3,594	" "
Assistant Surgeon General.......................	2,532	" "
Chief Clerk Surgeon General's Bureau.......	1,800	" "
Chief of Ordnance...................................	3,594	" "

Assistant Chief of Ordnance................................ 1,554 per annum
Chief Clerk of Ordnance Bureau................. 1,800 " "
Paymaster General.. 2,740 " "
Deputy Paymaster General............................. 2,144 " "
Additional Paymaster....................................... 1,950 " "
Chief Clerk Paymaster General's Bureau..... 1,800 " "
Commissary General of Subsistence............. 2,532 " "
Assistant Commissary General........................ 1,956 " "
Second Assistant Commissary General.......... 1,956 " "
Chief Clerk Commissary General's Bureau... 1,800 " "

GENERAL OFFICERS.

Lieutenant General..$720 00 per month
Aids-de-camp and military secretary to Lieutenant General, each............................ 170 00 " "
Major General... 445 00 " "
Senior Aid-de-camp to General-in-Chief....... 163 00 " "
Aid-de-camp, in addition to pay, etc., of Lieutenant or Captain...................... 24 00 " "
Brigadier General... 299 50 " "
Aid-de-camp, in addition to pay, etc., as Lieutenant... 11 00 " "

ADJUTANT GENERAL'S DEPARTMENT.

Adjutant General—Brigadier General..........$407 50 per month
Assistant Adjutant General—Colonel............ 211 00 " "
Assistant Adjutant General—Lt. Colonel...... 187 00 " "
Assistant Adjutant General—Major............... 163 00 " "
Judge Advocate General—Colonel................. 211 00 " "
Judge Advocate—Major..................................... 163 00 " "
Division Major.. 163 00 " "

INSPECTOR GENERAL'S DEPARTMENT.

Inspector General—Colonel..............................$211 00 per month
Assistant Inspector General—Major............... 163 00 " "

SIGNAL DEPARTMENT.

Signal Officer—Colonel......................................$211 00 per month

PAY DEPARTMENT.

Paymaster General... $288 33 per month
Deputy Paymaster General............................... 187 00 " "
Paymaster... 163 00 " "

PAY OF OFFICERS OF THE UNITED STATES. 221

OFFICERS OF THE CORPS OF ENGINEERS, TOPOGRAPHICAL ENGINEERS, AND ORDNANCE DEPARTMENT.

Chief of Ordinance—Brigadier General......$407 50 per month
Colonel.. 211 00 " "
Lieutenant Colonel..................................... 187 00 " "
Major... 163 00 " "
Captain... 129 50 " "
First Lieutenant... 112 83 " "
Second Lieutenant...................................... 112 83 " "
Brevet Second Lieutenant......................... 112 83 " "

OFFICERS OF MOUNTED DRAGOONS, CAVALRY, RIFLEMEN, AND LIGHT ARTILLERY.

Colonel..$211 00 per month
Lieutenant Colonel..................................... 187 00 " "
Major... 163 00 " "
Captain... 129 50 " "
First Lieutenant... 112 83 " "
Second Lieutenant...................................... 112 83 " "
Brevet Second Lieutenant......................... 112 83 " "

QUARTERMASTER'S DEPARTMENT.

Quartermaster General—Brigadier General..$407 50 per month
Assistant Quartermaster General—Colonel... 211 00 " "
Deputy Quartermaster General—Lt. Colonel 187 00 " "
Quartermaster—Major................................. 163 00 " "
Assistant Quartermaster—Captain............. 129 50 " "

SUBSISTENCE DEPARTMENT.

Commissary General of Subsistence—Brigadier General...$299 50 per month
Assistant Commissary General—Lt. Colonel.. 187 00 " "
Commissary of Subsistence—Major............ 163 00 " "
Commissary of Subsistence—Captain......... 129 50 " "
Assistant Commissary of Subsistence, in addition to pay, etc., as Lieutenant............ 11 00 " "

MEDICAL DEPARTMENT.

Surgeon General—Brigadier General..........$299 50 per month
Assistant Surgeon General........................ 211 00 " "
Medical Inspector General......................... 211 00 " "
Medical Inspector....................................... 187 00 " "
Surgeons of ten years' service.................. 199 00 " "
Surgeons of less than ten years' service... 163 00 " "

Assistant Surgeons of ten years' service....... 165 50 per month
Assistant Surgeons of five years' service...... 129 50 "   "
Assistant Surgeons of less than five years'
 service.. 112 83 "   "

Adjutant, Regimental Quartermaster, and
 Regimental Commissary, in addition to
 pay of Lieutenant, each.................................. 10 00 "   "

OFFICERS OF ARTILLERY AND INFANTRY.

Colonel..$194 00 per month
Lieutenant Colonel....................................... 170 00 "   "
Major.. 151 00 "   "
Captain... 118 50 "   "
First Lieutenant... 108 50 "   "
Second Lieutenant....................................... 103 50 "   "
Brevet Second Lieutenant............................ 103 50 "   "
Adjutant, in addition to pay, etc., of Lieut... 10 00 "   "
Regimental Quartermaster, in addition to
 pay, etc., of Lieutenant............................ 10 00 "   "

PAY OF NON-COMMISSIONED OFFICERS, PRIVATES, ETC.—CAVALRY.

Sergeant-Major.......................................$21 00 per month
Quartermaster Sergeant............................... 21 00 "   "
Chief Bugler... 21 00 "   "
First Sergeant... 20 00 "   "
Sergeant.. 17 00 "   "
Saddler Sergeant... 21 00 "   "
Commissary Sergeant................................... 21 00 "   "
Hospital Steward.. 30 00 "   "
Corporal.. 14 00 "   "
Bugler, or Trumpeter................................... 13 00 "   "
Ferrier and Blacksmith................................. 15 00 "   "
Private.. 13 00 "   "
Veterinary Surgeon...................................... 75 00 "   "
African under-cooks.................................... 10 00 "   "

ORDNANCE.

Sergeant...$34 00 per month
Corporal.. 20 00 "   "
Wagoner.. 14 00 "   "
Saddler.. 14 00 "   "
Private—first class....................................... 17 00 "   "
Private—second class.................................. 16 00 "   "

PAY OF OFFICERS OF THE UNITED STATES.

ARTILLERY AND INFANTRY.

Sergeant-Major	$21 00	per month
Quartermaster Sergeant	21 00	" "
Commissary Sergeant	21 00	" "
First Sergeant	20 00	" "
Sergeant	17 00	" "
Hospital Steward	30 00	" "
Corporal	14 00	" "
Artificer, Artillery	15 00	" "
Private	13 00	" "
Principal Musician	21 00	" "
Musician	12 00	" "
African under-cooks	10 00	" "

SAPPERS AND MINERS, AND PONTOONIERS.

Sergeant	$34 00	per month
Corporal	20 00	" "
Private—first class	17 00	" "
Private—second class	16 00	" "
Musician	12 00	" "
African under-cooks	10 00	" "

BRIGADE BANDS.

Leader	$45 00	per month
Four of the Band	34 00	" "
Eight of the Band	17 00	" "
Four of the Band	20 00	" "

MISCELLANEOUS.

Medical Cadets	$30 00	" "
Hospital Steward—first class	22 00	" "
Matron	6 00	" "

Female nurses 40 cents per day.

PAY OF THE NAVY OF THE UNITED STATES.

REAR ADMIRALS — ACTIVE LIST.

When at sea	$5,000	per annum
When on shore duty	4,000	" "
On leave, or waiting orders	3,000	" "
On Retired List	2,000	" "

COMMODORES — ACTIVE LIST.

When at sea	$4,000	per annum
When on shore duty	2,800	" "
On leave, or waiting orders	2,100	" "
On Retired List	1,600	" "

COMMANDERS — ACTIVE LIST.

When at sea	$2,800	per annum
When on shore duty	2,240	" "
On leave, or waiting orders	1,680	" "
On Retired List	1,400	" "

LIEUTENANT COMMANDERS — ACTIVE LIST.

When at sea	$2,343	per annum
When on shore duty	1,875	" "
On leave, or waiting orders	1,500	" "
On Retired List	1,300	" "

LIEUTENANTS — ACTIVE LIST.

When at sea	$1,875	per annum
When on shore duty	1,500	" "
On leave, or waiting orders	1,200	" "
On Retired List	1,000	" "

MASTERS — ACTIVE LIST.

When at sea	$1,500	per annum
When on shore duty	1,200	" "
On leave, or waiting orders	960	" "
On Retired List	800	" "

ENSIGNS — ACTIVE LIST.

When at sea	$1,200	per annum
When on shore duty	960	" "
On leave, or waiting orders	768	" "
On Retired List	500	" "
Midshipmen	500	" "
Fleet Surgeons	3,300	" "

SURGEONS.

For second five years after date of commission..................................$2,400 per annum

PAY OF OFFICERS OF THE UNITED STATES. 225

RETIRED SURGEONS.

Surgeons ranking with commanders............$1,100 per annum
Surgeons ranking with lieutenants............... 1,000 "   "

RETIRED PASSED AND ASSISTANT SURGEONS.

Passed..$850 per annum
Assistant... 650 "   "

PASSED ASSISTANT SURGEONS.

On duty at sea...$1,500 per annum
On other duty.. 1,400 "   "
On leave, or waiting orders......................... 1,100 "   "

ASSISTANT SURGEONS.

On duty at sea...$1,250 per annum
On other duty.. 1,050 "   "
On leave, or waiting orders.........................   800 "   "

PAYMASTERS.

On duty at sea—for fourth five years after
  date of commission................................$2,900 per annum

PAYMASTERS RETIRED.

Ranking with Captains..............................$1,300 per annum
Ranking with Commanders....................... 1,100 "   "
Ranking with Lieutenants........................... 1,000 "   "

ASSISTANT PAYMASTERS.

On duty at sea—after five years from date of
  commission..$1,500 per annum
On leave, or waiting orders.........................   800 "   "

CHAPLAINS,

To be paid as Lieutenants.

PROFESSORS OF MATHEMATICS.

On duty..$1,800 per annum
On leave, or waiting orders.........................   960 "   "

BOATSWAINS, GUNNERS, CARPENTERS, AND SAILMAKERS.

On duty at sea—for first three years' sea service from date of appointment...............$1,000 per annum

15

For twelve years' service and upwards......... 1,450 per annum
On leave, or waiting orders—for twelve years'
  sea service and upwards....................... 1,000 " "

CHIEF ENGINEERS

On duty—for first five years after date of
  commission..$1,800 per annum
After fifteen years from date of commission... 2,600 " "
On leave, or waiting orders, after fifteen years
  from date of commission....................... 1,500 " "

FIRST ASSISTANT ENGINEERS.

On duty..$1,500 per annum
On leave, or waiting orders....................... 900 " "

SECOND ASSISTANT ENGINEERS.

On duty..$1,000 per annum
On leave, or waiting orders....................... 750 " "

NAVY AGENT.

Commission not to exceed.......................$3,000 per annum
Navy Agent at San Francisco..................... 4,000 " "
Temporary Navy Agents...........................
Naval Storekeepers.................................

Officers of the Navy on Foreign Stations......$1,500 per annum
Engineer-in-Chief.................................... 3,000 " "
Naval Constructors................................. 2,600 " "
  "   "   when not on duty.......... 1,800 " "
Secretaries to commanders of squadrons..... 1,500 " "
Clerks to commanders of squadrons and com-
  manders of vessels.............................. 500 " "
At Navy Yards—Boston and New York....... 1,200 " "
At Navy Yard—Washington..................... 1,200 " "
At Navy Yards—Portsmouth, N. H., and
  Philadelphia...................................... 1,200 " "
At Navy Yard—Mare Island..................... 1,500 " "

YEOMEN.

In ships-of-the-line..................................$45 00 per month
In frigates... 40 00 " "
In sloops.. 30 00 " "
In smaller vessels................................... 24 00 " "

PAY OF OFFICERS OF THE UNITED STATES. 227

ARMORERS.

In ships-of-the-line	$30 00	per month
In frigates	25 00	" "
In sloops	20 00	" "

MATES.

Master's (Acting)	$40 00	per month
Boatswains	25 00	" "
Gunners	25 00	" "
Carpenters	25 00	" "
Sailmakers	20 00	" "
Armorers	20 00	" "
Masters-at-Arms	25 00	" "
Ship's Corporals	20 00	" "
Coxwains	24 00	" "
Quartermasters	24 00	" "
Quarter Gunners	20 00	" "

CAPTAINS.

Of forecastle	$24 00	per month
Of tops	20 00	" "
Of afterguard	20 00	" "
Of hold	20 00	" "
Coopers	20 00	" "
Painters	20 00	" "

STEWARDS.

Ship's	$30 00	per month
Officers'	20 00	" "
Surgeons', where ship's complement is 400 and over	40 00	" "
Surgeons', where ship's complement is 200 and under 400	33 00	" "
Surgeons', where ship's complement is under 200	25 00	" "
Paymaster's, where ship's complement is 240 and over	33 00	" "
Assistant Paymaster's, where complement is 100 and over	33 00	" "
Assistant Paymaster's, where complement is under 100	30 00	" "

NURSES.

Where complement is less than 200, one nurse. $14 00 per month
Where complement is over 200, two nurses,
each... 14 00 " "

COOKS.

Ship's..$24 00 per month
Officer's... 20 00 " "

MUSICIANS.

Masters of the Band.....................................$20 00 per month
First class.. 15 00 " "
Second class.. 12 00 " "

Seamen ....$18 00 per month
Ordinary Seamen... 14 00 " "
Landsmen... 12 00 " "
Boys...8-9 00 " "

FIREMEN.

First class..$30 00 per month
Second class.. 25 00 " "
Coal Heavers... 18 00 " "

MARINE CORPS.

Colonel Commandant..................................$3,186 00 per annum
Paymaster, with rank of Major.................... 2,154 00 " "
Adjutant and Inspector, with rank of
  Major.. 2,154 00 " "
Quartermaster, with rank of Major............. 2,154 00 " "
Assistant Quartermaster, with rank of
  Captain... 1,752 00 " "
Colonel... 2,529 00 " "
Lieutenant Colonel....................................... 2,239 50 " "
Major.. 2,010 00 " "

NOTE.—By a late act of Congress, the monthly pay of private soldiers has been increased three dollars, that of non-commissioned officers being proportionately advanced. And a tax of five per cent. was imposed on the salaries of commissioned officers, thus, indirectly reducing their pay.

SCHEDULE OF STAMP DUTIES.

	Stamp Duties.
Acknowledgment of deeds	exempt.
Affidavit	5 cts.
" in suits or legal proceedings	exempt.
Agreement or Appraisement, (for each sheet, or piece of paper on which the same is written)	5 cts.
Assignment or transfer of mortgage, lease, or policy of insurance, the same duty as the original instrument.	
" of patent right	5 cts.
Bank Checks, drafts or orders, &c., at sight or on demand	2 cts.
Bills of Exchange, (Foreign,) drawn in, but payable out of, the United States, each bill of three or more, must be stamped.	
For every bill of each set, where the sum made payable does not exceed one hundred dollars, or the equivalent thereof in any foreign currency in which such bills may be expressed, according to the standard of value fixed by the United States	2 cts.
For every additional hundred dollars, or fractional part thereof in excess of one hundred dollars	2 cts.
(Foreign,) drawn in, but made payable out of, the United States, (if drawn singly or in duplicate,) pay the same duty as Inland Bills of Exchange.	
[The acceptor or acceptors of any Bill of Exchange, or order for the payment of any sum of money drawn, or purporting to be drawn, in any foreign country, but payable in the United States, must, before paying or accepting the same, place thereon a stamp indicating the duty.]	
Bills of Exchange, (Inland,) draft or order, payable otherwise than at sight or on demand, and any promissory note, whether payable on demand or at a time designated, (except	

(229)

	Stamp Duties.
bank notes issued for circulation, and checks made and intended to be, and which shall be, forthwith presented for payment,) for a sum not exceeding one hundred dollars...................................	5 cts.
For every additional $100, or fractional part thereof...	5 cts.

[The warrant of attorney to confess judgment on a note or bond is exempt from stamp duty, if the note or bond is properly stamped.]

Bills of Lading, of vessels for ports of the United States or British North America..................................	exempt.
" or receipt for goods, to any foreign port.....	10 cts.
Bill of Sale of any vessel, or part thereof, when the consideration does not exceed five hundred dollars...	50 cts.
" exceeding $500, and not exceeding $1,000.	$1 00
" exceeding $1,000, for each $500, or fractional part thereof............................	50 cts.
" of personal property, (other than ship or vessel)	5 cts.
Bond, personal, for the payment of money. (See *Mortgage*.)	
" official...	$1 00
" for indemnifying any person for the payment of any sum of money, where the money ultimately recoverable thereupon is $1,000 or less..................................	50 cts.
" Where the money recoverable exceeds $1,000, for every additional $1,000, or fractional part thereof...........................	50 cts.
Bonds.—County, city, and town bonds, railroad and other corporation bonds, and scrip, are subject to stamp duty. (See *Mortgage*.)	
" of any description, other than such as are required in legal proceedings, and such as are not otherwise charged in this Schedule	25 cts.
Certificates of deposit in bank, sum not exceeding one hundred dollars..	2 cts.
" of deposit in bank, sum exceeding one hundred dollars.....................................	5 cts.
" of stock in an incorporated company........	25 cts.
" general...	5 cts.
" of record upon the instrument recorded...	exempt.

	Stamp Duties.
Certificates of record upon the book	exempt.
" of weight or measurement of animals, coal, wood, or other articles, except weighers' and measurers' returns	exempt.
" of a qualification of a Justice of the Peace, Commissioner of Deeds, or Notary Public	5 cts.
" of search of records	5 cts.
" that certain papers are on file	5 cts.
" that certain papers can not be found	5 cts.
" of redemption of land sold for taxes	5 cts.
" of birth, marriage and death	5 cts.
" of qualification of school teachers	5 cts.
" of profits of an incorporated company for a sum not less than $10 and not exceeding $50	10 cts.
" exceeding $50, and not exceeding $1,000	25 cts.
" exceeding $1,000, for every additional $1,000, or fractional part thereof	25 cts.
" of damage, or otherwise, and all other certificates or documents issued by any port warden, marine surveyor, or other person acting as such	25 cts.
Certified Transcripts of judgments, satisfaction of judgments, and all papers recorded or on file.	5 cts.

[N. B.—As a general rule, every certificate which has, or may have, a legal value in any court of law or equity, will require a stamp duty of 5 cts.]

Charter party, or letter, memorandum, or other writing between the captain, owner, or agent of any ship, vessel, or steamer, and any other person, relating to the charter of the same, if the registered tonnage of said ship, vessel, or steamer does not exceed one hundred and fifty tons	$1 00
" exceeding one hundred and fifty tons, and not exceeding three hundred tons	3 00
" exceeding three hundred tons, and not exceeding six hundred tons	5 00
" exceeding six hundred tons	10 00
Check, draft, or order for the payment of any sum of money exceeding $10, drawn upon any person other than a bank, banker, or trust company, at sight or on demand	2 cts.

Contract. (See *Agreement.*)

SCHEDULE OF STAMP DUTIES.

Stamp Duties.

Contract, Broker's.. 10 cts.
Conveyance, deed, instrument, or writing, whereby lands,
    tenements, or other realty sold, shall be
    conveyed, *the actual value* of which does
    not exceed $500.. 50 cts.
  "   exceeding $500, and not exceeding $1,000. $1 00
  "   for every additional $500, or fractional part
    thereof in excess of $1,000..................... 50 cts.
Endorsement of any negotiable instrument.................... exempt.
Entry of any goods, wares, or merchandise at any cus-
    tom house, either for consumption or
    warehousing, not exceeding one hundred
    dollars in value.................................... 25 cts.
  "   exceeding one hundred dollars, and not ex-
    ceeding five hundred dollars in value..... 50 cts.
  "   exceeding five hundred dollars in value.... $1 00
  "   for the withdrawal of any goods or mer-
    chandise from bonded warehouse.......... 50 cts.
Gaugers' returns, if for quantity not exceeding 500
    gallons, gross.. 10 cts.
  "   exceeding 500 gallons............................ 25 cts.
Insurance, (Marine, Inland, and Fire,) where the con-
    sideration paid for the insurance, in
    cash, premium notes, or both, does not
    exceed $10.. 10 cts.
  "   (Marine, Inland, and Fire,) exceeding $10,
    and not exceeding $50........................... 25 cts.
  "   (Marine, Inland, and Fire,) exceeding $50, 50 cts.
Insurance, (Life,) when the amount insured does not ex-
    ceed $1,000... 25 cts.
  "   (Life,) exceeding $1,000, and not exceed-
    ing $5,000.. 50 cts.
  "   (Life,) exceeding $5,000. .... $1 00
  "   (Life,) limited to injury to persons while
    traveling... exempt.
Lease of lands or tenements, where rent does not ex-
    ceed $300 per annum............................ 50 cts.
  "   exceeding $300, for each additional $200,
    or fractional part thereof in excess of
    $300.. 50 cts.
  "   perpetual, subject to a stamp duty as a
    "conveyance," the stamp duty to be
    measured by resolving the annual rental
    into a capital sum.
  "   clause of guaranty of payment of rent, incor-
    porated or indorsed, five cents additional.

SCHEDULE OF STAMP DUTIES.   233

                                                    Stamp Duties.
Manifest for custom-house entry or clearance of the
 cargo of any ship, vessel, or steamer for
 a foreign port, if the registered tonnage
 of such ship, vessel, or steamer does not
 exceed 300 tons................................ $1 00
 " exceeding 300 tons, and not exceeding 600
  tons.. 3 00
 " exceeding 600 tons............................. 5 00
Measurer's Returns, if for quantity not exceeding one
 thousand bushels................................ 10 cts.
 " exceeding one thousand bushels............... 25 cts.
Mortgage, trust deed, bill of sale, or personal bond for
 the payment of money exceeding $100,
 and not exceeding $500........................ 50 cts.
 " exceeding $500, for every additional $500,
  or fractional part thereof in excess of
  $500.. 50 cts.
Pawners' Checks.. 5 cts.
Pension Papers.—Powers of attorney, and all other pa-
 pers relating to applications for bounties,
 arrearages of pay, or pensions, or to re-
 ceipt thereof..exempt.
Passage Ticket from the United States to a foreign port,
 costing not more than $35..................... 50 cts.
 " from the United States to a foreign port,
  costing more than $35, and not exceeding
  $50.. $1 00
 " for every additional $50, or fractional part
  thereof in excess of $50....................... $1 00
Power of Attorney to sell or transfer stock, or collect
 dividends thereon................................ 25 cts.
 " to vote at election of incorporated company 10 cts.
 " to receive or collect rents..................... 25 cts.
 " to sell, or convey, or rent, or lease real estate $1 00
 " for any purpose................................. 50 cts.
Probate of Will, or letters of administration, where the
 value of both real and personal estate
 does not exceed $2,000......................... $1 00
 " for every additional $1,000, or fractional
  part thereof in excess of $2,000............ 50 cts.
 " bonds of executors, administrators, guardians, and trustees; are each subject to
  a stamp duty of.................................. $1 00
 " certificate of appointment..................... 5 cts.
Protest upon bill, note, check, or draft.................... 25 cts.

Stamp Duties.

Promissory Note.—(See *Bills of Exchange*, Inland.)
" deposit note to mutual insurance companies, when policy is subject to duty......exempt.
" renewal of, subject to same duty as an original note.

Quit Claim Deed, to be stamped as a conveyance, except when given as a release of a mortgage by the mortgagee to the mortgagor, in which case it is exempt.

Receipt for the payment of any sum of money or debt due exceeding $20, or for the delivery of any property...................................... 2 cts.
" for satisfaction of any mortgage or judgment or decree of any court............exempt.

Sheriff's return on writ or other process..............exempt.

Trust Deed, made to secure a debt, to be stamped as a mortgage.
" conveying estate to uses, to be stamped as conveyance.

Warehouse Receipt for any goods, wares, or merchandise not otherwise provided for, deposited or stored in any public or private warehouse, not exceeding $500 in value....... 10 cts.
" exceeding $500, and not exceeding $1,000. 20 cts.
" exceeding $1,000, for every additional $1,000, or fractional part thereof in excess of $1,000................................... 10 cts.
" for any goods, &c, not othewise provided for, stored or deposited in any public or private warehouse or yard................ 25 cts.

Writs and Legal Documents:
Writ, or other original process by which suit is commenced in any court of record, either of law or equity........................ 50 cts.
Writ, or other original process issued by a court not of record, where the amount claimed is $100 or over........................ 50 cts.
Upon every confession of judgment or cognovit for $100, or over, except in cases where the tax for a writ has been paid.. 50 cts.
Writs, or other process on appeals from justices' courts, or other courts of inferior jurisdiction, to a court of record.... 50 cts.
Warrant of distress, when the amount of rent claimed does not exceed $100........ 25 cts.

Stamp Duties.

Warrant of distress when amount exceeds $100 .... 50 cts.
Writs, summons, and other process issued by a justice of the peace, police or municipal court, of no greater jurisdiction than a justice of the peace in the same State .... exempt.
Writs, and other process in any criminal or other suits commenced by the United States in any State .... exempt.
Official documents, instruments, and papers issued or used by officers of the United States Government .... exempt.

GENERAL REMARKS.

Revenue stamps may be used indiscriminately upon any of the matters or things enumerated in Schedule B, except proprietary and playing card stamps, for which a special use has been provided.

Postage stamps cannot be used in payment of the duty chargeable on instruments.

It is the duty of the maker of an instrument to affix and cancel the stamp required thereon. If he neglects to do so, the party for whose use it is made may stamp it before it is used; but in no case can it be legally used without a stamp; and if issued after the 30th of June, 1864, and used without a stamp, it cannot be afterwards effectually stamped. Any failure upon the part of the maker of an instrument to appropriately stamp it renders him liable to a penalty of two hundred dollars.

Suits are commenced in many States by other process than writ, viz: summons, warrant, publication, petition, &c., in which cases these, as the original processes, severally require stamps.

Writs of scire facias are subject to stamp duty as original processes.

The jurat of an affidavit, taken before a Justice of the Peace, Notary Public, or other officer duly authorized to take affidavits, is held to be a certificate, and subject to a stamp duty of five cents, except when taken in suits or legal proceedings.

Certificates of loan, in which there shall appear any written or printed evidence of an amount of money to be paid on demand, or at a time designated, are subject to stamp duty as "Pomissory Notes."

The assignment of a mortgage is subject to the same stamp duty as that imposed upon the original instrument; that is to say, for every sum of five hundred dollars, or any fractional part thereof of the amount secured by the mortgage at the time of its assignment, there must be affixed a stamp or stamps denoting a duty of fifty cents.

When two or more persons join in the execution of an instrument, the stamp to which the instrument is liable under the law may be affixed and cancelled by any one of the parties.

In conveyances of real estate, the law provides that the stamp affixed must answer to the value of the estate or interest conveyed.

No stamp is required on any warrant of attorney accompanying a bond or note, when such bond or note has affixed thereto the stamp or stamps denoting the duty required; and whenever any bond or note is secured by mortgage, but one stamp duty is required on such papers, such stamp duty being the highest rate required for such instruments, or either of them. In such case, a note or memorandum of the value or denomination of the stamp affixed should be made upon the margin or in the acknowledgment of the instrument which is not stamped.

NATIONAL DEMOCRATIC PLATFORM
OF 1864.

Resolved, That in the future, as in the past, we will adhere with unswerving fidelity to the Union under the Constitution as the only solid foundation of our strength, security and happiness as a people, and as a framework of government equally conducive to the welfare and prosperity of all the States, both Northern and Southern.

Resolved, That this Convention does explicitly declare, as the sense of the American people, that after four years of failure to restore the Union by the experiment of war, during which, under the pretense of military necessity or war power higher than the Constitution, the Constitution itself has been disregarded in every part, and public liberty and private right alike trodden down, and the material prosperity of the country essentially impaired, justice, humanity, liberty and the public welfare demand that immediate efforts be made for a cessation of hostilities with a view to an ultimate convention of the States, or other peaceable means, to the end that at the earliest practical moment peace may be restored on the basis of the Federal Union of the States.

Resolved, That the direct interference of the military authorities of the United States in the recent elections held in Kentucky, Maryland, Missouri and Delaware was a shameful violation of the Constitution, and a repetition of such acts in the approaching election will be held as revolutionary, and resisted with all the means and power under our control.

Resolved, That the aim and object of the Democratic party is to preserve the Federal Union and the rights of the States unimpaired, and they hereby declare that they consider that the administrative usurpation of extraordinary and dangerous powers not granted by the Constitution, the subversion of the civil by military law in States not in insurrection, the arbitrary military arrest, imprisonment, trial and sentence of American citizens in States where the civil law exists in full force, the suppression of freedom of speech and of the press, the denial of the right of asylum, the open and avowed disregard of State rights, the employment of unusual test oaths, and the interference with, and denial of the right of the people to bear arms in their defense, is calculated to prevent a restoration of the Union and the perpetuation of the Government deriving its just powers from the consent of the governed.

Resolved, That the shameful disregard of the Administration to its duty in respect to our fellow-citizens who now are, and long have been, prisoners of war in a suffering condition, deserves the severest reprobation on the score alike of public policy and common humanity.

Resolved, That the sympathy of the Democratic party is heartily and earnestly extended to the soldiery of our army and sailors of our navy who are and have been in the field and on the sea, under the flag of their country, and in the event of its attaining power, they will receive all the care, protection and regard that the brave soldiers and sailors of the Republic have so nobly earned.

INDEX.

	PAGE.
Formation of Original Union...	5
Declaration of Independence	7
Constitution of the United States	12
Washington's Address to Colonial Congress upon receiving Commission as Commander-in-Chief	26
Washington's Address upon Resigning Commission as Commander-in-Chief	27
Washington's Inaugural Address	28
Washington's Farewell Address	32
History of the States	46
Missouri Compromise	67
Fugitive Slave Law	68
Kansas and Nebraska Act	74
Ordinance of 1787	85
Electoral Votes	92
General Remarks	112
Biographies of Ex-Presidents	113 to 144
Biography of Abraham Lincoln	145
Biography of John C. Fremont	151
Biography of Gen. George B. McClellan	155
Biography of Lieut. Gen. U. S. Grant	159
Biography of Andrew Johnson	163
Proposed Crittenden Compromise	165
Emancipation Proclamation	167
Letter explaining same	168
President Jackson's Proclamation to South Carolina Nullifiers	173
Platforms of 1860—1864	192 to 199
Speech of A. H. Stephens against Secession	200
Pay of United States Officers	218
Schedule of Stamp Duties	229
General Remarks	235

FLORENCE SEWING MACHINE!

THE BEST IN THE WORLD,

MAKES FOUR DIFFERENT STITCHES,

And has the Reversible Feed adapted for all kinds of Sewing.

SEND FOR CIRCULAR AND SAMPLE OF WORK.

J. W. SMITH, General Agent,

No. 17 Pennsylvania St., Indianapolis, Ind.

☞ LOCAL AGENTS WANTED.

THE HEAVENLY TOKEN:
A GIFT BOOK
FOR CHRISTIANS.
1 Vol. 12mo. 500 pages. PRICE $1.50

The publishers take great pleasure in presenting this volume to the Christian public, as one eminently calculated to do good.

In his preface, the author informs us that the work "is not designed as a systematic treatise, but as an humble essay on the great, the inexhaustible subject of the love of Christ, as manifested to a lost world." It is divided into four parts, under the following general heads: "The Love of Christ;" "Christ and Him Crucified;" "Wanderings of a Pilgrim;" "Immanuel's Land." These are subdivided into some eight or ten chapters each.

[FROM THE EDITOR OF THE "CHRISTIAN ADVOCATE."]

Having examined "The Heavenly Token," now being circulated in this community, I have no hesitancy in recommending the work to our people.
E. THOMSON,
Late President of the Ohio Wesleyan University.

[FROM THE NEW YORK CHRONICLE.]

In coming to the pages of this good book, after noticing so many of quite a different character, we feel our soul refreshed like a man who reaches a green, beautiful rivulet—irrigated oasis in a land where no water is, a land which is as the shadow of death. It is much in the strain of Doddridge's Rise and Progress of Religion in the Soul," or Baxter's "Saint's Rest," and like the latter book "was composed during a long perriod of recovery from a chronic disease, which brought the author to the gates of death, and well nigh terminated his life." It offers Christianity to the reader, not in any controversial aspect, not in any acute, metaphysical or philosophical form, not as gratifying curiosity by new revelations in reference to departed spirits or their abode, not in any of the phases of it in which so many are solely absorbed, but Christianity as embraced by one who has been slain by the law and made alive by Christ, as the balm of a wounded heart, as salvation for the lost, as life for the dead. And as the matter of this work is purely evangelical, so its style is eminently simple, direct, appropriate. It is made to bear with great force directly upon the conscience, and hence is hortatory, pungent, and powerful, stirring up the spiritual affections from their deepest fountains. We could wish that whatever books are given on the holidays, this one may accompany them as the crowning gift of all.

THE HEAVENLY TOKEN will be sent by mail to any part of the United States, on receipt of the price. ($1.50.)

500 AGENTS WANTED IMMEDIATELY to engage in the sale of the above work. One of our Agents has sold 500 copies in two months. For terms address,

ASHER & ADAMS,
INDIANAPOLIS, INDIANA.

MERRILL & CO.,

PUBLISH

INDIANA REPORTS,

The Soldier of Indiana in the War for the Union,

AND

BARBOUR & HOWLAND'S MANUAL

FOR ADMINISTRATORS, EXECUTORS AND GUARDIANS,

Etc., Etc., Etc.

They have the only Large Stock of

LAW AND MISCELLANEOUS BOOKS

In this State. They Wholesale and Retail

SCHOOL BOOKS AND STATIONERY,

ON THE BEST OF TERMS.

Order of

MERRILL & CO.,

GLENNS' BLOCK, INDIANAPOLIS.

www.ingramcontent.com/pod-product-compliance
Lightning Source LLC
Chambersburg PA
CBHW022007220426
43663CB00007B/1002